MANAGING WATER

Avoiding Crisis in California

Dorothy Green

University of California Press   Berkeley   Los Angeles   London

University of California Press, one of the
most distinguished university presses in the
United States, enriches lives around the world
by advancing scholarship in the humanities,
social sciences, and natural sciences. Its activities are supported by the UC Press Foundation and by philanthropic contributions from
individuals and institutions. For more information, visit www.ucpress.edu.

University of California Press
Berkeley and Los Angeles, California
University of California Press, Ltd.
London, England

Library of Congress Cataloging-in-Publication
Data

Green, Dorothy, 1929–
    Managing water : avoiding crisis in
California / Dorothy Green.
        p.   cm.
    Includes bibliographical references and
index.
    ISBN-13: 978-0-520-25326-1 (cloth : alk.
paper)
    ISBN-13: 978-0-520-25327-8 (pbk. : alk.
paper)
    1. Water-supply—California—Manage-
ment.   I. Title.
TD224.C3.G74   2007
363.6'109794—dc22   2007008265

Manufactured in the United States

10   09   08   07

10 9 8 7 6 5 4 3 2 1

The paper used in this publication meets
the minimum requirements of ANSI/
NISO Z39.48-1992 (R 1997) (*Permanence
of Paper*).∞

Cover photograph: A sign of drought, part
of the normal weather cycle in California.
Photograph by Rick Kattelmann.

In memory of Jack,
best friend, lover, and husband,
whose support made all things possible

CONTENTS

ACKNOWLEDGMENTS

This book would not be possible without the help of many, many people who have provided information and answered a million questions. They are too many to acknowledge. But a few have made major contributions that must be singled out for special thanks. Most importantly I must thank Heather Trim, Ph.D., former staff scientist to the Los Angeles and San Gabriel Rivers Watershed Council. She has given yeoman service to the successful completion of this book. She researched and wrote most of Chapter 4, "Drinking Water Quality," helped with formatting and editing, and has made contributions throughout. Her fine assistance is most appreciated.

Several interns helped with basic research. Richard Franks, a summer intern, provided much of the basic information in Chapter 1, "Los Angeles Area Water Supplies," and sketched out some of the issues in other parts of the book. Raphael Garcia contributed to Chapter 2, "Water Management: Who's in Charge?" Two early drafts were broadly circulated for comment and corrections within the water community and elsewhere. Comments about the need for a point of view, instead of an exposition about how the water world works, led to the development of the final chapter's concluding section, "Elements of a Sustainable Statewide Water Policy," which is the natural outgrowth of the book's contents.

The list of early commentators is long, but they must be acknowledged because of the tremendous benefits received due to their sometimes-detailed comments: Sharon Green and her staff at the County Sanitation Districts of Southern California; Tom Erb and staff at the Los Angeles Department of Water and Power; Mark Mackowski, the Upper Los Angeles River Area Watermaster; Jim Leserman of the Water Replenishment

District of Southern California; Chuck White and Bob Pierotti of the State Department of Water Resources; the Watershed Management Division of County Public Works; Susan Swinson of the U.S. Forest Service; Mary Ann Dickinson of the California Urban Water Conservation Council; Rebecca Drayce of TreePeople; Tom Ash of the Irvine Ranch Water District; Margaret Clark, Greg Taylor, Donald Berry of the San Gabriel River Water Committee; John Sullivan of Pitzer College; Kathy Caldwell now of CH2M Hill; and Darwin Hall of Cal State Long Beach.

Susan Cohen must also be recognized for her yeoman help with the graphics.

This final version probably still contains some factual errors. I accept all responsibility for the inaccuracies that are certain to have been included and for the point of view, which is my own. I continue to welcome all comments and criticism.

Dorothy Green

INTRODUCTION

[We found] a delightful place among the trees on the river.
There are all the requisites for a large settlement.

FR. JUAN CRESPI, *August 2, 1769*

About all that can definitely be said about the rainfall of
Southern California is that it is meager and unpredictable.

ALFRED CLARK, *War Over the San Gabriels*

The story of the state and especially of the Los Angeles area is the story of
water. Since its founding as a Spanish pueblo in 1781, Los Angeles has
engaged in a relentless pursuit for more water, even before it was needed,
in support of its ever-growing population and economy. Water and the
growth that it supports have been the driving forces behind the development of this semiarid land, for land without water is worth little, and land
with water is worth a great deal. It is only because of the foresight and hard
work of the visionaries who were responsible for local development (and
prospered because of it) that a population of almost 10 million people now
lives in an area that could never adequately sustain a population greater than
1 million with its own local water resources.

In this book, the term *Los Angeles Area* refers not to the city of Los Angeles, but to most of Los Angeles County, the part that lies south of the San
Gabriel Mountains. It includes the Los Angeles and San Gabriel rivers watershed and the small coastal watersheds from Palos Verdes to the Santa
Monica Mountains that drain to the Santa Monica Bay. Since the county
is home to about a third of the state's population, the Los Angeles area must
then be home to about 30%.

The same forces that developed the Southland also drove water development over most of the state, leading to the growth of many of its other
cities and the growth of an incredible agricultural industry that has

achieved great prominence in the nation and in the world. That development process was carried out in an ad hoc manner, to meet the needs and desires of local leaders and entrepreneurs. Only the direct economic costs and benefits were considered. The environmental impacts of dewatering one area to serve another were not a consideration. The thought that we might some day bump up against limits was unthinkable.

Now we are bumping up against limits. Each of our water supplies is unable to deliver as promised or expected. The environment, water quality, and endangered species concerns are now front and center, and the growing populations of the region and the state are all making increasing demands on this finite resource. Since dependence on imported water is greatest in southern California and therefore these limits are being felt here first, it can be instructive to the entire state to learn from Los Angeles' experience, and profit from what it has learned. The issues addressed are statewide, but, in order to understand better how the water world works, we examine the Los Angeles area in depth as a microcosm of the state.

In preparing for the future, everyone in the state is facing many difficult decisions regarding how best to allocate the limited water supply, how to think about sustainability for our economy and life style, and the needs of an abused environment. Making those decisions requires an understanding of today's water supply, its history, how it is managed, who is in charge, and what options are available to us as we plan for the future.

Water is critical to sustaining life itself, yet its importance in maintaining Los Angeles' economy and quality of life is not reflected in the very low price we pay to have this invaluable resource delivered to our homes and businesses.

As the issues are explored, here are some of the many questions that must be addressed. What are the current decision-making processes? How and by whom are the decisions about water use made? How and by whom should they be made? Are these decisions responsive to changing needs? Should they be left to our elected representatives? At which level of government—the state legislature? city councils and planning commissions? water agency boards? professional planners? Land use decisions such as where to permit development and how the land is developed impact our water supply. What role should water agencies play in land use decisions? What role should there be for citizen involvement in these difficult and important decisions?

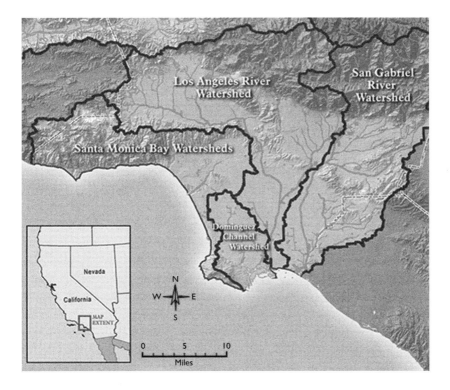

Figure 1. Map of Los Angeles Area. (SOURCE: Los Angeles and San Gabriel Rivers Watershed Council.)

We can meet the future of a growing California if water is used much more efficiently, if the management of that resource is better integrated and holistic, and if land use policies are tied to water availability. Growth should not take place in the most arid parts of the state, where more water is required to support our current life style, but should follow the principles of smart growth and watershed management. This means redeveloping the inner cores of our worn-out cities, where infrastructure already exists, around restored rivers, habitat, and parks.

Agriculture, though representing less than 3% of the state's economy, is still an important industry in the state and must be sustained while we restore our rivers and streams, protect endangered species, ensure healthful water quality, and provide for reliability that everyone can count on—all of this in a state that suffers from sporadic floods and droughts and now the uncertainty of climate change. We can meet this future while our established sources of supply are actually diminishing. We are that profligate and badly managed.

To do so requires an educated and informed citizenry. Because there are so many institutions, and because they operate below most people's radar screens, there has been little participation or even coverage by the media of these institutions, except on those rare occasions when there is scandal. Yet how and by whom our water supply is managed deserve close attention.

To set the stage, we begin by taking a quick look at the land of the region and at its climate.

A LAND AND WATER OVERVIEW

The Los Angeles River and the San Gabriel River were once unspoiled. Their waters ran freely and unpredictably across the alluvial plain that is the Los Angeles Basin. In some places the rivers flowed year-round above ground, providing the water needed for settlement. In other places the rivers went underground. They wandered in ever-changing courses, joining with springs from nearby hills to form wetlands, sloughs, or ponds, reaching the sea only in wet years. Together with the Santa Ana River floodplain, they created an artesian basin that covered nearly 300 square miles from Beverly Hills and Hollywood to Newport Beach. The names of local cities reflect this history: Artesia, Lakewood, Laguna (now called the City of Commerce), and Clearwater (now Paramount). On occasion, the Los Angeles River actually flowed out what is now the Ballona Creek instead of out to the Los Angeles Harbor area.

The Los Angeles River's ancient headwater was Encino Spring, in the San Fernando Valley. The drainage area of the Los Angeles River extends from the Santa Monica and the Santa Susanna mountains and the Simi Hills to the San Gabriel Mountains and south to the harbor. The mountains surrounding the San Fernando Valley are mostly only about 3,000 feet high, contrasting with 7,000-foot peaks in the San Gabriels. In the San Fernando Valley the river ran mostly underground and the landscape was drier than on the coastal plain. The land was dominated by live oaks and chaparral. Sediment at the eastern end of the valley, eroded off the San Gabriel Mountains, is as much as 1,000 feet thick. All of the areas around the smaller mountains and hills were once under ancient seas, as was the

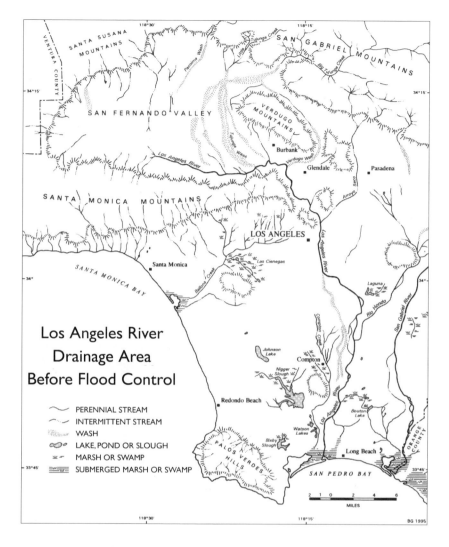

Figure 2. Los Angeles River drainage area as it once was. (SOURCE: Map by Blake Gumprecht.)

entire coastal plain all the way to what is now Pasadena and Pomona. At the Glendale Narrows, the groundwater was forced up above ground because of the granite bedrock, flowing seaward between the local mountains of Griffith Park and Glendale. It flowed above ground in the Narrows year-round, for many miles.

The ill-defined banks of both rivers below the Glendale Narrows and in and below the San Gabriel Valley were covered with a dense forest of willow and sycamore, elderberry, and wild grape. The dense undergrowth caused much of the coastal plain to be impassable. The ecosystems that evolved were rich biologically, filled with more than a hundred species of birds, deer, antelope, bear, coyotes, fox, and mountain lion. The rivers and streams teemed with fish. This extraordinarily rich ecosystem supported one of the largest concentrations of Indians in North America and, with European settlement, supported a productive agricultural economy dominated by vineyards, orange groves, and almost every fruit and vegetable known to man. In the 1880s and 1890s, shooting birds and catching fish for the table were major lucrative professions, and many duck clubs were established among the sloughs and marshes. Remnants of streams full of fish persisted as late as 1940, when a 25-inch-long steelhead trout was caught near Glendale.

The history of the region includes several ill-conceived but valiant efforts at trying to control the occasional floods of the Los Angeles and San Gabriel rivers, only to see these control efforts wash out, again and again—until, beginning in the 1930s, the Army Corps of Engineers and the County Department of Public Works built a series of dams in the mountains and in the flood plains and converted the rivers and streams into concrete storm channels.

Concrete storm channels provided two major benefits: They became smooth and straight avenues for stormwater to rush to the sea as quickly as possible, and they maximized the amount of land available for development. There has not been a damaging flood since the late 1930s. (See *The Los Angeles River: Its Life, Death, and Possible Rebirth* by Blake Gumprecht for more of this history.)

In order to understand the cycle of droughts and floods that plague the Los Angeles Area and the rationale behind this concrete storm drain system, we must understand the climate.

CLIMATE

The Los Angeles Area is well known for its sunny, moderate climate, classified as Mediterranean. Most rainfall occurs during the winter, with over 85% falling from November through March. Summers are usually hot and dry. In the coastal plain, moderate temperatures are the norm throughout

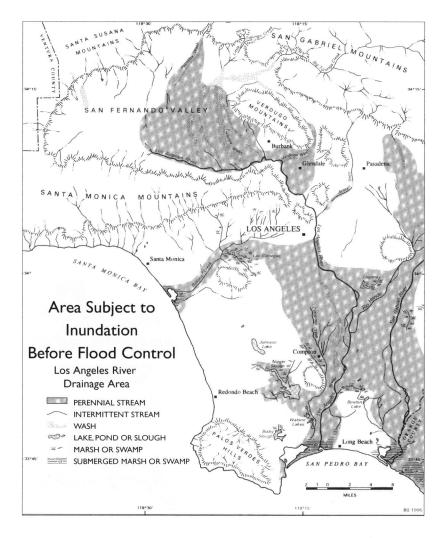

Figure 3. Los Angeles Area subject to inundation before flood control. (SOURCE: Map by Blake Gumprecht.)

the year. The inland valleys, on the other hand, experience greater fluctuations in temperature. Santa Ana winds can blow west from the Mojave Desert, usually between August and October, sometimes raising temperatures to over 100°. The amount of rainfall varies through relatively wet and dry years, with occasional droughts and occasional floods. There are no average water years. The last major drought occurred between 1987 and 1992.

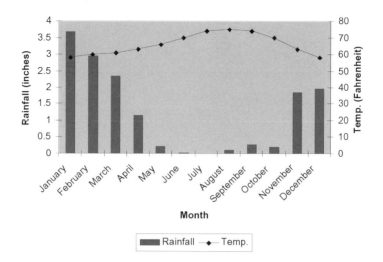

Figure 4. Average monthly precipitation and temperature at the Los Angeles Civic Center. (SOURCE: National Weather Service.)

Damaging floods, big enough actually to change the course of the Los Angeles River, were recorded in 1815, 1825, and 1889. Other destructive floods occurred in 1884, 1914, and 1938. Floods have caused extensive property damage, made hundreds of people homeless, and isolated communities, resulting in personal injury and loss of life. The great flood of 1913–14 left 177 people dead.

The destructive force of the floods was made even worse by conditions that exacerbated the situation. These conditions included the loss of riparian habitat along the edge of the rivers that had helped to contain the rivers. Habitat was removed to make room for farmland. The river banks were cut to link irrigation ditches to the river. And railroad companies built tracks next to the rivers, altering the natural drainage patterns.

Not only is rainfall in the Los Angeles area variable year to year, it is also variable geographically. The average annual precipitation varies from 15 inches in the Los Angeles Basin to 22 inches in the San Gabriel Mountains. It has been estimated that nearly 75% of the runoff in the Los Angeles Area is from the mountains.

Weather patterns in the Los Angeles Area are influenced by oscillations between the eastern Pacific high-pressure area and the northern hemisphere

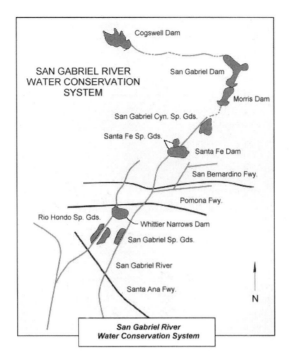

Figure 5. San Gabriel River conservation facilities, rivers, dams, etc. (SOURCE: Los Angeles County Department of Public Works.)

polar jet stream. Southern California gets most of its rain between September and March, when the jet stream tends to drift far enough south to drive these storms into the coastal mountains that stretch from Point Conception to the Mexican border.

During La Niñas, when the equatorial surface temperatures are relatively cool, the high pressure ridges stall, the jet stream is deflected north, and southern California almost always gets less rain than usual. The most devastating rains come from the west, bringing warm rain that has evaporated off a warm ocean, sometimes called the "pineapple express."

OUR RIVERS TODAY

The Los Angeles River today, now channelized, is 51 miles long. It originates in the western part of the San Fernando Valley, at the confluence of

Bell and Calabasas creeks, and discharges to the ocean at the Los Angeles/Long Beach Harbor after passing through 43 cities. The river retains some of its natural character for the only seven miles it flows through the Sepulveda Basin. The Sepulveda Basin is a multipurpose project designed to hold huge storm events on the rare occasions they occur. The basin is managed by the U.S. Army Corps of Engineers. Most of the time it serves many recreational and habitat functions. It contains two golf courses, many ball fields, a lake, picnic facilities, wildlife areas, and Japanese gardens built next to the Tillman Water Reclamation Plant.

The seven-mile portion of the river in the Glendale Narrows area is unlined (no concrete on the bottom) because of rising groundwater. The rising groundwater makes it impossible to line the bottom of the river in concrete because the geology of the Narrows constricts the subsurface flow, forcing the groundwater up into the riverbed. As a result, the narrows is one of the few places where the river provides habitat for wildlife: birds, plants, and fish. The river's estuary is also unlined downstream of Willow Street in Long Beach. There a wide variety of bird life thrives, feeding on the small crustaceans that grow on the concrete that is kept wet by the river just north of the estuary.

In addition to carrying floodwaters during the rainy seasons, the river carries water from two other sources: general urban runoff (the excess water that runs in the streets all year-round from landscape irrigation, car washing, hosing down sidewalks, etc.) and treated effluent from three wastewater treatment plants: the Tillman Plant in the Sepulveda Basin, the LA/Glendale Plant across from Griffith Park, and the Burbank Plant, which discharges to a tributary of the Los Angeles River.

There are spreading basins (ponds designed to capture stormwater and allow it to filter slowly into the ground) below Hansen Dam in the Tujunga Wash, a major tributary to the Los Angeles River. Stormwater is captured behind Hansen Dam and released to the spreading basins to infiltrate into the ground. The Los Angeles River does not have many places where spreading or percolation can occur, because of intense development and heavy clay soils that limit the amount of percolation in the western part of the San Fernando Valley and from Griffith Park south to the harbor.

The original City of Los Angeles was located on the east bank of the Los Angeles River, near the present North Broadway Bridge in downtown Los

Angeles, specifically because the river flowed year-round in that location. Competition for this limited amount of water became fierce as the region developed. In 1979, after many years in court, the water rights to the Los Angeles River were awarded to the city as Pueblo water rights, dating back to Don Gaspar de Portola, the Spanish governor of California when the city was founded. The water rights include all the native water from the entire San Fernando Valley watershed down to the confluence with the Arroyo Seco, except for sharing the groundwater in the small Sylmar Basin with the City of San Fernando. The court decision acknowledged the use of imported water and credited the overlying cities in the San Fernando Valley with 20% of the return flow of that imported water, which can be reclaimed from the groundwater basin.

The San Gabriel River today, 58 miles long, originates in the San Gabriel Mountains, where it is heavily used for recreational purposes such as fishing, picnicking, hiking, and swimming. Today, most of the upper San Gabriel River's water is stored in the Cogswell, San Gabriel, and Morris reservoirs, operated by Los Angeles County. These dams serve to store water both as flood protection and for drinking water supply. Some river water is served directly to customers, but most is stored so that it can be put into spreading grounds to percolate into the groundwater basin for later use. Both the Santa Fe Dam and the Whittier Narrows Dam are located below the mountains on the alluvial plain and serve mainly for flood control. But they both also provide large areas for a variety of recreational and habitat opportunities and pools that conserve water for recharge. The facilities behind these dams are closed only at those rare times when the space behind them is needed to provide temporary storage for very large storm flows. Both are operated by the U.S. Army Corps of Engineers.

Between the mountains and the City of Downey, located about six miles south of the Whittier Narrows Dam, the San Gabriel River is unlined (with no concrete on the bottom), and, with the use of inflatable rubber dams, serves as a recharge facility. One of the dams is also used to divert water into the San Gabriel River Coastal Spreading Grounds in Pico Rivera, and a radial dam is used to divert water into the spreading grounds along side the Rio Hondo in Montebello. The rubber dams can be deflated and the radial dam raised quickly during very large storms.

Besides stormwater, the river contains urban runoff (the excess water that flows off city streets even during dry weather) and reclaimed water from

Figure 6. Photo of Rindge Dam with waterfall off its face. (SOURCE: Jim Hutchison, U.S. Army Corps of Engineers, Los Angeles District.)

several county sanitation districts' water reclamation plants. Reclaimed water is highly treated wastewater from municipal sewage treatment plants. The lower San Gabriel River, starting at about Firestone Blvd., is a concrete-lined channel. The river empties into the ocean east of the Port of Long Beach, next to Los Alamitos Bay. The estuary has become industrialized with oil wells, refineries, and power plants. What is left of the estuary, now called the Los Cerritos Wetlands, is being studied for public acquisition and restoration.

Some of the water that flows off the mountains is captured by tunnels and treated and introduced into the local drinking water system. Most is diverted into areas where it is infiltrated into the ground.

Smaller channels and creeks empty into Santa Monica Bay. The largest is Ballona Creek, which is totally concrete and carries a significant load of urban runoff year-round. Several smaller creeks that flow out of the Santa Monica Mountains deliver runoff during wet weather. The largest of them, Malibu Creek, also delivers treated wastewater sporadically throughout the year. Malibu Creek was dammed many years ago to provide the local landowner, the Rindge family, with a water supply. Rindge

Dam is now totally silted up, and there is a waterfall off the dam face most of the year. Otherwise, many of the creeks that drain off the Santa Monica Mountains to Santa Monica Bay are still in mostly natural condition. Once the Rindge Dam on Malibu Creek and other impediments are removed on this and other creeks (being planned), spawning steelhead trout might yet flourish once again.

Chapter 1 | LOS ANGELES AREA WATER SUPPLIES

The almost total development of the Los Angeles Area was made possible only because of three giant aqueduct systems, built at public expense, that bring water from hundreds of miles away. The area continues to be dependent also on local rainwater and groundwater for about a third of its water supply. This chapter quickly reviews local surface water, groundwater, and the three aqueduct systems that import water to the Los Angeles Area, the reliability of each source, and the environmental and/or water quality constraints that apply to each. These are the sources on which the Los Angeles Area depends for its drinking water supply.

LOCAL SURFACE WATER: RIVERS, STREAMS, LAKES, AND RESERVOIRS

Surface water in the Los Angeles Area comes from the skies, in the form of rain or snow. This is the water that runs off into rivers and creeks, evaporates, is used by plants in their growing cycle, or infiltrates into the soil, replenishing our groundwater resources. The Los Angeles Area has two major river systems, the Los Angeles and San Gabriel rivers, and several large creek systems, Ballona and Malibu creeks being the largest. These rivers and creeks rise in the local mountains, where rainfall is much heavier than on the coastal plain. The average rainfall at the Los Angeles Civic Center is 15 inches a

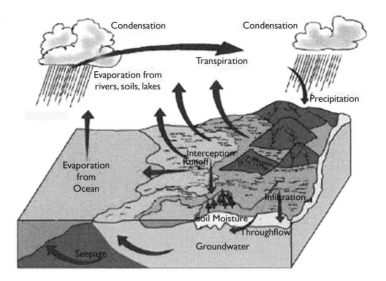

Figure 7. The hydrologic cycle. (SOURCE: Los Angeles City Bureau of Sanitation.)

year, whereas it rains as much as 40 inches a year on some of the peaks of the San Gabriel Mountains.

The Storm Drain System

The single-purpose storm drain system was built to contain and pass a capital storm. The system consists of an extensive network of underground storm drains connected to an above-ground system of concrete-lined channels that have replaced our native rivers and creeks. Reservoirs, check dams, detention and debris basins, and other facilities are also part of the storm drain system. They capture water for flood control purposes (holding peak flows until after the storm passes), or they capture water for later infiltration into the groundwater basins. With peak flows captured, the water can be released after the storm has passed and when there is more capacity in the storm channels. Then, water left in storage can be released slowly into spreading grounds or basins until it gradually percolates down into the ground and into the groundwater.

A *capital storm* or *flood* is defined by the Los Angeles County Department of Public Works as runoff from a 50-year-frequency-design storm falling on a saturated watershed over a four-day period. After it has rained for three days and the ground is fully saturated, the heavens open up and dump, in a 24-hour period, the amount of water that would be contained in a storm that could happen only once in 50 years. For example, in the foothills of the San Gabriel Mountains, where Pasadena, Azusa, and Glendora are located, the capital flood for which the storm drain system is designed would generate the following amounts of rainfall: 1.1 inches on the first day, 4.4 inches on the second, 3.9 inches on the third, and 11.0 inches on the fourth. (For more definitions, see the Glossary.)

In the 1920s, roughly 95% of the rain falling on Los Angeles either infiltrated into the ground or evaporated. Only 5% ran off to the sea. Today, with the extensive development and the paving over of our urban environment (as much as 80% of the land is now covered with roofs, roads, parking lots, patios, etc.) and the construction of the massive storm channel system, about 50% of stormwater runs off in the Los Angeles River drainage area, while 50% either infiltrates or evaporates. About 90% of the San Gabriel River's flow is captured for recharge into the groundwater supply. On average, only about 20% of the upper Los Angeles River native runoff is captured, due to a lack of sufficient spreading capacity and the prevalence of clay soils.

The concrete-lined channels that cross the Los Angeles Area carry rainwater to the Santa Monica Bay, the Los Angeles/Long Beach Harbor, or Seal Beach. During dry months, the flow is composed of urban runoff (the excess water that flows in our streets), effluent from water reclamation plants (sometimes called sewage treatment plants), and groundwater seepage. During a heavy rainfall, these channels become dangerous torrents flushing large quantities of stormwater, trash, debris, and pollutants to the ocean. They accomplish the single-purpose job they were designed to do well.

Spreading Basins

Spreading basins are large, shallow man-made pits or ponds where water is slowly allowed to percolate into the soil in order to recharge or replenish the underlying groundwater basins. Spreading basins are filled with stormwater that has been diverted into the spreading basins or held in reservoirs or lakes for future spreading. On average, nearly 279,000 acre-feet of water in Los Angeles County are returned to the groundwater supply in the county each year through spreading operations. Like surface water, the quantity of water diverted to spreading basins each year is affected by weather conditions. In water year 1997–98, a wet year, 444,000 acre-feet of water were spread. That number dropped to 172,000 acre-feet in water year 1998–99. Imported water and reclaimed water are also spread.

Reservoirs/Lakes

A large volume of surface water is held in reservoirs or lakes throughout the Los Angeles Area. Though the terms may be confused and interchangeable, a reservoir is always associated with a dam. Lakes, on the other hand, exist naturally, but many reservoirs have "lake" in their name. All major lakes within the Los Angeles Area are actually reservoirs. The lakes and reservoirs listed in Table 1 were created for a variety of purposes. Captured stormwater is conserved for later release into spreading grounds, where it percolates into the groundwater basin, increasing our drinking water supply. Stormwater runoff is captured to avoid flooding, stored, and later released to the ocean or to a spreading basin. Water imported from outside the region may be conveyed into reservoirs for the purposes of storage and/or regulation of flow to accommodate variability of demand. And any number of recreational activities, including fishing, swimming, and boating, may occur.

Role of U.S. Forest Service Land: The Angeles National Forest

An estimated 30% of the Los Angeles Basin's water supply comes from National Forest lands. The Angeles National Forest was among the first national forests established, and it was established with the prime purpose of protecting the water supply. The role that the forest plays as a major water source and the need to protect this precious water supply were recognized very early.

Two-thirds of the land area of the forest is considered to be sensitive watershed, due to land slopes that are greater than 60°, or steeper than the angle of repose. The mountains are so steep that rock and debris flows or mudslides are prevalent whenever the land becomes saturated with rainwater or is shaken by an earthquake.

Rainfall in the mountains varies wildly with elevation and location. It averages about 22 inches per year forestwide, with as much as 40 inches a year falling in the higher elevations. The trees and other vegetation in the forest use a significant portion of the total precipitation that falls on the forest. An estimated 230,000 acre-feet of water moves directly into the

TABLE 1. Major Reservoirs and Lakes in Los Angeles County

Name	Design Capacity (AF)	Management	Purpose	Water Source	Location
RESERVOIRS					
Big Dalton	1,053	LA County	Flood control, conservation	Stormwater	Big Dalton Canyon, 4 miles north of Glendora
Big Tujunga	6,240	LA County	Flood control, conservation	Stormwater	Big Tujunga Canyon, 10 miles northeast of Sunland
Brea	4,000	U.S. Army	Flood control	Stormwater	
Cogswell	12,298	LA County	Flood control, conservation	Stormwater	22 miles north of Azusa
Devil's Gate	4,601	LA County	Flood control, conservation	Stormwater	Arroyo Seco, northeast of La Verne
Eaton Wash	956	LA County	Conservation, debris storage	Stormwater	Northeast of Pasadena
Encino	9,800	LA City	Water supply	LA Aqueduct	Santa Monica Mountains
Fullerton	764	U.S. Army	Flood control	Stormwater	
Hansen	26,776	U.S. Army	Flood control	Stormwater	East San Fernando Valley
Hollywood	4,036	LA City	Water supply	LA Aqueduct	Hollywood Hills
Live Oak	250	LA County	Flood control, conservation	Stormwater	25 miles northeast of La Verne
Lopez	441	U.S. Army	Flood control	Stormwater	
Los Angeles	10,000	LA City	Water supply	LA Aqueduct	
Morris	39,300	LA County	Conservation	Stormwater	San Gabriel Canyon, 5 miles north of Azusa

Name	Capacity	Owner	Purpose	Water Source	Location
Pacoima	6,060	LA County	Flood control, conservation	Stormwater	Pacoima Canyon, 4 mile northeast of San Fernando
Puddingstone	17,398	LA County	Flood control, flow diversion, recreation	Stormwater	1 mile south of San Dimas
Puddingstone Diversion	148	LA County	Flood control, conservation	Stormwater	2 miles northeast of San Dimas
Santa Anita	1376	LA County	Flood control, conservation	Stormwater	2.5 miles north of Arcadia
San Dimas	1,496	LA County	Flood control, conservation	Stormwater	3 miles northeast of San Dimas
San Gabriel	53,344	LA County	Flood control, conservation	Stormwater	San Gabriel Canyon, 7.5 miles north of Azusa
Santa Fe	32,109	U.S. Army	Flood control	Stormwater	San Gabriel Valley on San Gabriel River
Sawpit	476	LA County	Flood control, conservation	Stormwater	2 miles north of Monrovia
Sepulveda	17,425	U.S. Army	Flood control	Stormwater	In San Fernando Valley
Stone Canyon	10,372	LA City	Water supply	LA Aqueduct	In Bel Air, Santa Monica Mountains
Thompson Creek	812	LA County	Flood control, conservation	Stormwater	3 miles north of Claremont
Westlake	9,600	Las Virgenes MWD	Water supply	Colorado River Aqueduct or State Water Project	
Whittier Narrows	67,060	U.S. Army	Flood control	Stormwater	On San Gabriel River between cities of South El Monte and Whittier

(continued)

TABLE 1. *(continued)*

Name	Design Capacity (AF)	Management	Purpose	Water Source	Location
LAKES					
Echo Park		City of Los Angeles	Recreation	Local runoff and groundwater	
El Dorado		City of Long Beach	Recreation	Local runoff, groundwater and recycled water	
Harbor Park		City of Los Angeles	Recreation	Local runoff (municipal water added when necessary)	
Malibu Lake		Private	Recreation	Local runoff	
Peck Road Park		LA County	Recreation, flood control, conservation	Runoff from San Gabriel Mountains	
Westlake		Private	Recreation	Local runoff and groundwater	

SOURCES: Los Angeles County Department of Public Works and Army Corps of Engineers.

Figure 8. Photo of Big Dalton Dam and Reservoir. (SOURCE: Los Angles Bureau of Sanitation.)

groundwater through deep percolation in the upland areas and along small ephemeral drainages. An additional 350,000 acre-feet of surface runoff is available on average for recharge downstream along the larger channels. This adds up to 580,000 acre-feet of water for recharge.

Capturing More Stormwater Runoff on Site

In order to maximize our use of local water, there have been several initiatives in recent years to increase the amount of stormwater infiltrated into the ground, on site, at an individual home, development, or neighborhood. The Los Angeles Regional Water Quality Control Board now requires that new construction (either new development or redevelopment) retain the first ¾ inch of storms within a 24-hour period on site or, minimally, that it be filtered before release, for the purpose of improving the quality of stormwater or urban runoff. About 80% of all local storms are of this size or smaller. Several local efforts have been launched to explore ways to capture more stormwater for recharge. See the "Watershed Management" section of Chapter 3.

Water Quality Concerns of Stormwater Retention

Due to concerns over possible contaminants found on city streets and in the air, studies are under way to assess the potential negative impacts of infiltrating stormwater into the groundwater supply through on-site infiltration. However, the U.S. Bureau of Reclamation has stated, "Research on the topics of urban stormwater runoff quality and of groundwater infiltration using the first three-quarters of an inch of a storm event indicate that on-site biological natural treatment along with existing and emerging technologies can keep the storm waters from polluting streams, bays, and estuaries while providing a useable water supply" (http://www.lc.usbr .gov/~scao/planpgm2.htm).

The Los Angeles & San Gabriel Rivers Watershed Council's Water Augmentation Study, Phase II Final Report, concluded: "Data collected to date indicate that there is no statistically significant degradation of groundwater quality from infiltration of stormwater-borne constituents. Groundwater quality has generally improved for most constituents at sites with shallow groundwater" (www.lasgrwc.org).

GROUNDWATER

The Los Angeles Area sits atop a relatively large water supply contained in a number of huge groundwater basins. These massive basins of water, which lie anywhere from a few feet to hundreds of feet below the surface, have been replenished for millions of years by the natural inflow of rainwater, which infiltrates the soil and percolates down to the groundwater table. The San Gabriel Valley and the eastern part of the San Fernando Valley are composed of sand and gravel that have washed off the mountains over the millennia. This alluvium has many spaces between the sediments, called *pore space*, where water is stored; because of the porous nature of the soils, these spaces can easily fill with water when it rains, and then it can be pumped up as needed. The San Gabriel Valley Basin can hold 3.2 million acre-feet of water. Within the state, only Shasta and Oroville dams, in northern California, hold more.

For eons, the groundwater beneath the Los Angeles Area remained untapped. At first, groundwater was available to anyone who possessed the means to access it. But as the population grew (and with it the demand for water) overpumping began to affect the groundwater basins adversely. Older, shallow wells ceased being productive. The water that had flowed from 1,596 artesian wells ceased to flow, and, in the case of the coastal groundwater basins, the associated decreasing pressure caused seawater to intrude into the groundwater basin and degrade water quality. No longer could shallow wells meet the needs of agricultural and municipal demands.

With the invention of the deep-well turbine pumps, groundwater became economically accessible in quantities that could sustain new industries and a larger population. These huge new pumps also laid the groundwork for more water wars.

Today, the Los Angeles Area receives 40–45% of its water supply from the ground. In 1998, 596,997 acre-feet were produced for use in the Los Angeles Area. In 1997, groundwater production was slightly higher, at 640,256 acre-feet, reflecting the variation in rainfall patterns.

Strategies for Managing Groundwater Basins

In response to the high demand placed on the groundwater basins as well as the reduction in natural recharge caused by urbanization (paving over the landscape), several strategies have evolved to maintain the integrity of the basins.

ADJUDICATION As the population of the Los Angeles Area grew and the groundwater was drawn down, methods for protecting the groundwater basins from overdraft had to be developed. Under current law, landowners can extract as much groundwater from under their property as they can put to beneficial use. The only way to deal with the conflicts that resulted from this tragedy of the commons (where water belonged to everyone and no one was in charge, and so everyone took without concern for the others) was to find a way to allocate not just the surface water, but the groundwater as well, to determine who has the right to pump how much water and to put into place a mechanism for keeping everyone honest. To manage groundwater better and to prevent further

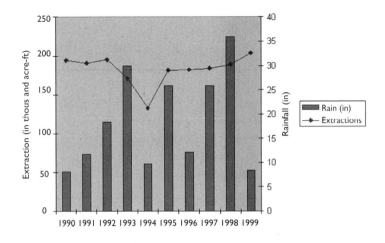

Figure 9. Groundwater extractions from and rainfall in the Central Basin, 1990–1999. (SOURCE: Central Basin MWD.)

water quality problems, most of the groundwater basins in the Los Angeles Area were adjudicated.

The courts defined which people or water agencies have rights to how much of the groundwater by allocating shares of ownership based on historic pumping records. Then a Watermaster is appointed to see that all those with permission to pump do not exceed their annual allocation. The role of the Watermaster can include such things as keeping track of water extractions, ordering replacement water (often imported water), overseeing recharge activities, and assessing water quality.

Adjudication is a long and difficult process. The Raymond Basin was the first groundwater basin in the state to be adjudicated. Today, according to the Association of Groundwater Agencies (AGWA), of the 21 groundwater basins that have been adjudicated, 7 are located in Los Angeles County, and 16 are located south of the Tehachapi Mountains.

SPREADING   The Los Angeles County Department of Public Works manages most of the spreading basins in the Los Angeles Area. The county entered into agreements with the Watermasters of the various groundwater basins to spread specific amounts of water. For example, in the Main San Gabriel Basin, the county signed a cooperative agreement with the Watermaster, in February 1975, to accept and spread up to 250 cubic feet per second (cfs)

Figure 10. Photo of Los Angeles County–operated spreading grounds. (SOURCE: County Public Works.)

of supplemental imported water. Over time, as the San Gabriel Valley population increased, the supplemental water deliveries have also increased. This imported water is directed into the same spreading basins into which the county also spreads captured storm water and reclaimed water. This requires careful timing and management.

The Department of Public Works operates 2,436 acres of spreading grounds and soft-bottom channel spreading areas. It assists in the operation and maintenance of 269 acres owned by others. An additional 656 acres are controlled and managed by other agencies. In addition to these facilities, a large portion of the San Gabriel River from Morris Dam to Whittier Narrows Dam has an unlined channel bottom that also infiltrates water into the ground and therefore returns an additional estimated yearly average of 84,161 acre-feet to the groundwater supply (www.ladpw.org).

INJECTION As groundwater levels in the coastal basins were pumped down below sea level, salty ocean water began to infiltrate into the fresh groundwater supply. This process is called *seawater intrusion*. To protect drinking water quality, wells were drilled along the coast, and fresh potable water mixed with reclaimed water is injected into the ground to recharge the coastal groundwater basins. The primary purpose of these injection wells is to protect the groundwater quality by forming a freshwater barrier between the intruding seawater and the groundwater supply. They also serve to replenish the basins with freshwater. In conjunction with the injection wells, observation wells are installed to monitor the salt content of the groundwater.

CONJUNCTIVE USE AND IN-LIEU REPLENISHMENT Conjunctive use is the practice of using surface water in conjunction with groundwater. In other words, when surface water is plentiful (late winter and spring), it is delivered to consumers, in preference to groundwater, and spread or put underground to replenish underground aquifers. Imported water is used to augment local water by replenishing the underground aquifers when surface water is plentiful. Then water stored underground can be pumped up for use when surface water is not available in the summer and fall. In other words, water is stored during the wet season against need during the dry season. Some groundwater managers are now encouraging and implementing conjunctive use to store not just wet-season water against dry-season need, but wet-year surpluses against dry-year need.

In-lieu replenishment is another form of conjunctive use, where a groundwater producer elects to participate in the seasonal storage program of the Metropolitan Water District of Southern California (MWD) and purchases surplus wet-season imported water at a cheaper rate in exchange for not taking a portion of its water rights for that year. This program

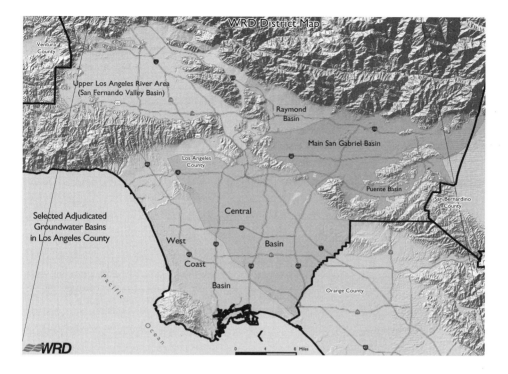

Figure 11. Map of adjudicated groundwater basins in Los Angeles County. (SOURCE: Water Replenishment District of Southern California.)

is designed specifically to encourage conjunctive use—to store imported water underground when it is plentiful against dry-season need. It encourages the use of local surface water supplies to meet local need while storing imported water underground during winter and spring months. In the West Basin and Central Coast Basins alone, a total of 23,516 acre-feet of groundwater were conserved in FY 1998–99 through in-lieu replenishment.

In addition to maintaining water supplies underground, the program is designed to replenish depleted areas of a groundwater basin where conventional recharge has proved inadequate; to increase the effectiveness of seawater-intrusion barriers by reducing nearby extractions; to reduce total annual extractions from the basin; and to help even out the demand for imported water by creating a market when there normally would be less demand for imported water. Residents use more water during the summer, after the winter rains have ended.

Figure 11 is a map of the major groundwater basins in the Los Angeles Area. The State Department of Water Resources publishes Bulletin 118 (updated regularly), which reviews the groundwater resources of the state, based on the reports from those who use groundwater (http://www.groundwater .water.ca.gov/bulletin118/).

MAIN SAN GABRIEL BASIN This 167-square-mile basin lies beneath the San Gabriel Valley, with Alhambra on the west, Monterey Park and the City of Industry to the south, San Dimas to the east, and Monrovia and Glendora to the north. The basin is composed of coarse sand and gravel that has washed off the mountains for millennia, creating an ideal condition for quick infiltration into the ground. In addition to natural percolation of rainwater and subsurface flow from smaller adjacent basins, the San Gabriel Basin is artificially recharged with an average of 110,000 acre-feet per year of stormwater that has been captured and put into spreading basins.

Water managers of the Main San Gabriel Basin seek to maintain the water level in the basin, as measured by the depth to water in the key well located in Baldwin Park, the middle of the basin. The optimal groundwater level is between 200 and 250 feet below the surface. Above 250 feet, imported water may not be spread, only local water, because otherwise there would be local flooding and, besides, local water is free. This key well water level can drop dramatically below 250 feet during periods of extended drought.

Though no recycled water is returned to the basin, the Upper San Gabriel Valley Municipal Water District is currently developing the Recycled Water Demonstration Project in order to be able to use recycled water from the San Jose Creek Water Reclamation Plant, operated by the County sanitation districts, as a future source of recharge for the basin. The storage capacity of the basin is estimated to be 8.6 million acre-feet.

Because much of the land overlying the Main San Gabriel Basin has been used for industrial purposes, especially during and immediately after World War II, when environmental concerns were minimal if even present, some of the groundwater in this basin has become contaminated with industrial solvents and the chemicals used to make rocket fuel. As a result, several Superfund sites are located in this basin.

RAYMOND BASIN This 40-square-mile basin in the Pasadena area is made up of the Monk Hill, Pasadena, and Santa Anita subbasins. The Raymond Fault separates the Raymond Basin from the Main San Gabriel Valley Basin to the southeast. In addition to natural recharge, surface water from the Arroyo Seco is diverted to spreading grounds in the basin. The first water was extracted in 1881, and by 1940 it was learned that the basin had been in overdraft since 1913. In 1944, this basin was the subject of the first basin-wide adjudication of groundwater rights in California.

PUENTE BASIN This 10,900-acre (17-square-mile) basin is tributary to the Main San Gabriel Basin and is hydraulically connected to it, with no barriers to groundwater movement. It is bounded by the San Jose Hills to the north and the Puente Hills to the south. It is not, however, within the legal jurisdiction of the Main San Gabriel Basin, though its management is reported through the Main San Gabriel Basin Watermaster.

CENTRAL BASIN This 277-square-mile basin lies in the southeastern part of Los Angeles County under the cities of Montebello, Cerritos, and Compton, among others, south of the Whittier Narrows Dam. Because a layer of impermeable material separates the groundwater supply from the surface, little of the basin's groundwater is replenished by the percolation of local rainfall. Most of the basin's natural replenishment occurs from surface inflow through the Whittier Narrows and groundwater flowing down-gradient from the Main San Gabriel Basin. Aggressive spreading and injection wells artificially replenish the basin with both imported and reclaimed water from the San Jose Creek, Whittier Narrows, and Pomona wastewater reclamation plants operated by the Los Angeles County Sanitation Districts.

Prior to 1961, groundwater from the basin satisfied most of the local water demand, but today, in spite of efforts to recharge the basin, more than half of the supply is met with imported water. In addition, a contamination plume from the Main San Gabriel Basin is beginning to migrate into the Central Basin through the Whittier Narrows.

WEST COAST BASIN This 160-square-mile basin lies to the west of the Central Basin. The two basins sit adjacent to one another, separated by the Newport-Inglewood Fault. Though no spreading occurs in the West Coast Basin because of the subsurface clay layers, substantial amounts of water spread in the Central Basin recharge the West Coast Basin as well. Two seawater-intrusion projects, built to prevent seawater from intruding into the underground drinking water supply, also return water to the basin through injection wells.

UPPER LOS ANGELES RIVER AREA   The Upper Los Angeles River Area (ULARA) is defined as the watershed of the upper Los Angeles River and its tributaries above the junction of the Los Angeles River and the Arroyo Seco. It includes the entire San Fernando Valley watershed. ULARA covers 513 square miles, of which 321 square miles are mountainous or hilly, with insignificant groundwater supplies. The relatively flat valley, encompassing 192 square miles, is underlain by four distinct groundwater basins.

1.   The San Fernando Basin (175 square miles), the largest of the four, underlies most of the San Fernando Valley. The native safe water yield from this basin has been determined to be 43,660 acre-feet per year. The cities of Los Angeles, Burbank, and Glendale have a right to extract imported return water from this basin averaging about 55,000 acre-feet a year.

2.   The Sylmar Basin (8.8 square miles) lies to the north. The safe yield is 6,510 acre-feet per year.

3.   The Verdugo Basin (6.9 square miles) lies to the east. The prescriptive right of the pumpers is 7,150 acre-feet per year.

4.   The Eagle Rock Basin (1.3 square miles), the smallest of the four, lies to the southeast. This basin has no significant native safe yield but can be replenished and drawn from.

Rainfall and surface runoff from the San Gabriel Mountains and the Tujunga, Pacoima, and Verdugo washes replenish the San Fernando Valley basins naturally. Stormwater runoff (and, perhaps soon, reclaimed water) is spread, contributing to their replenishment. The average annual amount of water spread to recharge the basins located below Hansen Dam in the Tujunga Wash is 26,171 acre-feet, but in 1998–99 only 14,662 acre-feet were spread because it was a dry year.

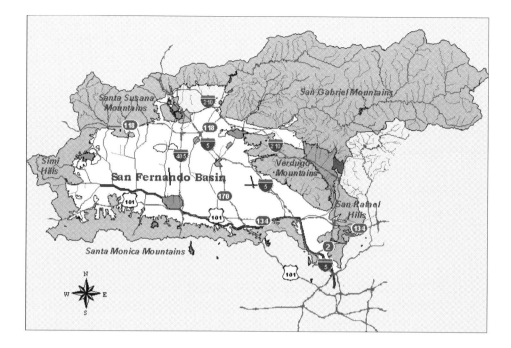

Figure 12. Map of San Fernando Valley groundwater basins. (SOURCE: Los Angeles Department of Water and Power.)

SANTA MONICA BASIN This 45-square-mile basin lies beneath the cities of Santa Monica, Culver City, and Los Angeles (West Los Angeles) and is not adjudicated. No spreading and no injection activities occur. The basin is divided into three subbasins, separated by north–south faults: the Coastal Subbasin, the Crestal Subbasin, and the Charnock Subbasin. Total production from Santa Monica Basin wells was 957 acre-feet in 1999. This number is far below its historical production of up to 9,000 acre-feet per year, due to extensive MTBE contamination, to be discussed later.

HOLLYWOOD BASIN This 15-square-mile basin lies beneath the cities of Los Angeles, Beverly Hills, and West Hollywood. Because of poor water quality and the small amount of water extracted from this basin each year, it has not been necessary to adjudicate it. The Hollywood Basin is located between two branches of the Hollywood Fault and encompasses six aquifers. The City of Beverly Hills pumped up to 3,500 acre-feet per year for 69 years, until 1976, when it closed down its wells and treatment facility in favor of buying all of its water from MWD. It maintains water rights to the basin, although it has no court-adjudicated rights. The city recently completed an advanced water treatment plant, utilizing reverse osmosis technology, to treat water extracted from the Hollywood Basin in order to reduce its dependence on imported supplies once again.

Eric Reichard of the United States Geological Survey (USGS), in a personal communication, considers the Central, West, Santa Monica, and Hollywood basins as parts of one large interrelated system.

Water Quality Concerns

The groundwater in many places has become contaminated by septic systems, agricultural chemicals, and industry. As a result, several Superfund sites are now located in the San Gabriel Valley and the eastern San Fernando Valley. Many wells that had been producing drinking water for local residents have been closed, and a plume of contamination is migrating under the Whittier Narrows Dam into the Central Basin. There are also concerns about rainwater infiltrating through contaminated soils in industrial places that have been identified as *brownfields*. See Chapter 4, "Drinking Water Quality," for a more detailed discussion of these issues.

IMPORTED WATER

The Los Angeles Area has large basins of groundwater lying beneath it, yet extractions from those basins fall far short of meeting the water needs of the current population. Any demand that local groundwater or surface water cannot meet is made up with water imported from outside the region by three major publicly financed aqueduct systems. These aqueducts are the Los Angeles Aqueducts, the Colorado River Aqueducts, and the California Aqueduct, which is part of the State Water Project. Each aqueduct system is overcommitted, being asked to deliver more water than it can. Each system is facing difficult environmental constraints. The Colorado River and State Water Project water also have water quality constraints.

Following a brief description of each system is a discussion of the reliability of each supply and the many pressures each is experiencing: environmental, water quality, and area of origin.

A detailed history of all of the aqueducts can be found in *The Great Thirst: Californians and Water—a History* by Norris Hundley. UC Press, 2001.

Los Angeles Aqueducts

The Los Angeles Aqueducts system is often associated with one man, William Mulholland. Never formally educated as an engineer, Mulholland taught himself hydrology at night, and because of his intelligence, determination, pragmatism and hard work, he became Superintendent in 1886 of the city's water system. In 1904, he traveled with others to the Owens Valley, 200 miles north of Los Angeles in search of water, to determine if it could be acquired and how best to move it to the city. The City then sent men to the Owens Valley to purchase farmland and their associated riparian water rights.

Then the city's residents had to be convinced to fund the aqueduct that would bring the water to their city. The Los Angeles Times' Chandler family and others with investments in the land that would be watered by the potential aqueduct launched a campaign that resulted in the city voting ten to one in favor of the project.

In 1905, this city of only 200,000 people approved a bond measure of $1.5 million to purchase land and water rights in the Owens Valley, the equivalent of $2 billion today. Two years later, voters approved a bond act for $23 million ($27 billion in today's dollars) to build one of the most impressive engineering feats in the nation—an aqueduct that would bring water from 233 miles away, so carefully engineered that no pumps are required. The aqueduct is gravity feed all the way.

Mulholland designed and supervised the construction, which he completed in nine years, ahead of schedule and under budget. This feat has often been compared to the difficulty of building the Panama Canal.

Since its completion in 1913, the aqueduct has been extended north to Mono Lake as part of a second aqueduct. The second Los Angeles Aqueduct, roughly parallel to the first, was completed in the 1970s, increasing the capacity to deliver water to the City of Los Angeles. The capacity of both barrels is 560,000 acre-feet a year. Three sources of water are sent to the City of Los Angeles from this region: Mono Lake's watershed, the Owens River, and Owens Valley groundwater.

The massive redistribution of water from the Owens and Mono basins to the City of Los Angeles has had both environmental and social consequences. Most residents of these eastern Sierra Communities are grateful to the city for purchasing most of the land in the region. There is very little development and no billboards on Highway 395. Others wish for more people and development.

Mono Lake is an ancient saline lake with no outlet. It supports a unique ecosystem of brine flies and brine shrimp that are the sources of food for an amazing number of birds on the Pacific flyway. They eat and rest at the lake before flying on. Islands in the lake provide safe nesting sites for one of the largest colonies of California seagulls. Four streams that fed Mono Lake were diverted into the aqueduct, sending a yearly average of 90,000 acre-feet to Los Angeles. As a result, the water level of the lake dropped as far as 17 feet below the desired level of 6,391 feet above sea level.

ENVIRONMENTAL CONSEQUENCES Diverting the streams and lowering the water level increased the salinity of the lake, threatening its ecosystem and exposing a land bridge to one of the islands within the lake. Predators could cross on the land bridge to attack nesting birds.

Law suits brought by the Audubon Society, the Mono Lake Committee, and CalTrout forced the State Water Resources Control Board to adopt regulations in 1994 restricting Los Angeles' diversion from the basin until Mono Lake water levels increased from approximately 6,376 to 6,391 feet above sea level. Even when such levels are reached, which is not expected to occur before 2015, the City of Los Angeles will be restricted to a yearly diversion of 30,000 acre-feet per year, one-third its historical average from Mono Lake.

The diversion of the Owens River to both local farmers and Los Angeles has dewatered the riverbed and the wetlands that were once a major feature of the valley, and it has turned Owens Lake into a dry lakebed. Owens Lake was once plied by steamships carrying lead and silver from the mines in the White Mountains on the eastern side of the lake. Dust storms originating on the dry lakebed surface significantly degrade the region's air quality.

Owens Valley groundwater has been pumped down, mined by both the city and local residents. Lowering the water table below the root zones of native plants has caused changes in the entire ecosystem of the valley. This situation has been resolved, thanks to cooperative pumping agreements between Inyo County and the Los Angeles Department of Water and Power (LADWP) to protect local agriculture and wildlife.

The LADWP is under court order to restore Mono Lake, rewater parts of the Owens River, restore some wetlands in the basin, and control the dust from Owens Dry Lake. It is experimenting with shallow flooding and growing salt-tolerant vegetation on the lake bed and is applying dust control measures over an ever increasing portion of the lake bed. These environmental restoration efforts are all using water that formerly was part of the city's water supply. The city has not been meeting court-ordered deadlines and has been sued to force compliance.

Over the next 20 years, the City of Los Angeles estimates that it will be able to take on an average 321,000 acre-feet per year through the Los Angeles Aqueducts, only about 57% of the 560,000-acre-feet capacity of the aqueducts, about a little more than a third less than it had been taking.

The Mono Lake Committee, working cooperatively with LADWP, was successful in identifying alternate sources of water needed to solve the basin's problems. They were also successful in securing both state and federal funding to help pay for them. The alternative sources include a massive toilet retrofit program for city residents, to reduce the amount of water used per flush from 5–7 gallons to 1.6 gallons per flush, and the construction of the East Valley Water Recycling Project, which will bring treated wastewater to the spreading grounds below Hansen Dam for recharge into the groundwater. In October 2001, LADWP reimbursed its customers for the 1 millionth ultralow-flow toilet.

To make up for the continuing shortfall in water needed to supply Los Angeles residents, LADWP purchases additional imported water from the Metropolitan Water District. The state is so plumbed, with connections between agencies and aqueduct systems, that water can be transferred from one agency to another with relative ease. However MWD's supplies are also under increasing pressure.

WATER QUALITY Because the source of water is essentially snow melt off the Sierra Nevada Mountains, Los Angeles Aqueducts' water quality is amazingly good, not heavily mineralized. It averages about 210 milligrams per liter total dissolved solids.

The Los Angeles Aqueduct was far from being fully exploited before the City of Los Angeles and others began looking for additional water supplies. The first surveying expedition for the Colorado River Aqueduct, led by William Mulholland, took place in 1923. The construction of such a massive project would require the backing of more than one city. In 1928, a total of 13 cities, including Los Angeles, banded together to lobby the state legislature to form the Metropolitan Water District of Southern California (MWD), the special district needed to build and manage the Colorado River Aqueduct. Three years later the residents of MWD's member cities passed a $220 million bond act to fund the aqueduct's construction. Construction began in 1932.

Over the next 10 years, a total of 35,000 men would endure the harsh California desert while constructing the 242-mile-long aqueduct, composed of 92 miles of tunnels, five pumping plants, and 144 underground siphons.

When completed in 1941, there were no takers for the Colorado River Aqueduct's water. A few wet years had replenished the groundwater supplies in the Los Angeles Area, and MWD was forced to offer water at no charge in order to build a user base. But the need for water in southern California grew as World War II progressed. A lot of the industry needed to support the war effort located to the Los Angeles Area. General Patton prepared his army for combat in North Africa by training in the Lower Mojave Desert, where he drew on the aqueduct to supply his troops. Other military bases were built in northern San Diego and Orange counties, which needed water. As a result, all of San Diego County joined MWD and brought with it its allotment of Colorado River water. The pipelines built to service these military bases provided the backbone water distribution system needed to accommodate the postwar population explosion in southern California.

As southern California grew with the postwar boom, MWD expanded its territory to include other cities and agencies. By 2000, MWD supplied water to 26 member agencies and 127 cities in six counties on the coastal plain from Ventura to the Mexican border

The Colorado River Aqueduct has the capacity to deliver 1.2 million acre-feet per year of Colorado River water. The Colorado River travels 1,440 miles through seven states (Utah, Wyoming, Colorado, New Mexico, Arizona,

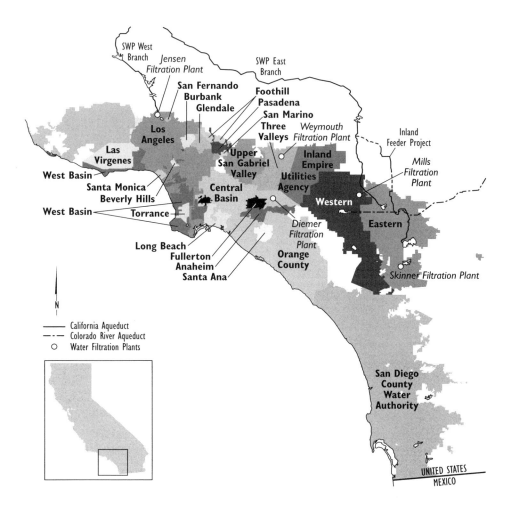

Figure 13. Map of the MWD service territory and member agencies. (SOURCE: MWD.)

Nevada, and California) and the Republic of Mexico. Its drainage area covers 244,000 square miles, including the hottest and driest regions of the Southwest. The reservoirs on the river can store four years of water in average rainfall years, and they serve to even out the wet-year/dry-year cycles.

THE LAW OF THE RIVER Attempts to negotiate the Colorado River's use among the seven states through which the river flows began as early as 1922 with

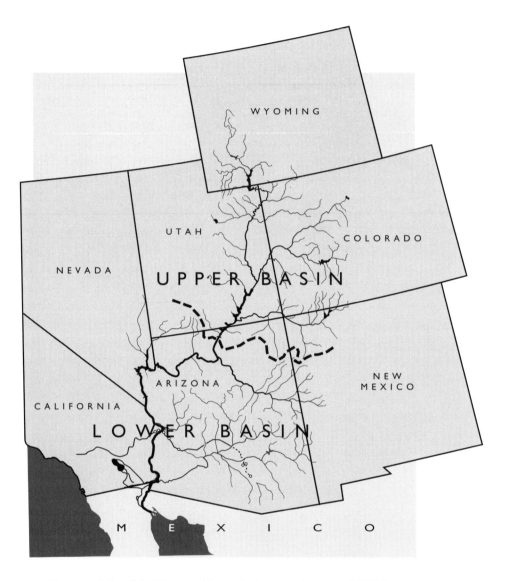

Figure 14. Map of the Upper and Lower Basin states. (SOURCE: MWD.)

the designation of the Upper and Lower Basin states. Six of these seven states signed the Colorado River Compact allocating 7.5 million acre-feet per year of Colorado River water to the Upper Basin and 7.5 million acre-feet to the Lower Basin States. Mexico was allocated 1.5 million acre-feet. The total so allocated equals 16.5 million acre-feet, which is more than the estimated annual average flow of the river, causing the river to be oversubscribed. The period chosen to determine the amount of water in the river was wetter than the long-term average. Records of precipitation and runoff have been kept for only 90–120 years in the West.

The compact plus numerous other laws, court decrees, regulations, and treaties developed over the years have collectively come to be known as the *Law of the River*. The Colorado River has been deemed the most controversial and regulated river in the country. This is not surprising considering that seven arid states, several Indian tribes, and the Republic of Mexico all claim a share of its water.

The Law of the River appropriates 4.4 million acre-feet of Colorado River water per year to the state of California for both agricultural and municipal uses. But California has been using on average about 800,000 acre-feet more than its annual allocation. Because the other states had not been using their full entitlement, MWD was able to keep its aqueduct full, delivering 1.2 million acre-feet a year despite a fourth-priority entitlement of only 550,000 acre-feet per year.

The United States Secretary of the Interior acts as the Watermaster for the river, and has the authority to declare surpluses or shortages. Since Arizona and Nevada are now taking their full entitlements, there is no more "surplus" for California.

THE 4.4 PLAN In December 2000, as one of his final actions as Secretary of the Interior and after many years of hard negotiations, Bruce Babbitt decreed that California must learn to live within its entitlement of 4.4 million acre-feet a year. To accommodate this transition, California was given until 2015 to develop alternative water supplies and conservation programs. During this period, the Secretary of the Interior will make additional supplies of water available to California using a negotiated set of interim surplus guidelines for Colorado River water from Lake Mead. MWD is now working hard to find ways to keep the Colorado River Aqueduct full or to find alternate sources of water under this decree.

TABLE 2. Colorado River Entitlements

Upper Basin States	7.50 million acre-feet
Colorado	
Utah	
Wyoming	
New Mexico	
Lower Basin States	7.500 million acre-feet
Arizona	2.800 million acre-feet
Nevada	0.300 million acre-feet
California	4.400 million acre-feet
California Allocations	
Agricultural Districts	3.850 million acre-feet
Palo Verde Irrigation District	
Yuma Project Reservation Division	
Imperial Irrigation District	
Coachella Valley Water District	
MWD	0.550 million acre-feet
California Surpluses (when available)	
MWD (was San Diego)	0.662 million acre-feet
Agricultural Districts	Any additional surplus

The most obvious place to look for more water is the Imperial Irrigation District (IID) in Imperial County. San Diego has negotiated with IID to buy water that farmers would conserve. The All American Canal that delivers Colorado River water to Imperial Valley farmers could be lined, saving water that has infiltrated into the ground into a groundwater basin that farmers south of the border have come to depend on. Or land could be fallowed, not farmed, eliminating farm worker jobs in a desperately poor county. Also at issue is the future of the Salton Sea.

ENVIRONMENTAL PROBLEMS CAUSED BY DIVERSIONS OF THE COLORADO RIVER The many diversions of the Colorado River, to farmers and cities that lie near the river or its aqueducts, have adversely impacted the river's wildlife and ecosys-

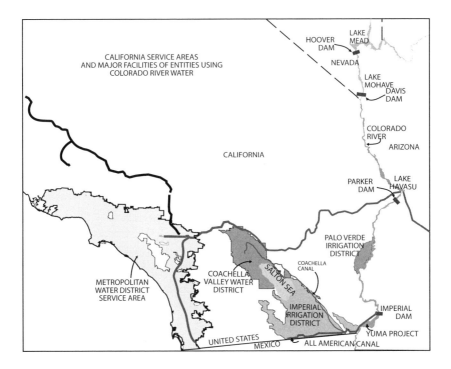

Figure 15. Map of the major facilities and water agencies served by the Colorado River. (SOURCE: MWD.)

tems. During most years, no water reaches the estuary or the Gulf of California. The river is all used up. This has resulted in a loss of 3,800 square miles of Baja California's wetlands, over 95%. The reduction in wetlands has endangered and disrupted the area's wildlife and the livelihood of its indigenous people. Birds migrating between the northern and southern hemispheres on the Pacific flyway no longer use the estuary as a stopover; many now stop at the Salton Sea. There are more than 50 species listed by the federal government as endangered in the Colorado River watershed.

The Salton Sea was formed in 1905 by a flood that redirected the entire Colorado River through existing irrigation ditches into the Salton Sink in the Imperial Valley. The Salton Sea is a sump with no outlets. Its only sources of water, aside from the limited amount of rainfall, are raw sewage and industrial waste from Mexicali and agricultural drainage from the Imperial and

Coachella valleys, where Colorado River water is used for irrigation. Yet, despite the sources of the inflow, the south end of the Salton Sea has become one of the most diverse bird hot spots in the world, hosting about 400 species, two-thirds of all bird species in the continental United States, more than 50 of them listed species or species of concern (www.saltonsea.ca.gov/environ.htm).

Efforts to restore the Colorado River watershed and the riparian and wetland habitats of Baja California parallel similar efforts in our own region. Some in the environmental community believe it is better to restore the estuary as a healthier place for birds on the Pacific flyway than to sink additional dollars into efforts to save the Salton Sea. A study funded by the Packard Foundation determined that the estuary has shriveled to one-tenth its historic size and needs an additional 30,000 acre-feet of water annually if it is to survive.

The Salton Sea, because of continual evaporation, is already 30% saltier than the ocean. It is destined to become even saltier. The increases in salinity will eventually kill off the existing ecosystem. Ways to preserve the Salton Sea and the wildlife habitat that has developed around it are being studied.

Any efforts to restore the Colorado River watershed and estuary will also require more water to be left in the system, which means a further reduction in the water supply available to cities and agriculture from this over-committed resource.

WATER QUALITY   The quality of the Colorado River's water has also suffered. Salt, or salinity, is an increasing water quality problem. Though occurring naturally, salt or mineral concentrations increase in water that is used by agriculture or when processed through wastewater treatment plants and returned to the river.

The Colorado River originates high up in the Rocky Mountains, where its salt concentration, usually expressed as total dissolved solids, or TDS, is only 50 milligrams per liter. Water taken from the Colorado River for irrigation purposes passes over and through the soil, dissolving mineral salts in its path, and then returns to the river as agricultural return flows. The river serves Las Vegas and other communities along the river with drinking water, which is returned as treated wastewater to the river. Finally, the river's water, captured behind a series of major dams, evaporates in the hot desert sun, further increasing its salinity. By the time it reaches the intake of the Colorado River Aqueduct at Parker Dam, the river's salt concentration has increased to a long-term average of 700 milligrams per liter.

This increase in salinity stands in the way of local water reclamation efforts because, as Colorado Aqueduct water is used, flushed down the sewer system, and reclaimed by local wastewater treatment facilities, it increases in salinity yet again. Once salt concentrations exceed 800–1,000 milligrams per liter, water is no longer serviceable for irrigation, groundwater recharge, or any other use unless put through an expensive reverse osmosis process to reduce the salt content.

The high salinity also causes the water to feel *hard*. This means that more soap is needed to wash, that scum or a ring appears around the bathtub, and that it is generally not as pleasant as water that is soft (has less mineral content). Because Colorado River water is so hard, MWD blends much of it with water from the State Water Project, which is much softer.

The State Water Project

The California State Water Project is a system of dams, 32 reservoirs and lakes, 25 power and pumping stations, and 662 miles of aqueduct designed to transport water from the northern portion of the state (the Sacramento River Watershed) to the central and southern portions of the state. The state Department of Water Resources manages the aqueduct, while MWD, which has contracted for 48% of the water, almost half, manages and distributes its share throughout its service territory, the coastal plain of southern California. The Kern County Water Agency contracted for 27% of the water, so both agencies together account for 75% of the water. The first deliveries to MWD occurred in 1972.

The California Aqueduct, the longest aqueduct in the world, requires a tremendous amount of energy to pump water up the San Joaquin Valley and over the Tehachapi Mountains and other mountains into southern California. The State Water Project is the single biggest user of eletricity in the state.

The State Water Project, as originally planned, would have cost approximately $4 billion, but, because then Governor Pat Brown determined such a price would never be approved by California voters, less than half the planned project was funded and built. As was the case in those days, environmental impacts were not considered and even economics were not given serious consideration. The engineering, however, was very well done.

TABLE 3. The Three Southern California Aqueducts

Aqueduct	Year Completed	Managed by	Length (miles)	Capacity (acre-feet/yr)	Can Deliver (acre-feet/yr)
Los Angeles	1913	LADWP	233	560,000	321,000
Colorado River	1941	MWD	242	1.2 million	550,000
California	1971	State DWR	600	4.2 million	1.86 million

What remains to be built of the State Water Project are (1) some way to take Sacramento River water through or around the Sacramento–San Joaquin Delta to the pumps in the south end of the delta, and (2) damming the north coast rivers and redirecting them to flow into the Sacramento River and to the delta. The peripheral canal, which would have taken Sacramento River water around the delta to the pumps, was soundly defeated at the polls in 1982, and damming the north coast rivers is no longer an option because they have been declared "Wild and Scenic," a federal designation that provides significant protection. As a result, less than half of the 4.2 million acre-feet (maf) a year the state signed contracts to deliver can actually be delivered. The half that cannot be delivered is called "paper" water, for it exists only on paper, in the service contracts. Service contracts are promises to deliver if the state can. They are not entitlements. Each contractor must pay for its share of the aqueduct system and the operations and maintenance, whether or not they get any water.

Stated another way, in California Department of Water Resources (DWR) Bulletin 160-98: "existing SWP facilities have . . . an 85% chance of delivering 2.0 maf to project contractors in any given year."

THE CENTRAL VALLEY PROJECT The State Water Project's impact on the environment cannot be examined without including the impacts of the Central Valley Project (CVP), since they are operated cooperatively. The CVP was built, starting in the 1930s, to provide irrigation for the entire Great Central Valley. It consists of 20 dams and reservoirs, mostly in the Sierra Nevada Mountains, starting with Shasta Dam on the upper Sacramento River, 500 miles of canals, and 11 power plants. It serves 250 long-term contractors, irrigating 3.4 million acres of farmland and supplying water to 3

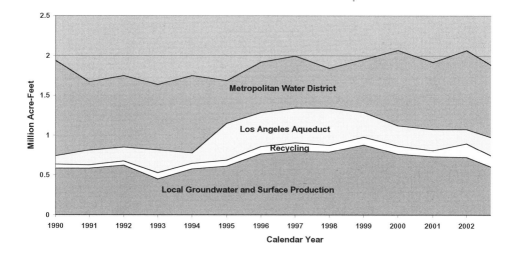

Figure 16. Historical Southern California water supply sources. (SOURCE: MWD.)

million people, and it generates enough power to serve 2 million house-holds. The watersheds of the Central Valley provide water for about a third of California's cropland and for about 50 cities in the valley and the San Francisco Bay area.

Both the CVP and the State Water Project divert water before it reaches the delta and pump water out of the delta. As much as 70% of the water that would normally flow through and out of the delta and out the Golden Gate is now either diverted before it gets to the delta to serve both agricultural and urban uses or pumped out of the delta into the two massive water delivery systems.

The Sacramento–San Joaquin Rivers Delta is a rare inland estuary that was once an enormous wetland filled with so many birds that the sky would darken when they were startled. This wetland supports over 750 species of plants and animals. A commercial salmon cannery was established on the Sacramento River in 1863, when, it is estimated, salmon numbered in the millions. The delta is the hub of the state's water system.

This extremely productive wetland was seriously impacted by the debris washed down off the mountains by hydraulic gold mining in the 1880s and by farmers who built levees and islands in the delta so that they could farm and feed the gold miners. The delta now consists of over 1,000 miles of waterways and islands. Over 95% of the original wetlands have been

Figure 17. Map of major water delivery systems statewide. (SOURCE: *California Water Plan Update*, Bulletin 160-2005.)

destroyed. Development of bedroom communities for the San Francisco Bay area is encroaching into the delta.

ENVIRONMENTAL AND WATER QUALITY PROBLEMS CAUSED BY WATER EXPORT FROM NORTHERN CALIFORNIA The construction of the Central Valley Project and the State Water Project and the subsequent movement of water from where it falls to where it is wanted have led to the almost-total consumptive use of the San Joaquin River. This once-mighty river, which in historic times flooded the entire San Joaquin Valley and often grew to be 10 miles wide, is now dry for as much as 70 miles of its length. It has been reduced to an agricultural sewer. The lower reaches are sometimes referred to as the "colon of the state," with essentially only agricultural drainage and other wastewaters entering the delta from the south.

An old state law requires that when dams are built in a river, water must be left to sustain the fishery. The courts have now ruled that Friant Dam, on the San Joaquin River above Fresno, has illegally diverted almost the entire flow of the river and that the river must be rewatered. The case is now the subject of serious negotiations between all of the interested parties.

Both supply systems, when built, were supposed to deal with the serious problem of groundwater overdraft in the Central Valley, but neither one has done so. The San Joaquin Valley has experienced the greatest volume of land subsidence in the world, due to overpumping. By the 1970s, 5,200 square miles of the valley had subsided more than a foot. The California aqueduct fell more than two feet between 1970 and 1994, and some places in the valley have subsided as much as 70 feet.

These two supply systems have also created massive environmental problems for the delta. Species that inhabit the lower end of the food web, such as phytoplankton, are at their lowest levels in history, and the ecosystem that fuels the estuary's web of life is experiencing such a low level of productivity that massive changes appear imminent. The little delta smelt, which once numbered in the hundreds of thousands, are so few in number that they could go extinct within the next year or two. Juvenile striped bass, threadfin shad, and long-fin smelt are also at historically low levels.

The three factors usually blamed for causing this crisis are toxins in the water from all the agricultural drainage and sewage treatment plants in the area, exotic species arriving in the ballast water of freighters coming

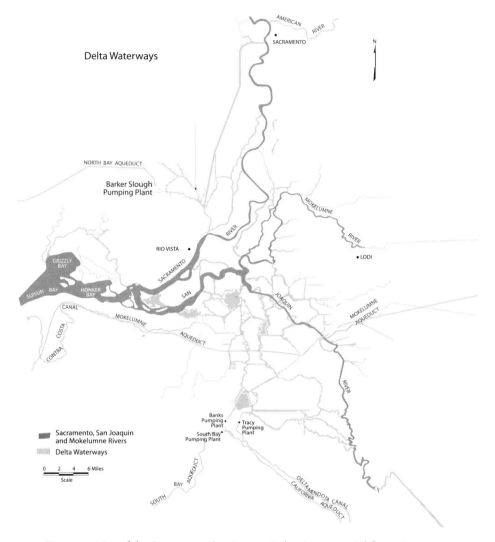

Figure 18. Map of the Sacramento–San Joaquin Delta. (SOURCE: California Department of Water Resources.)

into San Francisco Bay that have taken over habitat niches, and, most significantly, the loss of freshwater flow through and out of the delta. Other issues for the delta environment include water quality, the integrity of the levees, and impacts on the fisheries in the delta, in the bay, and out to sea.

Water quality in the delta is usually measured by how much salt is allowed how far upstream. Salt from the bay must be kept out of the delta and away from the pumps to protect water quality for delta farmers and for all of the cities that draw drinking water from the delta, not just southern California. Keeping saltwater out of the delta requires freshwater outflow. Besides salt, standards include dissolved oxygen, toxins, and flow. Water quality standards were established by the State Water Resources Control Board but were never enforced. A law suit was filed in the early 1990s to enforce state standards. The judge required that the USEPA establish federal standards. Its standards are more stringent than state standards. With the establishment of CALFED (see Chapter 2), most of the plaintiffs, expecting the standards to be enforced, dropped the suit. During the fall of 2005, the suit was revived to enforce the federal water quality standards.

Because the delta is composed of tule peat, from decaying tule reeds, the organic matter in the soil reacts with the chlorine used to disinfect drinking water to form trihalomethanes (THMs), which are suspected carcinogens. As a result, other disinfection chemicals must be used that create other disinfection by-products, with their own concerns. Runoff from both cities and agriculture and from sewage treatment plants adds its own toxins.

There is also a need to drain some 200,000 acres of farmland in the San Joaquin Valley, where large amounts of naturally occurring selenium leaches out of the irrigated farmland and where clay layers under the topsoil capture irrigation water and retain it in the root zones of crops. The federal government promised to build a drain, but there is nowhere to put the outlet. It cannot end in the delta, next to the pumps. It is too expensive to pump over the coastal mountains (to where?). Part of the drain has been built. It ends at the Kesterson Wildlife Refuge, where the selenium has been blamed for an environmental disaster that has resulted in malformed and dead birds and the poisoning of local wells. The alternative solution to this problem is to purchase and retire the land that should never have been irrigated in the first place.

Some of the delta islands are as much as 30 feet below sea level, because the tule peat soils have oxidized and blown away. Many of the levees were built out of the same tule peat soils and r.prapped with rock. They are maintained by a hodgepodge of agencies and private interests. Only some of them were engineered and are maintained by the Army Corps of Engineers or similar authorities. The levees are being undermined by burrowing animals and scoured by the strong tidal currents in narrow channels, boat wakes, high winter flows from the rivers, and the action of the pumps, causing reverse flows around some of the islands. These factors confuse fish searching for their spawning grounds and make the levees more susceptible to failure. Should a levee fail, and some predict that failure is inevitable, water will rush in to fill the island void. Most likely, this will be saltwater from the bay, destroying the island for future agriculture and negatively impacting water quality for the cities as well. Keeping the saltwater out would mean quickly releasing massive amounts of water contained upstream behind dams, greatly reducing statewide storage capacity, with no assurances that the released water would arrive in a timely manner.

Predictions regarding global warming all include rising sea level and more high-energy storms, which will only exacerbate the problems of levee integrity, where 95% of the native wetlands, which could buffer storms and sea level rise, have been destroyed. The inevitability of a major earthquake in or near the delta points to another disaster waiting to happen. Tule peat soils are subject to liquefaction in an earthquake. The levees have been predicted to fail within the next 50 years.

The water industry's response to all of these issues has been to increase pressure to build a peripheral canal around the delta to the pumps or to lay a pipeline through it so that they could pump out even more water. No one was asking how much water is needed to protect the health of the delta. Other circulating ideas include learning from the hurricane disaster that hit New Orleans so hard in 2005, where the wetlands that protected that city were destroyed by neglect and by a lack of understanding of the important role that wetlands play in providing a buffer against storm events. The state could buy some of the islands that are below sea level and restore some of the wetlands. There was a bill in the 2006 legislature to study reducing the amount of water exported from the delta. Reducing export would greatly improve water quality and support fish and wildlife as well as make the hub of the state's water system less vulnerable to sea level rise. It would also be cheaper than rebuilding the levees.

AREAS OF ORIGIN The environment and economy of those places from which the water is transferred are also impacted. Not only are the "areas of origin" concerned about the environmental impacts of dewatering, but the

TABLE 4. Summary of Shortfalls

Aqueduct	Year Completed	Managed by	Length (miles)	Capacity (acre-feet/yr)	Can Deliver (acre-feet/yr)
Los Angeles	1913	LADWP	233	560,000	321,000
Colorado River	1941	MWD	242	1.2 million	550,000
California	1971	DWR	600	4.2 million	1.86 million

people who live in those areas (mostly in the Sacramento River watershed) are also concerned about their own ability to grow and develop. In order to grow, they need to retain their own water supply and some control over their own futures.

CONCLUSION

Each of the sources of water on which the Los Angeles Area is dependent is oversubscribed, and most of the sources have water quality problems. Yet our communities continue to grow and farmers want to put more land under irrigation and/or control more water while the Endangered Species Act, restoration activities, and water quality constraints are reducing the amount of water available for consumptive use. Local surface supplies are contaminated by urban runoff. Parts of our groundwater basins are contaminated with industrial solvents, rocket fuel, and other pollutants and have been declared Superfund sites. Although much of our contaminated groundwater is being treated and put to beneficial use, it will require many years and a great deal of money to resolve this situation.

The Los Angeles Aqueducts deliver on average a third to 40% less than they have historically, because of air quality and habitat restoration efforts being undertaken in the Owens Valley and the Mono Basin. The Colorado River's supply to MWD is being cut back from 1.2 million to 0.55 million acre-feet a year by the Department of the Interior by the year 2015. And the State Water Project can only deliver, on average, less than half of the contracted amounts. During the 10-year period from 1991 to 2001, only an average of 1.86 million acre-feet was delivered, instead of the 4.2 million acre-feet in the contracts. Meanwhile demand increases to leave evermore water in rivers, streams, and the delta to restore fish and wildlife, wetlands, and riparian habitat. Some have likened this situation to that of a permanent drought.

The water industry continues to push for more reservoirs to store more water during high spring flows for later use. Industry leaders have been meeting in secret with state officials to amend State Water Project contracts and to plot how to extract even more water out of a very sick delta. Building more dams and diminishing the outflow through the delta will only create new environmental problems as well as exacerbate existing ones. The fisheries off the coast of the state are impacted by the lack of nutrients and freshwater outflow, and fishing associations are very active in water policy issues. The threat of global warming's raising the level of the sea and the fragility of the delta levees only exacerbate these concerns.

Chapter 5 addresses these and a host of other issues in the context of the entire state, since all systems are connected.

Chapter 2 | WATER MANAGEMENT

Who's in Charge?

> Most of the water in California is governed by archaic laws
> enforced by a labyrinth of special districts that would make
> the Byzantines proud.
>
> KOLE M. UPTON, *Chairman of the Friant Water Users Authority*

The California water world is highly fragmented. The Los Angeles Area
has hundreds of water agencies with many different management structures, different combinations of sources of water, different ways of operating, and different points of view toward being efficient. Almost all of these
agencies are unknown to the general public. People turn on the tap when
desired and get a bill at the end of the month, and that is where their interest ends. If we are to understand how water is delivered, managed, used,
and even misused, we must understand these agencies and the interrelationships between and among them. Without knowing them, how they
operate, and what functions they serve, it is impossible to hold any of them
accountable. We must know and understand them if we are to achieve a
truly integrated policy for managing our water resources, one based on coordination and cooperation.

Five different types of water agencies have water resource management
responsibility: water supply agencies, groundwater management agencies,
wastewater management agencies, stormwater management agencies, and
water quality agencies. As with many government agencies, each was
established by law to serve a single purpose. Nothing in the law requires
them to talk to one another or to cooperate and plan in an integrated way.

Some of these agencies serve combined functions. The Los Angeles County
Department of Public Works, for example, manages both stormwater and

water conservation (capturing stormwater for groundwater recharge) as well as delivering water directly to homes and businesses in some isolated parts of the county. The Las Virgenes Municipal Water District combines water supply, wastewater collection and treatment, and biosolids composting. The Los Angeles County Sanitation Districts collect and treat wastewater, distribute reclaimed water for reuse, and operate a variety of solid waste management and disposal facilities such as landfills.

In order to better understand the complexities of the institutions that manage various aspects of our water resources, this chapter explores the agencies in the Los Angeles Area as a microcosm of the state: their structures, functions, and interrelationships. There are so many agencies and so many different kinds that it is helpful to examine one area closely and then to explore the accountability issues that face the entire state. The five basic kinds of water agencies are as follows.

- *Water suppliers*—those public agencies and private providers responsible for the acquisition, treatment, and delivery of potable drinking water to residential, commercial, industrial, and a few agricultural customers, though agriculture does not need potable water. Some are wholesalers that provide water to other water purveyors. Others are retailers who serve water directly to customers. Some water suppliers also deliver highly processed reclaimed water for irrigation, industrial uses, groundwater recharge, and other indirect potable uses.
- *Groundwater management agencies*—those agencies responsible for the management of groundwater resources. Watermasters are court appointees who manage groundwater basins that have been adjudicated.
- *Wastewater management agencies*—those agencies responsible for the collection, treatment, and disposal of wastewater or sewage.
- *Stormwater management agencies*—those agencies responsible for the collection, treatment, and disposal of stormwater, as well as stormwater conservation and watershed protection.
- *Water quality agencies*—those agencies responsible for ensuring the healthfulness of drinking water, surface water, and groundwater.

And then there are various associations of water agencies that serve a variety of purposes.

The chapter ends with an examination of the one agency in the state established to develop an integrated planning process, CALFED. It has been totally ineffective because the political will to cooperate does not exist and because it had no funding source of its own.

WATER SUPPLIERS: WHOLESALE

There are many different types of water supply agencies, each kind with a different governance structure. Some are public agencies with elected boards of directors representing one-person one-vote. Some agencies base their vote on property ownership. Some are investor owned, while others operate as a mutual water company or a cooperative of local landowners. Some are operated by the city served, either directly by the city council or by appointees of the mayor with council approval. When elections for water district boards take place, the election only appears on our ballots when there is competition, when more than one person runs for an office. When an election actually takes place, less than 10% of those registered actually vote.

Historically, there has been little interest in water agencies and their policies and therefore there has been little media attention. People's interest extends as far as assurances that water will come out of the tap and is healthful and that water bills stay reasonably low. It is only in the past two decades that water quality issues have garnered headlines, thereby generating interest in water supply issues. The problems of getting polluters to take responsibility for cleaning up contaminated groundwater and the discovery of chromium 6 and perchlorate in some drinking water sources have been in the news. More recently, looming shortfalls from the Colorado River and the State Water Project have increased interest. Yet it is the rare individual who attends water board meetings solely for the purpose of being informed and having input into water policy decisions. Essentially all who attend have some kind of financial business before the agency.

Water wholesalers are those that sell water to other agencies (including other wholesale agencies), who then sell water to the public. Water retailers are those that sell water directly to residential, commercial, industrial, or agricultural customers. Most wholesalers in the Los Angeles Area buy imported water from the Metropolitan Water District. Many of them and many retailers have additional water supplies that come from local wells or rivers. Just about all of the wholesale agencies in the Los Angeles Area provide conservation services to their service territories and encourage water reclamation and reuse.

There are many different types of wholesale water suppliers in southern California. They include the U.S. Bureau of Reclamation, which is under the direction of the Secretary of the Interior, who manages the Central Valley Project in northern and central California and acts as Water master for the Colorado River. Reclamation has built many of the dams in the state. The Metropolitan Water District of Southern California (MWD) was formed by the state legislature to build and operate the Colorado River Aqueduct. It is the largest contractor for state water. Its board is composed of appointees from each of its 26 member agencies. Voting is based on the assessed value of the property within each member agency's district.

Municipal water districts in the Los Angeles Area are public wholesale agencies that purchase water from MWD and wholesale it to other water providers, who deliver directly to residents and municipalities. The Las Virgenes Municipal Water District serves users directly. Each district is governed by a five-person board of directors, elected by geographic area.

City water departments are publicly owned water utilities that are generally governed by city councils or sometimes by water commissions appointed by the mayor and/or the council.

Investor-owned utilities are private water companies that sell water for profit. The California Public Utilities Commission regulates their operations and levels of profit. They report to a board of directors, which is responsible to its shareholders. These investor-owned utilities are being bought up by foreign, multinational corporations headquartered in Europe.

Mutual water companies are run like cooperatives by the landowners served by the water company. Voting rights are generally based on the amount of land owned or the assessed value of the land owned. Irrigation districts generally are formed to serve farmland. Their governing boards are generally elected by the landowners served.

And county water districts are established to serve those areas in the county that are not served by any of the foregoing. The Board of Supervisors sets policy, rates, and governs.

The U.S. Bureau of Reclamation was formed by Congress and the Reclamation Act of 1902 specifically to provide water to serve family farms of 160 acres in order to settle the arid west. The Bureau of Reclamation built Hoover Dam and other facilities on the Colorado River and is governed by the Secretary of the Interior, who is charged with managing the Colorado River and acts as the Watermaster. The Secretary of the Interior implements the Law of the River, the series of treaties and agreements that have evolved over the years that divide the waters between the upper basin states, the lower basin states (which includes California), and Mexico. The Secretary of the Interior determines when or if there is surplus water on the river and how the surplus is to be distributed.

The Bureau of Reclamation has also built the Central Valley Project (CVP), a system of dams and canals that serve agriculture and some urban areas in the Great Central Valley. The CVP has been roundly criticized for serving farms of thousands of acres, in violation of the 160-acre limit. This limit has since been raised to 960 acres. It also has been accused of charging much less for water than the law requires, providing massive subsidies to farms, some of which also avail themselves of federal crop subsidies—double dipping. A 2005 study by the Environmental Working Group called *Virtual Flood* documents subsidies of $419 million a year, all of which goes to the largest and richest of the water districts in the Central Valley. The same study concludes that the federal government is promising an increase in taxpayer-subsidized water of 43% over the next 25 years as the original 40-year contracts come up for renewal. This is water that the Bureau of Reclamation cannot deliver without additional dams and severe damage to fish and wildlife. They are setting up these contractors to make windfall profits by selling the water for much higher prices. They are planning to deliver 5.1 maf a year, which they were only able to deliver once during the years 1990–2003. The average delivered in those years was 3.5 maf (www.ewg.org/reports/virtualflood/).

The Bureau of Reclamation also plays a more positive role, promoting conservation and developing additional water supplies like the major water reuse studies it has funded together with local water agencies in southern California and in the San Francisco Bay area and the water augmentation study with nine other partners in the Los Angeles Area (www.usbr.gov).

The California legislature created the Department of Water Resources (DWR) in 1956 (having evolved from a previous agency) to plan and guide the development of the state's water resources. As California grew, so did the mission of DWR. Its mission is to manage the water resources of California in cooperation with other agencies, to benefit the state's people, and to protect, restore, and enhance the natural and human environments.

DWR's stated goals to accomplish this mission are many. They are to prepare and update the California Water Plan (Bulletin 160) every five years to guide development and management of the state's water resources. They are to plan, design, construct, operate, and maintain the State Water Project to supply good-quality water for municipal, industrial, agricultural, and recreational uses and for fish and wildlife protection and enhancement. They are to protect and restore the Sacramento–San Joaquin Delta by protecting water quality and salinity in the delta, to provide water supplies for delta water users, to plan long-term solutions for environmental and water use problems facing the delta, and to administer levee maintenance reimbursements and special flood control projects.

DWR also regulates dams, provides flood protection, and assists in emergency management to safeguard life and property by supervising the design, construction, operation, and maintenance of more than 1,200 dams; to encourage preventive floodplain management practices. It maintains and operates Sacramento Valley flood control facilities; cooperates in flood control planning and facility development; and provides flood advisory information.

Additionally, DWR is charged to educate the public about the importance of water and its proper use; to collect, analyze, and distribute water-related information to the general public and to the scientific, technical, educational, and water management communities; and to serve local water needs by providing technical assistance, cooperating with local agencies on water resources investigations, supporting watershed and river restoration programs, encouraging water conservation, exploring conjunctive use of ground and surface water, facilitating voluntary water transfers, and, when needed, operating a state drought water bank.

DWR acted as the lead agency for purchasing electric power during the state's 2001 energy crisis because of its experience buying power for the State Water Project, the largest user/purchaser of electricity in the state. There is an interesting symbiosis between water and power. It takes huge amounts of energy to pump water out of the ground or over mountain ranges. According to the California Energy Commission, 19% of all the electricity consumed in California is used to pump and treat water. It also takes large amounts of cooling water to make electricity in a thermal power plant. Thermal power plants, such as oil, gas, coal, or nuclear, boil water to make steam to turn generators. The costs and management of either water or power directly impact the costs and management of the other (http://www .dwr.water.ca.gov/).

Metropolitan Water District of Southern California

The biggest water wholesale agency in California is the Metropolitan Water District of Southern California (MWD). It was established in 1928 by an act of the California State Legislature to provide supplemental water to the southern California coastal plain and to educate residents on water-related issues. It is also the largest contractor for water from the State Water Project, having contracted for 48% of its water. It sells imported water to 26 member agencies. It serves 13% of the land area and 90% of the people on the coastal plain from Ventura to the Mexican border. Its member agencies are cities, other municipal water districts, and one county water authority, San Diego. MWD supplies imported water to about 18 million residents in those six counties in a 5,200-square-mile service area. Ninety-two percent of its water is used for municipal and industrial purposes, 8% for agriculture. In the Los Angeles Area, 11 cities and six municipal water districts are member agencies.

The legislature created municipal water districts in 1911 to allow districts to "acquire, control, distribute, store, spread, sink, treat, purify, reclaim, recapture, and salvage any water, including sewage and storm water, for the beneficial use of users of the district." All but the Las Virgenes Municipal Water District in the Los Angeles Area, which is totally dependent on MWD for water, resell MWD and local water to other cities and other water agencies.

The founding cities of MWD included Anaheim, Beverly Hills, Burbank, Glendale, Los Angeles, Pasadena, San Marino, Santa Ana, Santa Monica, and Colton and San Bernardino (which withdrew in 1931). The cities of Compton, Fullerton, Long Beach, and Torrance joined in 1931. The City of San Fernando joined in 1971 after a severe earthquake. In addition to

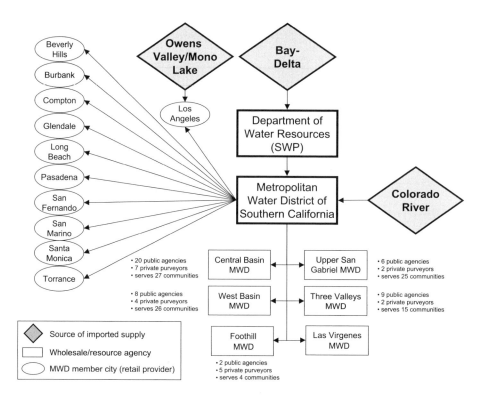

Figure 19. Institutional relationships between MWD member agencies and their retailers in the Los Angeles Area. (SOURCE: The author.)

these 14 member cities, there are 11 municipal water districts (six in this area) and one county water authority (San Diego).

Although MWD's mission was to ensure that all of the region's growing demand would be met by water imported from the Colorado River and from the State Water Project, a series of droughts, the passage and enforcement of the Endangered Species Act, increasing water quality concerns, and increasing competition for limited resources have forced the agency to rethink its mission and goals. MWD realized that instead of relying solely on new sources of imported water, it would better serve the region by offering financial incentives to encourage water conservation, the use of recycled water, and improved groundwater management—in other words, to increase dependence on local supplies. It has been successful in holding down the amount of water used despite increases in population.

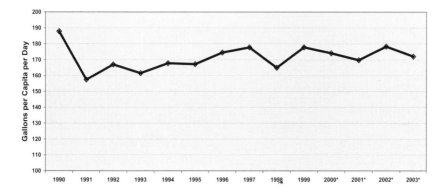

Figure 20. Per capita urban water use in Los Angeles County. (SOURCE: MWD.)

In 1996, MWD and its member agencies adopted southern California's first-ever Integrated Resources Plan (IRP). The goal of the IRP was vastly different than the historical engineer-driven planning that had dominated the agency since its creation. Rather than a single objective of ensuring reliability of supply through the construction of more dams and reservoirs, the agency adopted principles and objectives that included cost effectiveness, water quality, environmental protection, regional stewardship, and financial integrity. This process was also much more participatory and open than previous planning efforts and was designed to foster interdependence and cooperation between member agencies. These objectives resulted in a 20-year water plan that put a heavy emphasis on conservation, recycling, groundwater recovery, groundwater conjunctive use, storage, and voluntary water transfers.

MWD's mission statement adopted in 1992 reads: "The mission of the Metropolitan Water District of southern California is to provide its service area with adequate and reliable supplies of high-quality water to meet the present and future needs in an environmentally and economically sensitive way."

The IRP was updated in 2004 after a process that was not nearly as inclusive. The member agencies were closely involved, but public meetings were presentations made without participants having advance copies of the plan, so no real dialogue could be had. It concluded that MWD "will continue to provide for 100% reliability through 2025."

MWD's Board of Directors initially consisted of 51 directors. It was reduced to 37 in 2001 to streamline operations. Each member agency has at least one representative, with additional representatives and voting rights based on each agency's assessed property valuation. Each member agency selects or appoints its director(s) as it sees fit and is responsible for any compensation provided.

Historically, MWD was financed by a combination of property taxes and water fees. Property taxes were necessary in the early years, when bonds were sold to finance the construction of the aqueduct and other major capital improvements and there was not yet a user base to pay for the bonds. Now only about 11% comes from property taxes, as was projected for fiscal year 2005–2006. The City of Los Angeles has always been the member agency with the largest tax base, and therefore it has paid, over the years, the most in property taxes. As a result, it has the largest share of water rights, despite its modest needs since it has its own groundwater and aqueduct supplies. San Diego, with little to no groundwater, is almost totally dependent on MWD yet has had a much smaller entitlement to MWD water. This anomaly has driven San Diego to aggressively pursue the development of its own water supply, negotiating with Imperial Valley to bypass MWD and buy water directly. However, as San Diego county has grown, its percentage of water rights has somewhat evened out—as of June 2005, Los Angeles had 21.36% to San Diego's 16.16% assessed valuation.

MWD maintains one of the nation's most advanced water quality testing laboratories, located in La Verne, and operates five regional water treatment plants:

> The Joseph Jensen plant in Granada Hills (capacity 750 mgd or million gallons per day),
> The F. E. Weymouth plant in La Verne (capacity 520 mgd),
> The Robert A. Skinner plant in Winchester (capacity 520 mgd),
> The Robert B. Diemer plant in Yorba Linda (capacity 520 mgd),
> and the Henry J. Mills plant in Riverside (capacity 160 mgd).

It also has built and operates several large reservoirs. Lake Mathews, in Riverside County, is the terminus of the Colorado River Aqueduct, and Lake Skinner, at Winchester, is the terminus of the State Water Project. The newest reservoir, Diamond Valley Lake, near Hemet, has doubled the region's surface storage capacity.

MWD provides financial incentives for water management programs, such as local conservation, recycling, and groundwater recovery programs. It has developed several groundwater storage-banking programs with local agencies and irrigation districts in the Central Valley and near its Colorado River Aqueduct. It is working to better manage groundwater in its own territory. MWD is heavily involved in national and statewide drought and watershed planning. In 2000, MWD sponsored workshops on climate change, drought preparedness, and, together with the Los Angeles & San Gabriel Rivers Watershed Council and others, watershed management.

In 1999, SB 60, sponsored by then State Senator Tom Hayden, revised the Metropolitan Water District Act to formally include increased emphasis on sustainable, environmentally sound, and cost-effective water conservation, recycling, and groundwater storage. The bill also requires that MWD, in cooperation with other agencies, participate in watershed management, habitat restoration, and environmentally compatible community development utilizing the resource potential of the Los Angeles, San Gabriel, and other southern California rivers. Watershed management and all that it implies had not been a part of MWD thinking before this law was passed. MWD must report annually to the legislature its progress in meeting these new requirements. These SB 60 Annual Progress Reports to the California State Legislature are available online (www.mwdh2o.com).

Central Basin Municipal Water District

The Central Basin Municipal Water District (Central Basin) is a public agency that wholesales about 50,000 acre feet a year of MWD imported water to cities, mutual water companies, private companies, and investor-owned utilities in southeast Los Angeles County. Central Basin also delivers water used for groundwater replenishment and distributes reclaimed water from the County Sanitation Districts' water reclamation plants for irrigation, industrial use, and seawater barrier use in its region. In 2003–2004, about 65% of its water supply was local, 35% imported from MWD.

Central Basin was established in 1952 by a vote of the people to take advantage of imported water from the Colorado River. The underground water basin had been overpumped for years, an activity known as *groundwater*

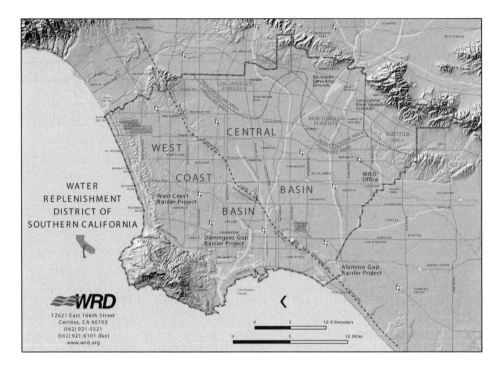

Figure 21. Map of Central and West Basin municipal water districts. (SOURCE: Water Replenishment District of Southern California.)

overdraft or *mining the groundwater.* District founders realized they had to curtail this activity in order to protect the groundwater from becoming contaminated by seawater. The groundwater basin was adjudicated in 1962, and the State Department of Water Resources was appointed Watermaster. Additional water needed to replace the water that had been and continues to be pumped out is purchased from MWD.

Central Basin, a member agency of MWD since 1954, serves 24 cities and several unincorporated areas within a 227-square-mile service area and a population of approximately 1.5 million residents. The Central and West Basin Water Replenishment District (now known as the Water Replenishment District of Southern California) was established shortly thereafter to ensure adequate groundwater supplies and to protect groundwater quality. Central Basin has 217,367 acre-feet a year of pumping rights, but the basin only has a safe yield of 120,000 acre-feet a year. The balance is made up by the Water Replenishment District. To optimize management costs, the Central Basin shares a small staff with its sister agency, the West Coast Basin Municipal Water District. It sells to 17 cities directly and to 14 other entities, mostly other water companies or districts (http://www .centralbasin.org/).

West Coast Basin Municipal Water District

Artesian wells and springs provided water for Inglewood and Long Beach in the 1870s. When they ceased flowing, wells were drilled ever deeper, until the 1920s, when water levels throughout the West Coast Basin dropped below sea level. Wells near Santa Monica Bay were abandoned because the water became too salty due to seawater intrusion. By 1932, the entire coastal aquifer was contaminated by seawater.

Lawsuits were filed in 1945 to adjudicate the basin and to establish control over pumping. West Coast Basin Municipal Water District (West Basin) was formed in 1947 to become a member agency of MWD and distribute imported water as an alternative to groundwater. The State Department of Water Resources has served as Watermaster since 1961. About 20% of its water is local, 80% from MWD. An alternate accounting method concludes that 20% of its water is local groundwater, 65% is from MWD, 7% is reclaimed and reused, and 7% is conserved.

The Los Angeles County Department of Public Works built and operates a line of 229 injection wells that parallels the coastline from Los Angeles International Airport to the Palos Verde hills, to keep additional saltwater out of the aquifer. Fresh potable water is injected to provide a barrier against seawater intrusion. West Basin operates a 1.3-million-gallon-per-day desalting plant in Torrance so that the salty groundwater captured behind this barrier can be treated and used.

West Basin has taken a leadership role in water reuse. It developed a broad-based local taxpayer coalition in support of a standby charge to fund the construction of an advanced tertiary wastewater treatment plant. It buys secondary treated wastewater from the City of Los Angeles' Hyperion Sewage Treatment Plant, further treats it to tertiary standards, and markets the reclaimed water. (See Chapter 4 for a description of these processes.) Deliveries began in 1995 for municipal, commercial, and industrial use. In 2003–2004, West Basin sold 24,500 acre-feet of reclaimed water to protect against seawater intrusion into the groundwater basin and for direct use to 203 sites. It produces five different qualities of water, depending on the end use to which it will be put—designer water. West Basin is also experimenting with new reverse osmosis membrane technology to be able to reduce the cost of seawater desalting, hoping that it will one day be competitive with imported supplies.

West Basin serves 17 cities, several of which also have their own water supplies, such as Torrance and Compton, and several unincorporated communities in the South Bay within a 185-square-mile service area. It serves approximately 850,000 residents, and has increased in population by 100,000 people since the early 1990s, yet its water usage has remained flat. A conservation master plan was due out in 2006. It sells directly to six cities and to seven other entities, including the Water Replenishment District, mutual water companies, investor-owned utilities, and others in southwest Los Angeles County (http://www.westbasin.org/).

Three Valleys Municipal Water District

The Three Valleys Municipal Water District (Three Valleys) supplements and enhances local water supplies with imported water from MWD; 40% is local, 60% is from MWD. Three Valleys was established in 1950 to serve 15 communities in the eastern part of Los Angeles County. About 600,000 residents within a 133-square-mile area are served. About 80% of the water purchased from MWD goes directly to Three Valleys' customers and about 20% is used to recharge the Main San Gabriel Basin. This imported water meets about half of the local water needs. Most of the rest comes from local groundwater sources together with a small amount of surface water from the San Gabriel River. Three Valleys operates one water treatment plant that has a capacity of 25 million gallons a day and three hydroelectric power plants that can generate as much as 1,000 kilowatts of energy. It depends on MWD's Weymouth Treatment Plant to treat the rest of the water it serves. It sells to seven cities and nine other entities (http://www.threevalleys.com/).

San Gabriel Valley Municipal Water District

The San Gabriel Valley Municipal Water District was incorporated on August 17, 1959. It is made up of four cities in three noncontiguous parcels covering 27 square miles: Azusa, Alhambra, Monterey Park, and Sierra Madre. The district is not a member of MWD. It chose instead to contract directly with the state in 1962 for delivery of 25,000 acre-feet (later amended to 28,800 acre-feet) of State Water Project water. The district built two pipelines to deliver water from the state's Devil Canyon power plant, located north of the City of San Bernardino, for purposes of groundwater recharge in the Main San Gabriel Basin. The sole use for the imported water is to replenish the groundwater basin for the four cities, each of which has its own wells and distribution system. Contracting is done through the Watermaster, who manages pumping rights. Its five-member board is elected by districts, which often follow city boundaries, based on population. This water district also has a hydroelectric power plant that makes energy from its state water as it flows downhill. The power is distributed by Southern California Edison (http://home .onemain.com/~ymcvicar/).

Upper San Gabriel Valley Municipal Water District

The 144-square-mile Upper San Gabriel Valley Municipal Water District (Upper District) was formed by voters in the San Gabriel Valley at an election held on December 8, 1959, to help solve water problems in the rapidly developing San Gabriel Valley. The Upper District played a vital role in determining water rights within the Main San Gabriel Basin by acting as plaintiff in the 1973 court case that resulted in the adjudication of the Main San Gabriel Basin. A Watermaster was ordered by the court to administer and enforce the pumping rights of those who were parties to the settlement. On March 12, 1963, residents of the district voted to annex to MWD so that they could purchase supplemental water to spread, to make up for historical overpumping.

Upper District buys and spreads MWD water and serves 25 communities in the San Gabriel Valley, many of which also have their own groundwater supply. It provides about 80% from MWD and 20% from local resources. The retailers who purchase water through the Main San Gabriel Basin Watermaster pay the MWD bill plus 5% to the Upper District for management services. These services include providing local conservation and reuse programs for its retailers. Upper District has been planning a pipeline to bring reclaimed water to local spreading grounds as a way of increasing its local water supply. This project is on hold as water quality issues are being pursued and alternative ways of meeting its goals are explored.

The appearance of volatile organic compounds (VOCs) in many water wells in the district was first discovered in 1979, which led to the creation of several Superfund sites. The district uses its Rate Stabilization Fund to help finance cleanup efforts in the valley and then to pursue the responsible parties to recoup expenditures. (See Chapter 4, on drinking water quality, for a discussion of these issues.) It serves 10 cities directly and 24 other entities, mostly other water companies (http://www.usgvmwd.org/).

Foothill Municipal Water District

The Foothill Municipal Water District (Foothill) is a small wholesale water agency serving supplemental imported water from MWD since 1953 to four foothill cities—Altadena, La Cañada Flintridge, La Crescenta, and Montrose—and a part of Glendale. Foothill serves a total of about 80,000 residents within a 22-square-mile service area, providing 55–60% of these communities' water. About 40% is local water; 60% is from MWD. This supplemental water is both served directly and injected into the groundwater basin for storage and future use. Foothill provides management services to the Raymond Basin Watermaster. All the land is essentially fully developed and is 90% residential. Seven retail agencies serve 80,000 people (http://fmwd.com/).

The Committee of Nine, or the San Gabriel River Water Committee

The San Gabriel River Water Committee, or the Committee of Nine, was formed in 1889 to secure a safe and reliable water supply from the San Gabriel River and to protect the rights to and interests in the river on behalf of committee members. It was created as a result of an 1889 Compromise Agreement between parties with an interest in San Gabriel River water and sought to quell nearly a century of conflict over water use. The agreement was so well planned that it is still in effect today. The Compromise Agreement established the committee to administer the division of the waters of the San Gabriel River. Buyouts have reduced the number of entities today to five: the Azusa Agricultural Water Company, the Azusa Valley Water Company (a subsidiary of the City of Azusa), the California-American Water Company, the Covina Irrigating Company, and the Monrovia Nursery Company.

The committee has surface water rights to 135 cubic feet per second of runoff, the precipitation and snowmelt that becomes stream flow and collects behind the San Gabriel Dam on the San Gabriel River. All water flow above this amount belongs to the San Gabriel Valley Protective Association, including any water stored behind Cogswell, San Gabriel, and Morris dams. All three of these dams are operated by the county. The Committee of Nine has no storage rights behind any of the dams.

The San Gabriel Valley Protective Association (see next subsection) allows the Committee of Nine to utilize a portion of their storage rights behind San Gabriel Dam as a courtesy to store water temporarily. This courtesy storage is capped at 2,000 acre-feet between November 15 and April 15. It increases to 6,000 acre-feet between April 16 and November 14. Any water remaining in courtesy storage on November 1 of each year is transferred to the Protective Association. The Committee of Nine uses their courtesy storage to supplement the river flow in the summer and fall, when the river flow falls below its needs. The Committee of Nine can borrow additional water from the Protective Association when their courtesy storage is exhausted. They repay this amount the following winter, when inflow to the dam typically exceeds its water needs.

The Committee of Nine can pump groundwater as allocated/permitted by the San Gabriel Basin Watermaster. It also buys water from MWD as needed. The Azusa Valley Water Company and the Covina Irrigating Company have surface water treatment plants that supply potable drinking water to more than a quarter-million people in the San Gabriel Valley.

The Committee's Board of Directors consists of nine people representing the current five entities. Regular monthly meetings are routinely supplemented with subcommittee meetings. There is no compensation, for all board members are volunteers. There is one full-time employee and one part-time employee.

The San Gabriel Valley Protective Association

The San Gabriel Valley Protective Association (Protective Association) is composed of a 22-member board elected by all of the water entities that draw from the San Gabriel River, from the mountains to the sea. It holds the water rights to the entire river, granted by the State Water Resources Control Board. It is a nonprofit association that meets perhaps once a year to serve the following functions: hold and maintain the state water rights permit, measure the water elevation in the key well, and report this to the county. Its Distribution Committee meets quarterly to determine how to distribute the water that has been conserved behind the county's dams.

Covina Irrigating Company

Covina Irrigating Company is a mutual wholesale nonprofit that evolved from agricultural roots. It is a member of the Committee of Nine. It has a nine-member board, elected by its shareholders, representing Covina, Glendora, Valencia Heights, the Southern California Water Company, the Suburban Water Company, and the Valley County Water District. The City of Azusa is a shareholder but has alternate sources of water. Its provides supplemental water, 70–75% drawn from the San Gabriel River Canyon, with the balance pumped from three active wells located in Baldwin Park. It has two additional wells that are now contaminated with nitrates. It operates its own water treatment plant, located on Arrow Highway, between Grand and Glendora boulevards in Glendora, and serves high-quality water.

WATER SUPPLIERS: RETAIL

What follows is a sampling of retail agencies that serve the Los Angeles Area. They include most of the original MWD member agencies, some of the investor-owned utilities, and a few others. To better understand the role of each of these agencies, we also need to understand how efficient they are and how well they are actively seeking to maximize their own local resources. A nonprofit called the California Urban Water Conservation Council (CUWCC) was formed to develop, quantify, and price various conservation strategies and best management practices (BMPs). As part of our cursory overview of each agency, their participation in this nonprofit is mentioned. Some cities, such as Los Angeles, Burbank, Glendale, Long Beach, and Torrance, have also developed recycled-water projects to reduce their dependence on imported water. The two largest agencies' efforts at conservation and reuse, Los Angeles Department of Water and Power and MWD, are dealt with in Chapter 3, on water use efficiency.

There are so many retail agencies that to cover all of them, even as superficially as done here, is not possible and would not contribute significantly to our understanding of the institutional barriers facing the management of our water resources or the variety of responses to the need for greater efficiency. There are, for example, 48 retail water purveyors just in the San Gabriel Valley and 372 public water systems in the county.

City of Los Angeles Department of Water and Power

The Los Angeles Department of Water and Power (LADWP) is the largest municipal utility in the country. It currently serves water and power to over 3.8 million residents. It is financed by the revenue generated from the sale of water and electricity. Water and power bonds are used to finance capital projects. A five-member commission establishes policy for LADWP. Commissioners are appointed by the mayor for five-year terms and approved by the city council. The commissioners, however, really serve at the pleasure of the mayor.

LADWP became a municipal water agency in 1902, with William Mulholland serving as the first water superintendent. He quickly assessed Los Angeles' growth and worked to enlarge the Los Angeles River system and build more storage reservoirs and main lines. Mulholland also realized that conservation was integral to ensuring an adequate water supply for the city's residents. He installed water meters early on to help curtail wasteful consumption.

The City of Los Angeles operates a complex system that includes the two Los Angeles Aqueducts, water treatment facilities, seven reservoirs, located mostly in the Hollywood Hills, and 12 hydroelectric facilities that generate 250 megawatts of electricity. It stores both stormwater and imported water underground in the eastern San Fernando Valley, with assistance from County Public Works, which operates most of the spreading grounds in the county. As one of the original MWD member agencies, the city buys supplemental water from MWD. It has the following sources of water supply: 11–32% in a dry year from the Los Angeles Aqueduct and the Owens Valley and Mono Basin; 37–46% from MWD in an average year, up to 57–65% in dry years; 12–15% local groundwater; 10% reuse; and 8–9% stormwater capture. Less than 10% of the city's water came from MWD before the Mono Lake decision that requires the restoration of the lake, the Owens River, and wetlands.

Los Angeles has Pueblo Water Rights that date back to King Carlos III of Spain, which include a native safe yield of 43,660 acre-feet per year from the San Fernando Valley groundwater basin and return-water rights (the

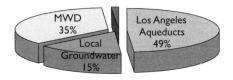

Figure 22. Pie chart showing Los Angeles city supply system.
(SOURCE: LADWP.)

imported water that infiltrates into the ground) of 20.8% of all the imported water used in the valley. In addition, the city has water rights to 15,000 acre-feet per year in the Central Basin, 3,255 acre-feet per year in the Sylmar Basin, 1,500 acre-feet per year in the West Coast Basin, and approximately 500 acre-feet per year in the Eagle Rock Basin.

The City has 66 active wells, which averaged about 92,400 acre-feet per year in the 1990s. LADWP has developed water recycling projects in cooperation with the city's Bureau of Sanitation, which has responsibility for collecting and treating wastewater. LADWP has sole authority to sell water in the city and therefore must work cooperatively with the City Bureau of Sanitation to market reclaimed water. The city charter limits LADWP to selling water only within the city limits, except for those few places where it makes more sense to serve the locality through LADWP's infrastructure, and then it must levy a surcharge. Five percent of LADWP's revenue is returned to the city council in lieu of taxes (http://ladwp.com/).

Las Virgenes Municipal Water District

The Las Virgenes Municipal Water District provides potable water, recycled water, wastewater services, and biosolids composting to the cities of Agoura Hills, Calabasas, Hidden Hills, and Westlake Village and neighboring unincorporated areas of Los Angeles County, which include most of the Malibu Creek upper watershed. A few small local mutual water companies and some private wells had been using what little local groundwater exists in the area. However, this local groundwater is high in sulfur or manganese and is not potable. Las Virgenes is totally dependent on MWD. Established in 1958, it serves a population of over 65,000 across a 122-square-mile area in western Los Angeles County. It is the only fully integrated system in the Los Angeles Area, installing and operating both a drinking water treatment and delivery system and a wastewater collection and

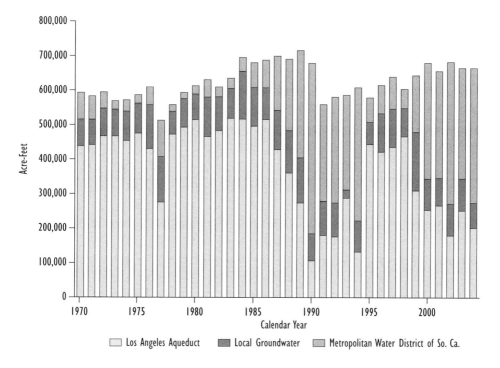

Figure 23. Historical water supplies for the City of Los Angeles, by source. (SOURCE: LADWP.)

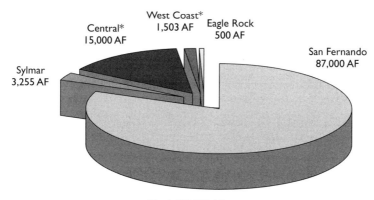

Total: 107,258 AF per year

*Groundwater basins outside the Upper Los Angeles River Area boundries.

Figure 24. Pie chart showing annual groundwater entitlements for the City of Los Angeles. (SOURCE: LADWP.)

treatment system. It serves 600 customers with reclaimed water. It also operates a state-certified water quality laboratory to ensure that both potable and recycled water meet state and federal guidelines.

Las Virgenes composts the biosolids from its wastewater treatment facility together with wood chips. In a final attempt to complete all cycles, it uses the methane gas that is a by-product of its composting operation to energize two fuel cells that then produce enough electricity to run the composting operation. The fuel cells can generate enough power to serve the average needs of 300 households. The wastewater, composting, and fuel cell facilities are operated in cooperation with the Triunfo Sanitation District, which serves the Ventura County part of the Malibu Creek watershed (http://lvmwd.com/).

City of Azusa

The City of Azusa is one of the original Committee of Nine and therefore takes about a third of its water supply directly from the San Gabriel River. It has a plant to treat this local surface water. It owns about 12 wells, all of which are above any of the contamination sites in the San Gabriel Valley. Well water is only chlorinated before being served. A small amount of treated water from MWD is added to its system via the Upper San Gabriel Valley Municipal Water District. The city is a member agency of both the Upper District and of the San Gabriel Valley Municipal Water District, which is not part of MWD.

Azusa Light and Water is managed by the mayor and city council. It also provides trash services. Azusa's own water department doubled in size after purchasing the Azusa Valley Water Company, which had already purchased others, thereby giving it three votes on the Committee of Nine. It also serves parts of Glendora, Covina, West Covina, Irwindale, and some unincorporated county. Azusa has not signed on to the conservation BMPs, but it has passed city ordinances to encourage conservation and a landscape ethic (http://www.azusalw.com).

City of Beverly Hills

The City of Beverly Hills covers an area of 5.69 square miles and serves about 32,000 people plus another 9,200 people in neighboring West Hollywood. The city originally had its own water system, pumping out of the Hollywood aquifer. However, this water is hard (high in total dissolved solids) and does not taste good and therefore needs treatment. After a number of years of being totally reliant on MWD imported water, the city has reinstated its own water system, hiring a private contractor to design, build, and operate a new water treatment plant as part of a whole new public works facility. The new treatment plant became operational in June 2003 and pumps about 3,500 acre-feet a year from its four wells to meet about 14% of current water demand; MWD supplies the rest. The city's wastewater is sent to Los Angeles' Hyperion for treatment. It has signed on to the conservation BMPs, is offering rebates for low-flow toilets and washing machines, and is working with MWD on its landscape training program. It has also put into place a tiered billing system: The more you use, the more you pay per 100 cubic feet of water (http://www.beverlyhills.com/).

City of Burbank

Burbank has a population of 105,000 people. It also has its own wastewater collection and treatment facility, where it treats about two-thirds of its own sewage, sending the balance to Los Angeles' Hyperion Treatment Plant. The City of Burbank uses about half MWD water and half from its own wells. These 10 wells are all located within or next to a Superfund site, and the water from all 10 wells is treated and then blended with MWD water to ensure that it meets drinking water standards. It has an active reuse program, using reclaimed water for cooling water in its own power plant and for irrigating parks, golf courses, schools, its own municipal dump, and Caltrans freeway landscaping. It is implementing all the conservation BMPs (http://www.ci.burbank.ca.us/Departments/deptsa.htm#Public%20Works).

City of Compton

The City of Compton serves an area of 7.81 square miles and a population of over 93,000 people. It participates in managing the local groundwater with the Water Replenishment District, getting about 47% from underground, with the balance from MWD. It has five active wells and a sixth that is inactive because trace amounts of the solvent TCE were found. They are old, having been built in the 1950s and '60s. Compton has signed on to implement the conservation BMPs, but it is doing none of them. Compton serves water to about 70% of the city. The rest of the city is served by three private companies (Park Water Company, Southern California

Water Company, and the California Water Service Company) and by two mutual water companies (Midland Park Trust and Sativa Water) (http://www.comptoncity.org/).

City of Glendale

The City of Glendale serves an area of 30.6 square miles and a population of almost 200,000 people. In 2004, it got 72% of its water from MWD, 26% from local groundwater, and about 2% from local surface water. All the native water in the San Fernando Basin has been granted to the City of Los Angeles as pueblo water rights, but Glendale is entitled to pump 20% of its total usage as return flow from imported water that has been used within the city. Unfortunately, the City of Glendale overlies a Superfund site, and its wells were shut down in 1980 due to contamination from PCE, TCE, and other industrial solvents. In September 2001, an air stripping facility was turned on to clean the water at this Superfund site. Chromium 6 was discovered in the treated water, and the city council debated and studied the issue for months until agreeing that five parts per billion (ppb) would be acceptable in its drinking water supply. The standard is now 50 ppb for total chromium. There is no separate standard for chromium 6. Glendale has aggressively pursued treatment technology to deal with the chromium 6 issue, with grants from the American Water Works Association, the big national trade association, and from USEPA. Glendale's wells in the Verdugo Basin contain nitrates, so their water is blended with MWD supplies to bring the nitrates to acceptable levels.

Together with the City of Los Angeles, Glendale owns its own sewage treatment facility in the Glendale Narrows on the Los Angeles River. It has built a regional reclaimed water distribution system that includes Pasadena and a part of Los Angeles, serves 50 sites at this time with reclaimed water, and is meeting about 5% of its demand with reclaimed water. This translates into reuse of 20% of the wastewater, or 1,627 acre-feet a year. The rest is discharged to the Los Angeles River. Glendale would like to extend its reclaimed water system to serve Scholl Canyon Landfill, where it can be used for dust control. Pasadena would like eventually to build a pipeline to bring reclaimed water to serve the Rose Bowl. These projects are dependent on finding financing. Glendale is doing all of the conservation BMPs (www.ci.Glendale.ca.us).

The City of Long Beach is the fifth-biggest city in the state. It formed its own water agency in 1911 and took over a number of small agencies in 1933 that were competing and duplicating services within the city. In response to a growing population and increasing pressures on limited groundwater resources, it created a Board of Water Commissioners to manage the system, made up of five members appointed by the mayor and approved by the city council. It is one of MWD's original member agencies. About 74% of the city's demand is for potable water. About 45% of this demand is met with groundwater and 55% with MWD's imported water. About 8% of the demand is for reclaimed water, which is used in industry and irrigation. Finally, the remaining 18% of the city's demand is met by conservation. The conservation and reuse efforts have been so successful that although the city's population has increased by 25% in the last 20 years, its demand for potable water has decreased from about 74,000 acre-feet per year to roughly 70,000.

The city's service area overlays part of the Central Groundwater Basin. It participated in the adjudication of both the Central and West Coast basins that ended in 1963, when the city's legal pumping rights were established. The Long Beach Water Department has since purchased additional pumping rights, and today it can pump 32,500 acre-feet a year, the most of any pumper in both the Central and West basins. It also participated in the successful lawsuit (which came to be known as the Long Beach Judgment) guaranteeing that a minimum amount of surface and subsurface water would flow from the San Gabriel Valley to replenish the Central Groundwater Basin.

The city entered into a conjunctive use agreement with MWD to inject potable water off-season into new wells that could serve both to replenish the groundwater and to recover water for later use. The Water Replenishment District recharges the Central Basin aquifer in the Whittier Narrows area. It takes between 50 and 100 years for that recharged water to find its way down to Long Beach's wells. In partnership with the Water Replenishment District, it has built and is now operating a project that conserves about 3,000 acre-feet of imported water a year by treating reclaimed water to drinking water standards and then injecting this polished water, in lieu of imported drinking water, to prevent seawater from migrating into and spoiling the freshwater of the Central Basin. It is a signatory to and is doing all of the conservation BMPs.

Because the groundwater under the city is drawn from what was once an ancient tropical forest, the water is colored and unappetizing, though it is healthful. To eliminate the color, which also left bathtub rings, the city built a groundwater treatment plant in the 1950s, which was totally rebuilt in the 1990s. The treatment plant uses a nanofiltration technology to produce high-quality water that it now bottles for sale. To operate the treatment plant, it built its own state-of-the-art water quality laboratories, managed by certified personnel. The city is now experimenting with further developing its nanofiltration technology for ocean desalination. They expect to use 70–80% less energy than the traditional reverse osmosis technology, for a cost savings of 20%. They are also experimenting with a slow through-the-sand intake system for its proposed desalination system, which would be less damaging to the ocean environment.

The city built and maintains its own sewage collection system, which connects to the County Sanitation Districts' wastewater treatment facilities. When the County Sanitation Districts were looking for a site to build a sewage treatment plant, Long Beach city leaders sold County Sanitation a site for cash and for the first right of refusal to all of the tertiary treated wastewater it would generate. Long Beach began to experiment with marketing reclaimed water in the 1980s. It sells about 5,000 acre-feet a year of reclaimed water for commercial and irrigation purposes (http://www .lbwater.org/).

City of Pasadena

The City of Pasadena is an original member of MWD. It covers 26 square miles, and has a population of 160,000 people. About 60% of its water supply comes from MWD, the balance from local groundwater in the Raymond Basin. Pasadena captures surface runoff from Eaton Canyon and the Arroyo Seco for spreading in its own spreading grounds. Pasadena has an agreement with Glendale to purchase up to 6,000 acre-feet a year of its reclaimed water from the LA/Glendale facility, and hopes to be able to build the infrastructure to make use of this water when funding is available. It has signed onto the conservation BMPs and is doing all of them. It has just installed 340 waterless urinals as part of a pilot program, is involved in commercial conservation, especially restaurants, and offers landscape classes (www.pwpweb.com) (http://www.ci.pasadena.ca.us/waterandpower/).

City of Torrance

The City of Torrance is an original member of MWD, covers 19.54 square miles, has a population of 105,000 people, and serves 78% of the city. The rest of the city is served by the largest investor-owned utility west of the Mississippi, California Water Services Group. The city delivers both potable and reclaimed water. Its water system is governed by the mayor and city council, who appoint a seven-member commission (members serve staggered four-year terms) to provide advice. MWD is now supplying about 92% of its potable water supply.

Torrance is working together with the Water Replenishment District to clean up a bubble of saltwater that has intruded into its groundwater basin. They have built a desalter on city property, funded in part by MWD's Local Projects Program. Torrance has also entered into an agreement with West Basin, which supplies 7,000 acre-feet a year of reclaimed water to the Mobil Oil refinery. Torrance has added an additional 20+ customers for irrigation water as West Basin builds onto its backbone purple pipe system that will eventually reach Palos Verdes. According to the CUWCC website, Torrance is a signatory but has done none of the conservation BMPs (http://www.ci.torrance.ca.us/).

City of San Marino and the California-American Water Company

The City of San Marino is an original member of MWD. Almost all of its water, however, is served by California-American Water Company (Cal-Am), which has been bought out by RWE Thames Water, a Germany-based multinational water company that claims to be the world's third-largest water provider and the largest in the United States. A small part of the city is served by the Sunnyslope Mutual Water Company. The city council appoints the MWD director, and Cal-Am's engineer represents the city at MWD member agency managers meetings. Before acquisition by RWE Thames, Cal-Am served more than 10 million people in 23 states, including the communities of Baldwin Hills, Duarte, Bradbury, and El Monte and parts of Rosemead, San Gabriel, and Temple City. It was a wholly owned subsidiary of the American Water Works Company (www.amwater.com), previously the largest publicly traded U.S. corporation devoted exclusively to the business of water and wastewater. Cal-Am is one of the Committee of Nine; as such it has access to the San Gabriel River. It owns and manages the Fish Canyon Spreading Grounds and operates wells in the area, all of which are west of the plume of contamination in the basin. Neither the city nor Cal-Am has signed onto the BMPs (http://www.ci.san-marino.ca.us/ and http://www.calamwater.com/awpr1/caaw/default.html).

City of Santa Monica

The City of Santa Monica is also an MWD original member agency. It serves a permanent resident population of 90,000 and a daytime population of over 300,000 residents, tourists, and workers. Historically it pumped enough of its own groundwater from the unadjudicated coastal basins to meet 70% of its needs, purchasing 30% from MWD. However, with the discovery of MTBE in its groundwater, 10 wells were shut down, five of which are still closed. The oil companies who were guilty of contaminating the groundwater are paying to clean it up and for the additional MWD water Santa Monica needs to purchase. The ratio is now 82% MWD water, 18% from wells. Historically, Santa Monica has had to treat its groundwater because of high TDS (total dissolved solids), using ion exchange to soften the water. In the early 1980s, TCE was also discovered in the groundwater, and an air stripping facility was added to the treatment.

The city is implementing all of the conservation BMPs, has built a facility just inland from the Santa Monica Pier to treat urban runoff in some of its worst storm drains, and is using this treated water for landscape irrigation. The city also requires that all new construction infiltrate the first three-quarters of an inch of any storm in a 24-hour period on site. This is to reduce the amount of urban runoff that drains onto the beach. It does not recharge the aquifers from which it pumps, since those aquifers are outside of the city limits, and it takes water many, many years to travel so far underground (http://santa-monica.org/).

American States Water Company

American States Water Company (AWR), the parent company of a variety of subsidiaries that serve the regulated water industry, is traded on the New York Stock Exchange. The regulated water industry (investor-owned utilities, or IOUs) is regulated by the California Public Utilities Commission. The subsidiaries include the Southern California Water Company, now known as the Golden State Water Company, and the American States Utility Services. It provides communities with individually tailored service contracts ranging from meter reading, customer service, and system maintenance to full operations service. Its philosophy is "to continue to implement long-term strategies through its subsidiaries, to increase shareholder value by earning the authorized rate of return for its utility operations, and to increase overall earnings through selective nonregulated activities." It serves 127,000 people (9,300 meters) in Central Basin, West Coast Basin, San Gabriel Valley communities, and Culver City, with about 45% local water and 55% from MWD (www.aswater.com).

Southern California Water Company, Renamed,
as of October 1, 2005, Golden State Water Company

The Golden State Water Company is a wholly owned subsidiary of American States Water Company and serves six MWD agencies, 29 cities, and several unincorporated communities in Los Angeles County, with more than 100,000 customer connections. On average, it delivers 41% of the water it serves to its own customers from 64 active company-owned wells. The remaining water supply is surface water purchased from MWD through the West Coast Basin and Central Basin Municipal Water Districts. It is one of the larger investor-owned utilities in the region. It is working with the Water Replenishment District (see later in this chapter) to provide wellhead treatment to some of the wells that suffer from volatile organic compounds (VOCs), arsenic, or other contamination. The company took a leadership role by going to the California Public Utilities Commission and, by carefully describing all facets of its water conservation program, persuaded them to include the money spent on conservation in its rate base. It is implementing all of the conservation best management practices and serves on the advisory committee to help write the California Water Plan B160-05 (http://www.aswater.com/Organization/Company_Links/Regions/Region_2/region_2.html).

California Water Services Group

The California Water Services Group (Cal Water) is the parent company of California Water Services Company, a wholly owned subsidiary. It also provides services to the nonregulated water industry. Cal Water claims to be the largest investor-owned water utility in the western United States and the third-largest in the nation. It serves over 2 million people in 100 communities, including, in the Los Angeles Area, Dominguez, East Los Angeles, Hawthorne, Hermosa/Redondo, and Palos Verdes. It is a signatory and is doing all of the BMPs (www.calwater.com).

Southwest Water Company

The Southwest Water Company provides a full range of water and public works services, from water supply and wastewater treatment to multifamily residence utility billing. Much of its work is performed under contract with cities, municipal utility districts, and other government entities. It serves 2 million Americans in 35 states. It owns and operates the regulated public water utility Suburban Water Systems (www.suburbanwatersystems.com), an investor-owned utility serving Los Angeles and Orange counties. It serves a population in the Los Angeles Area of about 261,000 through a water distribution system that includes 31 reservoirs, 14 wells, 116 booster pumps, and more than 800 miles of pipeline, distributing about 52,000 acre-feet of water a year in the San Gabriel Valley and Central Basin areas. It is not a signatory to the conservation BMPs (www.south westwater.com).

This sampling of water supply agencies suggests the wide variety of types of agencies, how they are structured, and how they function. With this bewildering arrangement it is no wonder that it has been impossible to plan in a comprehensive or integrated way to maximize our local resources, as recommended by a variety of planning processes.

GROUNDWATER MANAGEMENT AGENCIES

Texas and California are the only states to have no laws requiring groundwater management, despite the fact that when more water is pumped out of the ground than is replenished, either by nature or man, the land can subside or cave in to fill the void created. Ideally, groundwater should be managed by determining the safe yield of the basin (how much water can safely be pumped out without destroying the storage capacity of the groundwater basin) and then allocating pumping rights to those owning land over the basin—much like what happens when groundwater is adjudicated. In this way, the underground storage capacity is not compromised and buildings and roads above ground are protected from damage caused by settling of the earth.

Managing for safe yield is purely voluntary in California, except in the basins that have been adjudicated. This has resulted in the tragedy of the commons in many parts of the state, with every person looking out for him- or herself and pumping the resource without concern for what the future might hold. There are places in the San Joaquin Valley where the land has subsided 75 feet, yet agribusiness has successfully blocked any serious attempt at state-mandated management. A recent attempt, AB 3030, encourages existing agencies, such as boards of supervisors or voluntary associations of local agencies, to develop groundwater management plans.

There has been no state review of groundwater overdrafts since 1980. Current state estimates of overdraft, as stated in the California Water Plan B 160-05, is about 2 million acre-feet a year. Only when groundwater overdrafts and competition between those with the pumps have become intolerable have people gone to court to resolve the issues of long-term sustainable management. For groundwater information from DWR, see www.groundwater.ca.gov/dwr_publications/.

Watermasters

The Watermasters' job is to oversee and enforce the water rights in the adjudicated groundwater basins. Watermasters can be court-appointed management boards, the State Department of Water Resources, or an individual. During the process of adjudication, pumping rights are established based on the safe yield (how much water can safely be pumped out each year), replenishment sources and procedures, and a management structure. Some agencies perform some Watermaster functions. The Los Angeles County Department of Public Works, through its operation of spreading basins, injection wells, and other facilities, replenishes the groundwater. The Water Replenishment District of Southern California performs groundwater management and water quality functions in cooperation with County Public Works in the Central and West Coast basins. Together all of these adjudicated basins provide over 600,000 acre-feet of groundwater supply each year to the Los Angeles Area.

The functions of Watermasters are many. They include:

- Managing and controlling the withdrawal and replenishment of water supplies in the basin,
- Determining the annual operating safe yield for the next fiscal year and notifying each of the pumpers of his or her shares,
- Acquiring imported water from MWD and spreading replacement water as needed,
- Coordinating local efforts to preserve and restore the quality of groundwater in the basin,
- Assisting and encouraging regulatory agencies to enforce water quality regulations affecting the basin,
- Collecting data about production, water quality, and other relevant data from producers, and
- Preparing an annual report of Watermaster activities, including financial activities, and summary reports of pumping and diversions.

Here is an example of groundwater managers' consideration of water quality: In 1991, the Watermaster for the Main San Gabriel Basin asked the court for authority to limit groundwater extractions in order to prevent the spread of contamination.

The Water Replenishment District of Southern California

By 1945, due to the large population growth in the Los Angeles coastal plain, the groundwater in the Central Basin and West Coast Basin was severely overdrafted and problems with seawater intrusion began. Two groups, the West Basin Water Association (1946) and the Central Basin Water Association (1950) formed to find ways to limit groundwater extractions, to provide new water, and to create an exchange water pool in order to provide groundwater pumping rights for users. In 1947 the West Coast Basin Municipal Water District was formed, and in 1952 the Central Basin Municipal Water District was formed, to join MWD and to distribute water from the Colorado River. In 1959 these Water Associations helped to create the Central and West Basin Water Replenishment District, later renamed the Water Replenishment District of Southern California (WRD). The Department of Water Resources is the Watermaster for

TABLE 5. Adjudicated Basins and
Watermasters in the Los Angeles Area

Groundwater Basin	Final Decision	Watermaster
Central Basin	1965	Department of Water Resources, Southern District
West Coast Basin	1961	Department of Water Resources, Southern District
Upper Los Angeles River Area	1979	A qualified hydrologist appointed by the California Superior Court
Main San Gabriel Basin	1973	Nine-member board nominated by water purveyors and water districts, appointed by the California Superior Court
Raymond Basin	1944	Raymond Basin Management Board
Puente Basin	1985	Three appointees (consultants)

SOURCE: From www.agwa.org/adjud_basins.html.

West and Central basins, but WRD plays a significant role in managing this groundwater and works cooperatively with DWR.

The 420-square-mile Water Replenishment District of Southern California manages groundwater for approximately 4 million residents in 43 cities in southern Los Angeles County. A five-person elected board of directors oversees the Replenishment District. The Water Replenishment District protects the basins by purchasing imported replacement water from Central Basin for spreading and injection into the ground and reclaimed water from the County Sanitation Districts to be spread at facilities owned and operated by the Los Angeles County Department of Public Works. Spreading is accomplished by diverting water into large earthen basins at the Rio Hondo and the San Gabriel River Spreading Grounds, located in Montebello and Pico Rivera.

Three sources of water are utilized for replenishment at the spreading grounds: (1) imported water purchased from the Central Basin Municipal Water District, (2) treated reclaimed wastewater purchased from the

ITEM	WATER YEAR Oct 1 - Sep 30		
	2003-2004	2004-2005 [a]	2005-06 [a]
Total Groundwater Production	248,334 AF	245,025 AF	252,931 AF
Annual Overdraft	(135,686) AF	(75,639) AF	(107,726) AF
Accumulated Overdraft	(702,100) AF	(660,247) AF	

Quantity Required for Artificial Replenishment for the Ensuing Year		
Spreading		
Imported for Spreading in Montebello Forebay		27,600 AF
Recycled for Spreading in Montebello Forebay		48,000
	Subtotal Spreading	75,600
Injection		
West Coast Basin Barrier		19,000
Dominguez Gap Barrier		13,400
Alamitos Barrier		3,800
	Subtotal Injection	36,200
In-lieu	Subtotal In-lieu	10,303
	Total	122,103 AF

Source and Unit Cost of Replenishment Water for the Ensuing Year		
Recycled Water	Oct-Dec	Jan-Sep
Spreading (CSDLAC - San Jose Creek)	$ 21.31 /AF	$ 21.31 /AF
Spreading (CSDLAC - Whittier Narrows)	$ 7.00 /AF	$ 7.00 /AF
Injection (WBMWD - West Coast Barrier)	$ 450.00 /AF	$ 450.00 /AF
Injection (LA-Terminal Island - Dominguez Barrier)	$ 431.00 /AF	$ 431.00 /AF
Injection (WRD-Alamitos Barrier)	$ 286.00 /AF	$ 286.00 /AF
Imported Water		
Spreading from CBMWD	$ 238.00 /AF	$ 238.00 /AF
Injection - Alamitos (includes $5/af Long Beach surcharge)	$ 448.00 /AF	$ 458.00 /AF
Injection - Dominguez Gap & West Coast (includes $93/af WBMWD surcharge prior to 1/1/06, $92/af after)	$ 536.00 /AF	$ 545.00 /AF
CBMWD Contract Rate for Spreading	$828,000	
WBMWD Water Service & Capacity Reservation Charges	$ 51,287	$ 175,013
In-lieu		
Central Basin Met Member Agency (Long Beach, Compton, Los Angeles)		$ 137 /AF
CBMWD Customer		$ 174 /AF
West Basin Met Member Agency (Torrance, Los Angeles)		$ 137 /AF
WBMWD Customer		$ 168 /AF

Figure 25. Groundwater conditions and replenishment summary of the Water Replenishment District of Southern California. Note estimated values (a).

Los Angeles County Sanitation Districts, and (3) stormwater runoff diverted from the adjacent Rio Hondo and San Gabriel River. Its primary source of revenue is assessments on water pumped from the Central and West Coast basins. It works closely with the State Department of Water

Resources, which serves as the Watermaster for the two basins. It also has some authority and responsibility for water quality and provides well-head treatment for those agencies that contract for that service. It publishes an annual Engineering Survey and Report that reviews all of its activities (http://www.wrd.org/).

The Water Replenishment District has partnered with the United States Geological Survey to conduct a study of the Central and West Coast basins to determine how best to operate and protect the basins. The study involves quantifying the various characteristics of the basins, creating computer models, and developing a planning mechanism for future actions, focused particularly on the recharge activities and the seawater intrusion problem. Multiple depth-monitoring wells have been drilled and sampled in order to develop a three-dimensional picture of the basins (http://pubs.usgs.gov/fs/2002/fs086-02).

Department of Water Resources: Watermaster
Service for Central and West Coast Basins

In 1946, the courts asked the Department of Water Resources to study the boundaries and geohydrologic characteristics of the West Coast Basin. In 1962, the Water Replenishment District of Southern California initiated the process of adjudication of the Central Basin, and by 1965 the courts had appointed the Department of Water Resources (DWR) as the official Watermaster for the two basins. The department receives monthly reports from those who pump the groundwater and creates a water rights account. DWR shares responsibility with the Replenishment District to record all groundwater extractions, and they share concerns over protecting the groundwater resource (http://www.dpla.water.ca.gov/sd/watermaster/watermaster.html).

Upper Los Angeles River Area Watermaster

The Upper Los Angeles River Area (ULARA), commonly referred to as the San Fernando Valley Basin, contains four separate groundwater basins— the San Fernando Basin, the Sylmar Basin, the Verdugo Basin, and the Eagle Rock Basin. Management efforts in ULARA started 80 years ago, when the area first began to use water delivered by the Los Angeles Aqueduct for agricultural purposes. In the 1930s, water from the Owens River was artificially recharged into the basin for later pumping. In 1955, litigation began over water rights in ULARA. In 1962, a detailed study of the geology and hydrology of the Los Angeles River and the groundwater basins was filed with the court. In 1979, the final court judgment awarded the City of Los Angeles the Pueblo Water Rights to all surface and subsurface waters within the San Fernando Basin and all tributary waters to the Los Angeles River within ULARA.

It also awarded Los Angeles, Burbank, and Glendale the right to capture return water, which is the portion of imported water served within the basin that percolates back into the groundwater. The judgment also adjudicated water rights within the Sylmar, Verdugo, and Eagle Rock basins. The court appointed a Watermaster, Mel Blevins, to enforce the judgment and manage the basins within ULARA. He has since been replaced by Mark Mackowski, headquartered in the Los Angeles Department of Water & Power building. The Watermaster was given water quality authority in 1993, which means he can make demands on the Regional Water Quality Control Board to do its job as the local water quality enforcer.

Main San Gabriel Basin Watermaster

The Main San Gabriel Basin Watermaster was created in 1973 by the California Superior Court of Los Angeles County to administer the basin's adjudicated water rights and to provide a basinwide governing body for managing the water resources. Of the Watermaster's nine-member board of directors, six are elected by the water producers, two by the Upper San Gabriel Valley Municipal Water District, and one by the San Gabriel Valley Municipal Water District. The Main San Gabriel Basin provides groundwater to two MWD member agencies—the Upper San Gabriel Valley Municipal Water District and the Three Valleys Municipal Water District—as well as the San Gabriel Municipal Water District. It also serves 35 other public and investor-owned water supply agencies, 15 industrial customers, four governmental agencies, and eight agricultural and golf course pumpers. Additionally, 45 private people or companies either pump directly or lease their water rights to other parties.

In 1983, the agencies interested in optimizing groundwater recharge formed a group called the Groundwater Replenishment Committee and began to meet together on a regular basis to discuss groundwater recharge needs. In 1993, this group agreed to coordinate deliveries of local and imported water and to identify future needs and potential future recharge facilities. The Upper District, Three Valleys, MWD, and the County Department of Public Works, working cooperatively, have identified the gravel pits next to the San Gabriel River as additional potential recharge areas.

For the past 20 years the Watermaster, the Upper District, and MWD have operated under a Cyclic Storage Agreement. Under this agreement, surplus imported water is stored in the basin and extracted when supplies are short. The long-term annual average amount of water that has been stored has been 85,000 acre-feet. In 1990, the Watermaster asked for and got from the court the right to limit extractions to help prevent the spread of contamination and to expedite superfund remediation (www.watermaster.org).

Puente Basin Watermaster

The Puente Basin is connected hydraulically to the Main San Gabriel Basin. It was adjudicated separately in 1985, and two consulting engineers act as Watermaster. There are five pumpers from this basin, who pump on average a total of about 1,000 acre-feet a year. The safe yield has been determined to be between 1,500 and 3,000 acre-feet a year. The only source of water is natural recharge, and the water quality of the basin is not potable. The water is too high in total dissolved solids and is used for irrigation only.

The western end of the basin is contaminated with volatile organic compounds (VOCs). That part of the basin is located in the Puente Operable Unit Superfund site. Therefore, pumpers must have an alternate potable water supply. They are the Walnut Valley Water District and the Roland Water District, which also use imported water, the City of Industry, which still has a little agriculture left and also has wells in the Main San Gabriel Basin, the Industry Urban Development Agency, and the Los Angeles Royal Vista Golf Course. The Puente Narrows Agreement, an addendum to the Main San Gabriel Basin court decision, requires a minimum flow from the Puente Basin to the Main San Gabriel Basin of 588 acre-feet per year. Under the agreement the subsurface flow passing from the Puente Basin to the Main San Gabriel Basin is constantly monitored at two wells, one on either side of the Puente Narrows. The Puente Basin Watermaster publishes her report in conjunction with the Main San Gabriel Basin's Watermaster report.

Groundwater from the Raymond Basin serves several cities and communities in the San Gabriel Valley and surrounding foothills: Pasadena, Alhambra, San Marino, and La Cañada Flintridge. It is a subwatershed of the Arroyo Seco, a tributary to the Los Angeles River. Its first wells were drilled in 1881 for agriculture and the expanding cities. In 1937, due to severe overdrafting, Pasadena brought legal action against Alhambra. As a result of that lawsuit the first California adjudicated basin was created. The adjudication spelled out an action plan to establish the basin's safe yield and pumping rights. The State Department of Water Resources acted as Watermaster during this period. In 1984, the basin's governance was changed, with the Watermaster responsibilities being reassigned to the 10 entities that pump 1,000 acre-feet a year or more from the basin. The Foothill Municipal Water District provides management services. The Raymond Basin Management Board represents the interests of five cities or parts of cities and five other entities (http://www.iinet.com/~rbmb/).

Los Angeles County Department of Public Works

County Public Works is not a Watermaster, nor does it have control over any of our groundwater basins. However, it does play a very important role in managing local groundwater because, together with the Army Corps of Engineers, it is in charge of managing stormwater and therefore manages most of the spreading grounds in the county.

The Los Angeles County Flood Control District was created as part of the 1915 Flood Control Act. The purpose of the agency was "to provide for the control and conservation of the flood, storm, and other waste waters of said district, and to conserve such water for beneficial and useful purposes by spreading, storing, retaining, or causing to percolate into the soil within said district, or to save or conserve in any manner, all or any of such waters, and to protect from damage from such flood or stormwater, the harbors, waterways, public highways, and properties in said district." The Flood Control District was merged with the Los Angeles County Road Department and portions of the Los Angeles County Engineer on January 1, 1985, to become the Los Angeles County Department of Public Works (County Public Works).

It operates sewer systems and airports, administers local public transit programs, manages capital projects for other county departments, meets and monitors environmental requirements, and provides general engineering services and building regulation services for unincorporated parts of the county. It also provides contract services to many cities in the county. It is governed by the County Board of Supervisors.

County Public Work's chief functions concerning water are to control flooding for safety and to conserve stormwater runoff and other waters. It also retails water to isolated parts of the county, is a signatory, and is doing all the BMPs. It has developed a master plan for the Los Angeles River and is developing a master plan for the San Gabriel River watershed.

SPREADING ACTIVITIES The county manages 15 dams, 301 debris retaining structures, 28 spreading basins, 75 stream-gauging stations, and 14 reservoirs in Los Angeles County. Stormwater is captured behind the dams at the mouths of mountain canyons and then released gradually throughout the year and diverted to spreading basins for groundwater recharge. This diverted surface water is given first priority for spreading. Imported and other water is spread as a lower priority. Spreading operations occur throughout the year.

The amount of surface water recharged for local use depends on weather conditions. In 1998, over 23,000 acre-feet of surface water were used for municipal purposes. But in 1996, a drier year, that number dropped to approximately 13,000 acre-feet. County Public Works, in water year 2002–2003 (a water year is usually defined from October 1 to September 31), spread 100% of the rainfall index: 134,611 acre feet of stormwater, 81,129 acre-feet of imported water, and 42,640 acre-feet of recycled water. Los Angeles County conserved during the 2002–2003 hydrology year 134,611 acre-feet of local stormwater runoff that would otherwise flow to the sea, 81,129 acre-feet of imported water, and 42,640 acre-feet of recycled water. The water is directed to 28 groundwater recharge areas or spreading grounds in the Los Angeles area consisting of unlined river bottoms, spreading basins, and pits.

INJECTION County Public Works also operates a series of injection wells to protect groundwater basins near the coast from seawater intrusion. The West Coast Barrier Project consists of 153 injection wells and 296 observation wells and stretches south from the Los Angeles International Airport to Palos

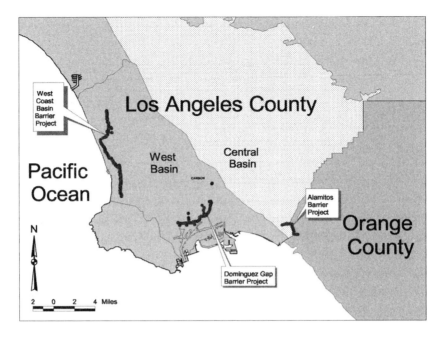

Figure 26. Map of the three barrier projects. (SOURCE: County Public Works.)

Verdes. In water year 2003–2004, a total of 13,000 acre-feet were recharged through these injection wells; 28% was reclaimed.

The Dominguez Gap Project barrier sits adjacent to the Dominguez Channel and consists of 41 injection wells with 107 observation wells. In water year 2003–2004, a total of 6,089 acre-feet of imported and recycled water was injected through these wells from the West Coast Basin.

The Alamitos Barrier project forms a small cup just to the northeast of the Long Beach Marina. It has 43 injection wells, 175 monitoring wells, and four extraction wells, recharging a total of 6,000 acre-feet in water year 2003–2004. Recycled water was purchased from the Water Replenishment District, and imported water from the Long Beach Water Department.

WASTEWATER MANAGEMENT AGENCIES

Wastewater collection and treatment and the discharge of the treated effluent in the Los Angeles Area are the responsibility of the Sanitation Districts of Los Angeles County and the City of Los Angeles' Bureau of Sanitation. The City of Burbank operates a small wastewater treatment plant, and the City of Glendale, in conjunction with the City of Los Angeles, owns and operates the treatment plant located in the Glendale Narrows. The Las Virgenes Municipal Water District delivers drinking water and collects and treats wastewater. For information about reclamation and reuse programs for each, please see Chapter 3, on water use efficiency. Discharges from wastewater treatment plants are closely regulated by the Regional Water Quality Control Board, which implements the federal Clean Water Act on behalf of the United States Environmental Protection Agency.

Sanitation Districts of Los Angeles County

The Sanitation Districts of Los Angeles County (County San) comprise a federation of 25 independent special districts serving the wastewater and solid waste management needs of about 5.1 million people, or about half the residents of Los Angeles County. Its service area covers approximately 810 square miles and encompasses 78 cities and unincorporated territories within Los Angeles County. Its role is to construct, operate, and maintain facilities to collect, treat, and dispose of sewage and industrial wastes and to provide for disposal and management of solid wastes at its own local landfills, including refuse transfer and resource recycling. Local sewers and laterals that connect to County San's trunk sewer lines are the responsibility of local jurisdictions, as is the collection of solid wastes.

The Sanitation Districts operate 11 wastewater treatment facilities, 10 of which are classified as water reclamation plants. The eleventh, the Joint Water Pollution Control Plant in Carson, treats to full secondary standards and discharges to the ocean. Six of the ten are in the Los Angeles Area, and five treat municipal wastewater to tertiary standards while recycling 44.5% of the reclaimed water for a variety of applications. Wastewater treated to tertiary standards is suitable for many uses, such as landscape and agricultural irrigation, industrial process water, recreational lakes, wildlife habitat, and groundwater replenishment. Reclaimed water not directly reused is discharged to the Rio Hondo or the San Gabriel River or one of its tributaries.

Wastewater solids removed by these plants are returned to the sewer for further processing at the Carson facility, where the biosolids are removed

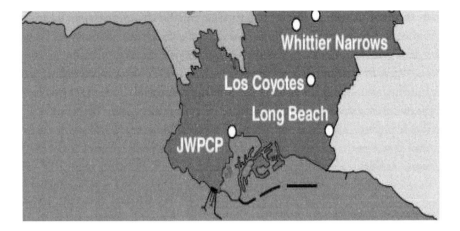

Figure 27. Map of the County Sanitation District's sewage treatment plants.

for a variety of beneficial uses. County San also operates a number of state-of-the-art water quality laboratories and is experimenting with ultraviolet technology to reduce the need for chlorine and therefore the disinfection by-products associated with chlorine (www.lacsd.org).

City of Los Angeles Bureau of Sanitation (City San)

The Los Angeles wastewater system serves over 4 million people in Los Angeles (85%) and 29 contract cities (15%) that are next to or surrounded by the City of Los Angeles. The system contains more than 6,500 miles of sewer pipelines and four wastewater treatment plants that can process approximately 550 million gallons of flow each day. The plants are located in the Sepulveda Basin in the San Fernando Valley, one jointly operated with the City of Glendale in the Glendale Narrows on the Los Angeles River, on Terminal Island in the harbor, and one of the biggest in the world, the Hyperion plant, located just south of Los Angeles International Airport, at the beach.

The Bureau of Sanitation is also responsible for the collection, transport, and disposal of stormwater. The city operates a system of constructed channels, debris basins, pump plants, storm drain pipes, and catch basins to divert stormwater to the ocean. Many of the smaller storm drains' dry-weather flows are now diverted from Santa Monica Bay into the sewer system to Hyperion in order to protect ocean water quality.

During the past couple of years, major efforts have been made to coordinate the operation of each of the various divisions of the Bureau of Sanitation. They have developed, together with a cross section of the city's residents (environmental, business, and community leaders), an Integrated Plan for the Wastewater Program (IPWP), a master plan that will integrate management of drinking water supply, wastewater, and stormwater as the city plans for its future growth. This effort puts City San at the forefront of comprehensive planning because, by fully educating a cross section of the community to the problems and tradeoffs that will need to be made, it has built support for a more enlightened approach that has resulted from examining multiple resources together and adopting multipurpose solutions.

City San also provides trash pickup and recycling, with a goal of recycling 70% of its solid waste. It cocomposts green waste with waste from the zoo into a fine fertilizer and soil amendment and provides workshops for residents in composting (www.lacity.org/SAN/).

Las Virgenes Municipal Water District

Las Virgenes is the only fully integrated system in the Los Angeles Area, installing and operating both a drinking water treatment and delivery system and a wastewater collection and treatment system. It has 500 customers for reclaimed water and composts the biosolids that are the by-product of the sewage treatment process, converting it into a fine fertilizer and soil amendment that is made available free every Saturday morning to its customers. The treated effluent from its Tapia Wastewater Treatment Plant is discharged down Malibu Creek, except for seven months of summer, late spring, and early fall, when the Regional Water Quality Control Board has forbidden this activity in order to protect water quality in the creek and at Surfrider Beach, at the mouth of the creek. Las Virgenes has not been meeting this regulation. Nutrients discharged during the shoulder months cause algae blooms in the creek. The only alternative is to discharge any water it cannot reuse effectively down a tributary to the Los Angeles River (http://www.lvmwd.dst.ca.us/).

City of Burbank Sanitation Department

The City of Burbank operates a small water reclamation plant where it treats 9 million gallons a day of the city's wastewater. It discharges both directly and indirectly to the Burbank Western Channel, indirectly after use as cooling water at the Burbank Steam Power Plant. Whatever wastewater it cannot treat goes into the sewers that connect with the City of Los Angeles, which provides treatment under contract. Of the 330,000 million gallons recycled, 50% was used for cooling water in the steam plant, 30% to irrigate a golf course, 10% on its landfill, and 10% for other uses (http://www.ci.burbank.ca.us/PublicWorks/index.htm).

STORMWATER MANAGEMENT AGENCIES

United States Army Corps of Engineers

The U.S. Army Corps of Engineers (Army Corps) administers a wide variety of programs, of which stormwater management is one of the most important. The Army Corps operates many of the major dams in the area, including Santa Fe and Whittier Narrows dams on the San Gabriel River and the Hansen and Sepulveda Basin dams on the Los Angeles River system. These dams have large basins associated with them that are used for recreational and habitat purposes as well as for stormwater storage during very large storms. The Army Corps is responsible for the maintenance of sections of local rivers, including stretches of the Los Angeles and San Gabriel rivers.

The Army Corps is the last word on modeling stormwater flows and determining the 100-year flood plain, here and across the nation. In addition, the Army Corps issues permits for stream bank alteration under the federal Clean Water Act. Whenever a developer or other entity wants to build along one of the rivers or tributaries and needs to make changes to the channel, they must fulfill Army Corps requirements, including, in some cases, mitigation for the removal of wetlands or riparian habitat. The Army Corps also now has a mandate to do environmental restoration, which includes wetlands and riparian habitat restoration, to provide for recreational opportunities in their facilities, and to work cooperatively with local communities (http://www.usace.army.mil/).

Los Angeles County Department of Public Works (County Public Works)

The Department of Public Works was formed on January 1, 1985, from the former County Road Department, a portion of the Department of County

Engineer Facilities, and the County Flood Control District. Together with the Army Corps, the county manages the massive storm drain system that drains our region to prevent flooding. Many cities build and manage their own internal storm drains that feed into the larger ones managed by the county and the Army Corps. Others depend totally on the county for this service.

County Public Works, as part of its storm water management program, operates numerous dams designed to reduce peak flows by capturing water temporarily until the storm subsides and water can safely be released to the downstream storm channels. These same dams are also designed to capture and hold stormwater for release after the storm has passed in order to put that water into spreading grounds and into our underground aquifers. The county operates almost all of the spreading grounds in the county and the seawater barrier injection wells.

The county established a Watershed Management Division in August 2000 and is now incorporating watershed management thinking into its operations, developing multipurpose projects that can store stormwater where it falls, recharging the groundwater to augment our drinking water supply, improving the quality of urban runoff, and returning moisture content to the soil in support of habitat near our rivers and streams. The Watershed Division, together with TreePeople and Montgomery Watson Harza, is retrofitting an entire neighborhood or subwatershed—Sun Valley, in the eastern end of the San Fernando Valley—to prevent local flooding by capturing all stormwater from a capital event and infiltrating it on site. In addition, the Division is planning to rebuild the parking lot at its headquarters building in Alhambra to demonstrate many of the best management practices to infiltrate stormwater. It has taken the lead in developing and helping local cities to implement the Regional Water Quality Control Board's regulations to address stormwater pollution from new development and redevelopment by the private sector called Standard Urban Stormwater Mitigation Plans, or SUSMPs.

Caltrans

California's transportation agency, Caltrans, has built and manages the drainage systems for all freeways and state roadways and has implemented a Stormwater Management Program. Rainwater washes pollutants from highways, streets, and gutters into the storm drain system. Highways typically contribute products of combustion, brake and tire dust, oil and grease, litter, and other materials that get flushed through the storm drain system to California's rivers and lakes and the ocean. The program consists mainly of installing filters or other mechanisms to remove oil and grease and trash from the runoff. The program is updated annually to guide all aspects of Caltrans' stormwater activities. The Stormwater Management Program also includes research, monitoring, training, and public education (http://www .dot.ca.gov/).

Cities and Other Agencies

Many cities have their own internal storm drain systems that connect to the county's and the Army Corps'. Other cities are dependent on these agencies to provide stormwater services. Two that are providing leadership in stormwater management are the Cities of Los Angeles and Santa Monica.

CITY OF LOS ANGELES The City of Los Angeles built and maintains its own internal storm drain system. It has trained all of its city employees about the benefits of managing stormwater wisely and has an outstanding public education program. Los Angeles was first to rebuild a city parking lot to retain stormwater on site. The city has its own laboratories to test water quality in the storm drain system and at the beach and is diverting a number of smaller drains away from the beach to Hyperion for treatment in order to protect ocean water quality.

SANTA MONICA Santa Monica is also providing stormwater management leadership. It has built the Santa Monica Urban Runoff Facility (SMURF), which gives advanced primary treatment to dry-weather runoff from some of the most contaminated storm drains that formerly drained onto the beach. This treated water, about 300 acre-feet a year, is of good enough quality to use for freeway and other landscape irrigation and some industrial uses. Because the drains captured for treatment originate beyond the Santa Monica city limits, both the city and county of Los Angeles have helped to fund this innovative educational facility, located just inland

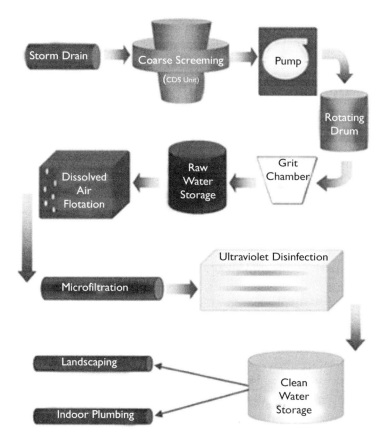

Figure 28. Diagram of the Santa Monica Urban Runoff Facility (SMURF). (SOURCE: City of Santa Monica.)

from the Santa Monica Pier. Santa Monica has also mandated that, with all new construction and remodeling, the first three-quarters of an inch of storm water that falls in a 24-hour period must be captured where it falls and put underground, even in the downtown area, where buildings are built from lot line to lot line, both to reduce the volume of urban runoff and to improve water quality at the beach. This applies not just during construction but also as a permanent way of reducing runoff in the city.

LOS ANGELES & SAN GABRIEL RIVERS WATERSHED COUNCIL The Los Angeles & San Gabriel Rivers Watershed Council has been at the forefront of promoting watershed management, starting with better stormwater management but including a multitude of other policies that promote multipurpose projects to provide multiple benefits. It has brought together 10 agencies to determine how much stormwater can be captured for recharge where it falls in order to add to our underground drinking water supply. Managing stormwater in this way results in reducing the need continually to add on to our storm drain system as the city continues to grow and be paved over, improves water quality in our drains and rivers, and gets moisture back into the ground in support of native habitat. The cooperating agencies are the U.S. Bureau of Reclamation, the California Department of Water Resources, the Metropolitan Water District of Southern California, the Water Replenishment District of Southern California, the Los Angeles Regional Water Quality Control Board, the Watershed Management Division of the County of Los Angeles, the City of Los Angeles Watershed Protection Division, the Los Angeles Department of Water and Power, the City of Santa Monica, and the Watershed Council (www.lasgrwc.org).

WATER QUALITY REGULATORY AGENCIES

United States Environmental Protection Agency

The federal Clean Water Act of 1972 authorized an essential set of core programs that the United States Environmental Protection Agency (USEPA) administers in order to protect and restore both surface water and groundwater quality. Water quality standards are determined by USEPA and administered by state agencies under federal guidance and guidelines.

POINT SOURCES Federal water quality standards regulate the quality of discharges from point sources, those sources with a known outlet that discharge directly to rivers, streams, or the ocean. Point sources include wastewater treatment plants and many kinds of industries that discharge out of a pipe. Wastewater treatment plants may adopt local standards necessary to protect the biological treatment process of treating the wastewater from upsets, to ensure compliance with discharge permits, to prevent pass-through of pollutants to the environment, and to protect the quality of the biosolids produced. These standards are called *pretreatment*. (See description of the sewage treatment process in Chapter 4.)

NONPOINT SOURCES   When the Clean Water Act was reauthorized in 1987, nonpoint source pollution, which is water from diffuse sources such as agricultural runoff, street or urban runoff, and malfunctioning septic systems, was added to USEPA's responsibilities. Urban runoff is a major nonpoint source of pollution and the largest source of ocean pollution in the area. Nonpoint water quality standards were not enforced until a lawsuit was brought by environmental groups in the Los Angeles Area. The settlement of this suit requires that new stormwater permits be issued that regulate trash, bacteria, nutrients, heavy metals, and other contaminants. Discharge permits and enforcement are left to local agencies (the Regional Water Quality Control Boards in California) but given oversight by USEPA (http://www.epa.gov/).

Four key themes were articulated in the USEPA Clean Water Action Plan adopted in February 1998. First, a watershed approach should be used to restore and sustain the health of rivers, lakes, coastal waters, and wetlands. Second, improving state and tribal standards is a key step toward protecting public health, preventing polluted runoff, and ensuring accountability. Third, encouraging natural resource stewardship or conservation of cropland, pasture, rangeland, and forests that are in private and public hands can protect water quality. Federal natural resource agencies are essential to this effort. And fourth, fostering an informed citizenry and officials, who are essential, by providing accurate and timely information about the health of watersheds, beaches, fish, and drinking water is the foundation of a sound and accountable clean water program.

State Water Resources Control Board and Regional Water Quality Control Boards

The State Water Resources Control Board (State Board) establishes water quality standards statewide and is in charge of managing water rights. It hears appeals from Regional Board rulings. Five full-time State Board members are appointed by the governor and confirmed by the state senate (http://www.swrcb.ca.gov/).

Nine Regional Water Quality Control Boards (Regional Boards) were established in 1967. The mission of the Regional Boards is to develop and enforce water quality objectives and implementation plans that will best protect the beneficial uses of the state's waters, recognizing local differences in climate, topography, geology, and hydrology. Each Regional Board has nine part-time members appointed by the governor and confirmed by the senate. Regional Boards develop *basin plans* that determine the beneficial use of each water body. They issue waste discharge requirements (discharge permits), take enforcement actions against violators, and monitor water quality. The ongoing challenge for both State and Regional Boards is protecting and enforcing the many beneficial uses of both surface water and groundwater, taking into consideration the needs of industry, agriculture, municipal districts, and the environment.

The Los Angeles Regional Water Quality Control Board covers most of Los Angeles and Ventura counties. It conducts the following broad range of activities to protect ground and surface waters under its jurisdiction. It addresses regionwide and specific water quality concerns through updates of the Water Quality Control Plan (Basin Plan) for the Los Angeles Region. It prepares, monitors compliance with, and enforces discharge permits called Waste Discharge Requirements, including NPDES (National Pollution Discharge Elimination System) permits. It implements and enforces local stormwater control efforts. It regulates the cleanup of contaminated sites that are already polluted or have the potential to pollute ground or surface water. It enforces other water quality laws, regulations, and waste discharge requirements.

It also coordinates with other public agencies and groups that are concerned with water quality, informs and involves the public on water quality issues, prepares a biennial water quality assessment, and develops and enforces total maximum daily loads (TMDLs), which are essential plans that determine how much of each pollutant the receiving waters can assimilate (www.waterboards.ca.gov/losangeles/).

Department of Health Services

Appointed by the governor, the State Department of Health Services' director heads one of the largest departments in state government, with over 5,000 employees working in the Sacramento headquarters and over 60 field offices throughout the state. The Department of Health Services is one of 13 departments within the State Health and Welfare Agency.

The Department's Division of Drinking Water and Environmental Management promotes and maintains a physical, chemical, and biological environment that contributes positively to health, prevents illness, and ensures protection of the public through the regulation and monitoring of public water systems, wastewater reclamation projects, disposal of low-level radioactive waste, shellfish production and harvesting operations, and medical waste generators. This division is also responsible for administering the federal Safe Drinking Water Act, for maintaining the scientific expertise of the drinking water program, and for carrying out its administrative functions (http://www.dhs.ca.gov/).

San Gabriel Basin Water Quality Authority

The San Gabriel Basin Water Quality Authority was established to coordinate the Superfund cleanup of the San Gabriel Valley. A Joint Powers Authority was established by USEPA, at first composed of the most important agencies in the region to foster consolidation and cooperation and to find and manage the funding needed to do the job. Then in 1993, the legislature stepped in, formed the San Gabriel Valley Water Quality Authority, and gave it taxing authority. The board of the Water Quality Authority is composed of one representative each from the Three Valleys Municipal Water District, the Upper San Gabriel Municipal Water District, and the San Gabriel Valley Municipal Water District. Two seats are for local cities, one with pumping rights, one without; and one seat is reserved for water producers that are investor-owned utilities and serve water in the basin.

Its enabling legislation requires the development of a basinwide groundwater quality management and remediation plan to characterize basin contamination and to develop and implement basin cleanup. It is also responsible for public information and for preventing contaminated groundwater from spreading under the Whittier Narrows Dam into the Central and West Coast basins. This is complicated, because the sources of contamination must be identified, and the people responsible must pay for the cleanup. The authority's biggest problem is determining who will pay for the cleanup.

Identifying those responsible from before the Clean Water Act was written has proven to be very difficult. Nitrates were first discovered in the east end of the basin in 1974. By 1979, the solvents TCE and PCE were discovered, and in 1984 four Superfund sites were identified. By 1990, Sierra

Club members challenged all of the water district directors who were up for reelection in the San Gabriel Valley. This was the first time there were any challenges since 1972. Local church groups also organized to protest the slowness of cleanup. The responsibility for cleanup had been given to the Main San Gabriel Basin Watermaster to coordinate, but it was taking too long to assemble the necessary money to do the job.

ASSOCIATIONS OF WATER AGENCIES

Water agencies have come together to form various water agency associations to serve a variety of functions. Historically they have promoted the formation of the various municipal water districts and the Water Replenishment District in order to solve local water problems. These associations have no management or regulatory function. They serve to keep members informed, to share and disseminate information, to lobby the state legislature, and to socialize. Below are some of these associations.

- The *American Water Works Association* is the largest nationwide association of water agencies and the dominant water force nationally and in most states (http://www.awwa.org/).
- The *Association of California Water Agencies (ACWA)* is the largest statewide. It was originally established to provide low-cost insurance for water agency directors and employees. It holds two major conferences a year in various parts of the state and plays a major role in lobbying the state on water policy matters. ACWA doubles as a government agency, since all of its members and employees are water district officials and they get health care and pensions under the state system, and a nonprofit agency when it wants to avoid freedom of information inquiries (http://www.acwa.com/).
- *The Association of Ground Water Agencies* is a relatively new southern California association. It completed a study of the storage potential of our local underground aquifers (www.agwa.org).
- The *Central and West Basin Association of Pumpers*
- The *California Water Association of Investor-Owned Utilities* is made up of investor-owned utilities that serve about 20% of the state's water. There is also a national association.

- The *San Gabriel Valley Water Association* is a coalition of water agencies; it meets quarterly. It is most concerned with water quality issues and the Superfund cleanup in the valley.
- The *Southeast Water Coalition (SEWC)* was formed by a group of cities to address the migration of contaminated groundwater from the San Gabriel Valley into the Central Basin.
- The *Groundwater Resources Association of California* (www.grac.org)
- The *Water Industry Coordinating Council* coordinates these national water efforts: the Association of Metropolitan Water Agencies (only the big agencies); the National Association of Water Companies (the private companies); the National Rural Water Association (farmers); and the National Water Resources Association (the western agencies).

WATER MANAGEMENT ACCOUNTABILITY

The complexity of water management in the Los Angeles Area is illustrated by the multitude of water institutions that have evolved, both in quantity and in kind.

There are hundreds of agencies in the Los Angeles Area because of how the region grew and developed over time. Single-purpose agencies were established to deal with specific issues as they arose, just as the county has evolved to contain 88 different cities, many of which have their own water delivery systems. Each of these agencies has its own board of directors and staff. As the region has grown into one large urbanized area, this proliferation of agencies raises questions about just how efficient and effective they can be, especially as water quality regulations continue to become more stringent over time. Duplication of boards, staffing, etc., and the sheer economies of scale would suggest the need for consolidations. With so many of them doing different things at different levels, how can a citizen even begin to understand all these agencies or even where she or he can go to find out?

Different kinds of water agencies have different management structures. Most water districts, municipal water districts, and irrigation districts have publicly elected boards of directors to set policy, hire and fire the general manager, and determine the agency's budget. The boards also determine their own compensation and perks of office. Water agency directors are usually elected to serve four-year terms. When vacancies do occur, which has been rare, the remaining directors fill the vacancy, so there are almost always incumbents running for reelection. If there are no challengers, then the election doesn't even appear on our ballots. This is beginning to change because of the recent prominence of water quality issues and because of the popular 2000 movie *Erin Brockovich*, both of which have stimulated some press coverage and some interest in the affairs of water agencies.

Little media coverage means little attention. Because the day-to-day issues before these agencies are in themselves not exciting, there is little if any news coverage unless a scandal or a major water quality issue arises. People cannot be interested in what they know nothing about. Therefore, it is the rare citizen that attends board meetings to learn what is going on. Those who do attend invariably have financial business before the board.

Directors are often provided with health, dental, and life insurance, and a car allowance, and sometimes they are even provided with retirement benefits. Directors are usually paid a per diem, an amount for each meeting attended. This per diem can be used to cover committee meetings, prayer meetings, dinner meetings of various philanthropic or political associations, and attendance at water conferences held at resort hotels for a week at a time, several times a year. These perks can add up to $10,000 or $20,000 a year or more per director. Newspapers have reported improprieties relating to the amount of money or perks given to a few elected directors, such as acting and flying lessons. The *Sacramento Bee* ran a series of articles on this subject in November 2003. Of course there are many directors who take their jobs seriously and are fine public servants. Others are in it for the prestige or the perks or to use their elected position as a stepping-stone to a more visible public office.

As drinking water quality standards continue to become more stringent, it will be more and more difficult for water districts to provide the treatment required. Very small water agencies, those that serve fewer than 200 connections, are regulated by the county health department but under state supervision and are exempt from some water quality requirements. To cope with the costs associated with meeting water quality standards as well as with other infrastructure needs, agency directors find it difficult to raise rates and still get reelected. Economies of scale would suggest that it makes more sense to work cooperatively to install regional water treatment facilities.

Some local water distribution and wastewater collection systems are old and crumbling, built 100 years ago. Small agencies especially find it hard to raise the capital and/or the water rates needed to repair or replace old infrastructure and get reelected. An easy answer for smaller water systems is to sell the system or to hire out the operation and maintenance to multinational companies that are everywhere, scouting to buy up whatever they can and promising to do the job more economically. (See Chapter 5.)

The directors who benefit from the perks mentioned earlier are covetous of their prerogatives, which can add up to a substantial amount of money, so they press for the need to maintain local control. This is true even when the control they speak of is personal. Local control is sought by cities and by agencies at every level of government, yet there are benefits to be gained by close cooperation and/or consolidation.

Communication, Cooperation, and Coordination

By necessity, each of the several hundred agencies in the Los Angeles Area is first and foremost concerned about its own needs and responsibilities. Inertia, concerns about turf, mistrust of others, and a lack of concern on the part of some to the broader needs of the region have proven to be obstacles that are beginning to be overcome as water agencies confront declining resources and increasing demand. The concept of working across media or across agencies is also beginning to gain acceptance, especially in those cities or agencies where multiple jurisdictions already exist and where there are thoughtful leaders, mostly in the larger agencies. These need to be encouraged. Some examples follow.

The Los Angeles & San Gabriel Rivers Watershed Council has successfully brought together 10 agencies around one table to work cooperatively in studying how we might augment our drinking water supply by infiltrating stormwater where it falls. The study's first objective was to show that the quality of groundwater would not be negatively affected by infiltrated urban runoff and air pollution. Agencies include water supply agencies, stormwater management agencies, a water quality agency, groundwater management agencies, and cities.

The County of Los Angeles' Watershed Management Division is working cooperatively with the local Sun Valley community, with the nonprofit TreePeople, and with consultants to totally retrofit this subwatershed tributary to the Los Angeles River. The goal is to retain all stormwater in a capital event within the subwatershed, restore habitat, improve water quality, and eliminate the need to build a $42 million concrete storm channel.

The City of Los Angeles is working on an integrated wastewater, water supply, and stormwater planning process that is involving many people from all across the city. These people, drawn from lists of civic leaders compiled by all the City Council offices, have invested over a year and a half to learn all of the ins and outs of running such a complex system and the trade-offs that need to be considered when designing future systems. Costs, jobs, environmental benefits, and public health benefits are some of the issues being balanced, as well as the benefits of an integrated systemic approach to resource management versus just building facilities to meet each separate future need.

The city of Santa Monica has successfully completed a project that takes runoff from two of the most polluted storm drains, which formerly drained onto the beach, and is giving this water advanced primary treatment. It is then good enough in quality to be used for irrigating freeway landscaping, parks, schools, etc., and for some industrial process water purposes, replacing a similar quantity of imported water. Santa Monica has been able to do this because it has its own water delivery system and manages its own stormwater and because it was able to work cooperatively with the City and County of Los Angeles, who helped fund the project.

Cooperation for the Future

What follows are some other examples of how better communication and cooperation might work in the future.

Water suppliers have not always coordinated with wastewater agencies in resource planning, and vice versa. This is most apparent in water conservation programs. Water supply agencies, because they have not typically spoken to sanitation districts, have calculated the cost effectiveness of their conservation programs based on the avoided costs of new water supplies alone. It is also important to calculate the avoided costs of new wastewater treatment facilities that would not have to be built and maintained as the volume of wastewater decreases. Another advantage in having one agency that manages both water supply and wastewater management functions is not having to decide which agency owns the reclaimed water, the water supply or wastewater treatment agency.

Water suppliers and water quality agencies don't speak the same language. Water quality agencies, in an effort to prevent any degradation of groundwater quality, have put more stringent restrictions on the quality of water to be spread into the ground than on imported drinking water supplies.

Historically there has been great mistrust between groundwater management agencies and water supply agencies. This mistrust has led to a lack of willingness to manage groundwater resources in conjunction with surface supplies. As a result, storage in local groundwater basins has not been maximized. Efforts by the legislature to mandate groundwater management have not been successful. It is only recently that local, not statewide, groundwater storage capacity has been the subject of a comprehensive study, one performed specifically to determine how best to coordinate conjunctive use. The last assessment of our groundwater resources by the state was done in 1980. The legislature has only been able to make groundwater management permissive.

There currently are no provisions for allocating a designated amount of water to maintain habitat that already exists in the rivers, nor are there provisions for allocating water for wetlands or fish. These considerations need to be included in any planning for future water uses. The environment must have dedicated water rights, too.

THE CALFED PROCESS

The state tried to find a coordinated, comprehensive way to solve all of the problems in the delta in a public and transparent process called CALFED. It grew out of an effort by leaders among the urban water management agencies, who worked to find common ground among the three different interest groups in the state, each of which has veto power in the state legislature: agriculture, the urban sector, and environmentalists. These three interest groups are all adept at lobbying for their points of view, and they are usually able to block any legislation with which they disagree. The urban leaders began to talk to people in each of the other two groups, searching for a way to establish better communications and to end the gridlock in something called the *three-way process*.

At about the same time, Felicia Marcus was appointed head of USEPA Region IX, in San Francisco. She quickly realized that there was no policy coordination among any of the federal agencies with responsibility in the delta. Besides EPA, there are the Army Corps of Engineers, U.S. Fish and Wildlife, the Bureau of Reclamation, the National Oceanic and Atmospheric Administration, the Bureau of Land Management, and others. So she put together something called Club FED, standing for the Federal Environmental Directorate, to develop a unified voice from the federal government. The state had to follow suit, bringing together the many state agencies, and they then all merged with the three way process to form CALFED.

CALFED was created as a cooperative, interagency working group composed of 23 state and federal agencies to address the water supply, demand, and environmental problems associated with the San Francisco Bay and Delta. Four basic problem areas were identified: ecosystem quality, water supply reliability, water quality, and levee system integrity. They recognized that these problems and their solutions are all interrelated.

CALFED explored a wide range of alternatives to deal with these problems and, after many years of study and review and with the participation of a broadly representative public advisory committee and a scientific advisory committee, adopted *California's Water Future: A Framework for Action,* also known as the Record of Decision or ROD, in August of 2000. This 57-page document outlines an extensive and integrated water management plan that includes hundreds of specific actions. The eight key components of the plan include ecosystem restoration, watersheds, water management, storage (which means building more dams and reservoirs and/or storing more water underground), conveyance, water use efficiency, drinking water quality, water transfers, levee system integrity, and good science. CALFED has spent about $3 billion on projects to restore the delta ecosystem, on helping local watershed groups develop watershed management plans, and on various public education efforts.

CALFED was originally governed by a committee of representatives from each of the government agencies, which did not work out very well. It is now governed by the Bay Delta Authority, a part-time seven-member board. Five members are appointed by the governor from various regions of the state. And one each is appointed by the Speaker of the Assembly, and the President Pro Tem of the State Senate. The Bay Delta Authority has oversight functions only. It has no regulatory authority or taxing authority, so many of its recommendations have not been implemented. The large Public Advisory Committee and the Scientific Advisory Committee continue their functions. Much of the funding that has supported its programs so far has come from bonds passed by the voters: Propositions 40, 50, and 204.

The principle that the users or beneficiaries should pay for the projects and programs that would be developed by CALFED was adopted early on. However, there has been great resistance on the part of both agriculture and the urban water community to pitch in and actually pay for what they want done. Instead they have gone to both the state and federal governments, demanding that taxpayers foot the bill, with poor results. Others have challenged in court the environmental documentation that supports the ROD.

The ROD EIR/EIS was declared insufficient by the Third Circuit Court of Appeals in the fall of 2005 because it does not consider reducing pumping from the delta as an alternative, nor does it identify sources of water to fill the proposed new dams, nor does it evaluate the Environmental Water Account established to help restore habitat and fish.

The governance of CALFED has also been challenged because of its lack of effectiveness. The delta ecosystem is changing dramatically, water quality standards have never been enforced, and a levee failed in June 2004 without any obvious cause, probably a burrowing animal. It took $40 million just to pump out the island, Jones Tract, and repair the levee. Overall damage done to other infrastructure and buildings was estimated at $90 million to $100 million. Yet the land farmed is worth only $20 million to $30 million. Since 1980, 27 delta islands have partially or completely flooded, including Jones Tract.

Governor Schwarzenegger finally asked the Little Hoover Commission to investigate why the agency has not been successful, and to recommend a different governance structure and/or other ways to make this agency more effective. See Chapter 5 for more on CALFED. For history, structure, committees, etc., visit http://calwater.ca.gov.

CONCLUSION

The region has developed over time, so there are now many different water agencies providing us with many different needed services. Because of the great number of agencies, it is difficult if not impossible for the people to become knowledgeable about the agencies and their roles, responsibilities, and effectiveness and therefore to be able to hold them accountable. Better communication, coordination, cooperation, and perhaps consolidation, along with more comprehensive messages from them, would make it much easier for the public to understand and follow water issues and concerns.

Economies of scale suggest that it takes the financial resources of larger agencies to treat water economically and to raise the capital needed to repair and/or replace old, worn infrastructure. These economies of scale make smaller purveyors tempting targets for takeover by private investors who are willing to make investments up-front to build a water business and sometimes willing to promise more than they can deliver. For those who favor retaining direct public control over our water resources, consolidation of some of these agencies should be seriously considered.

The proliferation of agencies also suggests the need for regional if not statewide planning—a statewide water policy—to bring some coherence to how water is managed. CALFED has proven to be ineffective because the political will truly to solve all the problems does not exist and because it lacks an independent funding source.

Other existing planning processes are explored in Chapter 5 along with their effectiveness. None have any teeth.

Chapter 3 | WATER USE EFFICIENCY

> With technologies and methods available today, farmers
> could cut their water needs by 10–15%, industries by
> 40–90%, and cities by a third with no sacrifice of economic
> output or quality of life.
>
> SANDRA POSTEL, *Global Water Policy Project*

The biggest and best source of *new* water, the one most people believe to
be the most cost effective, the cheapest, the most readily available, and the
most secure method of supplying the Los Angeles Area and the state with
water to meet the needs of our growing population, is to use our local water
resources much more efficiently. Efficiencies include conservation, reclamation and reuse (which is considered a new water supply by some),
conjunctive use of surface water and groundwater, watershed management,
which includes better utilization of stormwater, the development of a
landscape ethic, and better management of our dams and spreading grounds,
all described in this chapter. Also described is ocean desalinization.

The California Constitution, Article X, Section 2, requires that all uses
of the state's water be both reasonable and beneficial. It prohibits the waste
and unreasonable use, method of use, or method of diversion of water. The
State Water Resources Control Board, as part of its water rights authority
and responsibilities, can condition a water right on appropriate conservation. This authority was applied in the 1980s to agricultural runoff that was
raising the level of the Salton Sea and flooding neighboring agricultural
lands. The State Board issued a Cease and Desist Order that required more
agricultural conservation to stabilize the water level in the sea. Therefore,
if the constitution is to be followed, as well as our common sense, the biggest
and most dependable source of new water available is to use what we have
as efficiently as possible.

Many studies have concluded that we can greatly reduce our dependence on imported water and accommodate the increased population growth, both within the region and statewide, by fully implementing these efficiencies. However, if we are to achieve the savings that are possible, there must be carrots and sticks added to the programs that are now available. Almost all efficiency programs are voluntary at this time. Each water agency must find it in its own self-interest to put into place the programs outlined in this chapter. Without the carrots provided by the Metropolitan Water District of Southern California (MWD) and the resources of most of the municipal water districts, most of the smaller agencies in the Los Angeles Area would not implement any of them.

Some of the reasons are explored in Chapter 2, but the primary reason seems to be their unwillingness to acknowledge that spending money on efficiencies makes economic sense. They are unwilling to budget the money needed. When each agency is dependent on water sales for its income, it does not find it in its self-interest to spend money in order to have less product to sell. This, despite the fact that efficiencies are the cheapest "new" sources of water available.

The best argument for not promoting as much efficiency as possible is that, with the installation of low-flow showerheads, washing machines, and toilets, for example, there will not be the same opportunities to save or cut back on usage during the next drought. This is called "hardening the demand." This argument is specious, since the easiest cutbacks during times of drought are simply turning the water off when brushing teeth or shaving or washing dishes or vegetables, taking shorter showers, and not flushing the toilet after every use—just being careful not to waste.

CONSERVATION: CURRENT PRACTICES

The efforts to conserve water in California were mostly initiated as the result of the last drought, which, for the first time, caused water shortages in both the agricultural and urban sectors. Until the drought of 1987–92, there had always been some "surplus" as then defined in the system. The Endangered Species Act was not yet being implemented on the scale that it is being implemented today, nor were water quality standards. Water was thought wasted if it flowed to the sea.

TABLE 6. Indoor Water Use in California

End Use	% of Total Use
Toilets	32
Showers	22
Washing Machines	14
Dishwashers	1
Leaks	12
Faucets	19

SOURCE: From *Waste Not, Want Not: The Potential for Urban Water Conservation in California.* The Pacific Institute, November 2003.

As the state comes to grips with the problems of restoring the Sacramento–San Joaquin Delta, providing for a reliable water supply of good quality, and protecting the delta levees, a coalition of state and federal agencies, each with some responsibility in the delta, came together with environmental groups and both urban and rural water agencies to form CALFED. CALFED has adopted conservation as one of its principal goals. It has been exploring ways to certify those who are conserving as a prerequisite to receiving state grants or low-interest loans.

Although only the residential sector is given close examination in this book, there is also great room for improvement in the industrial sector. Conservation in industry becomes highly technical and specific to each industry, so it is more difficult to assess. However, MWD's experience in offering a subsidy to those industries that can become more efficient in their water use has been amazing. All the money set aside for this subsidy is immediately spoken for. Because agriculture has almost disappeared in the Los Angeles Area, this sector is not discussed here but in Chapter 5.

California Urban Water Conservation Council (CUWCC)

Since the 1987–92 drought, some cities and water districts in California have made water conservation a high priority by seeking to eliminate wasteful practices. To assist in this goal, urban water agencies throughout California joined with environmental groups and other water professionals to form the nonprofit California Urban Water Conservation Council (CUWCC).

They signed a Memorandum of Understanding (MOU) in 1991 that details 14 best management practices (BMPs) designed to conserve water that each signatory promised to implement. This council also works to identify additional best management practices and to quantify the savings that can be obtained from each. It acts as the conservation clearinghouse for the state and as a brain trust of sorts for the signatory agencies. It is totally voluntary.

Implementing these best management practices has already led to successes that can be measured. Despite a population increase of slightly over 35% (or nearly 1 million people) since 1970, current water use in the City of Los Angeles has grown by only 7%. Per capita usage has been reduced by 15%. The entire MWD service territory now uses about the same amount of water as it did 20 years ago, despite a comparable increase in population. Eight of the BMPs account for 85% of the savings at 50% of the cost of new water.

CUWCC's Best Management Practices (BMPs).

Because each area has unique needs, water agencies are not required to use the programs exactly as outlined but can adapt them to their needs as long as their program is as effective. All members of CUWCC are required to submit a progress report to its website once every two years. The report is accepted via the web in order to keep an accurate and organized database that can be used easily to assess the progress of different areas and agencies. The results of these filings are available for all to see (www.cuwcc.org). The 14 best management practices follow.

1. *Water survey programs for single-family and multifamily residential customers.* Provide the highest 20% of water users with incentives and/or alternative household appliances (toilets, showerheads) that will result in less water consumption.

2. *Residential and commercial plumbing retrofit.* Offer ultralow-flush toilets (ULFTs) to homeowners to replace their existing toilets. The state prohibits the sale of toilets using more than 1.6 gallons per flush. Therefore ultralow-flush models are now required on all new construction in the state. A bill pending before the legislature as this is written would require that toilets be replaced whenever a home is

sold. This is now required in the cities of Los Angeles and Santa Monica. Toilet flushing accounts for almost a third of all indoor water used.

3. *System water audits, leak detection, and leak repair.* Conduct an audit, at least once every three years, to compare the meters of the water suppliers to those of their customers to determine if there are leaks in the system. When cost effective, leaks are repaired.

4. *Metering of all old and new connections and the institution of commodity rates.* Meters are required on all new connections, and water bills must be based on volume of use. Meters must be installed in those parts of the state that are not currently metered, such as Fresno, Sacramento, and Stockton.

5. *Large landscape conservation programs and incentives.* Identify and contact all irrigators of large landscapes (e.g., golf courses, green belts, common areas, schools, parks, cemeteries), offering them information about how to irrigate more efficiently and about the use of native plants. Water agencies must also provide follow-up audits at least once every five years and provide multilingual training and current information necessary to carry out the program. A state law has since been passed requiring the use of drought-tolerant landscaping in large landscaped areas.

6. *High-efficiency washing machine rebate programs.* Support local, state, and federal legislation to improve the efficiency of washing machines, because high-efficiency washing machines save water and energy and lessen the load on wastewater treatment plants. If an energy or wastewater utility in the agency's territory offers a rebate for the purchase of such a machine, then the water agency must also provide a rebate, unless the maximum rebate offered by the others is less than $50. Washing machines account for approximately 25% of all water used indoors.

7. *Public information programs.* Promote water conservation through public speaking and the media, by inserting educational material into water bills, and by listing individual customer use, in gallons per day, on bills. Coordinate with other government agencies, industry groups, and public interest groups in promoting water awareness.

8. *School education programs.* Work with school districts in the water supplier's service area to provide educational material and instructional assistance to promote water awareness.

9. *Commercial and industrial conservation programs.* Identify and contact the top 10% of industrial and commercial customers, offering audits and incentives sufficient to achieve implementation of water-saving practices. Provide follow-up audits at least once every five years.

10. *Wholesale agency assistance programs.* Provide local assistance, because of the greater financial ability of most wholesale agencies over many of the smaller retail agencies.

11. *Conservation pricing.* Provide incentives to customers to reduce average use. This may involve an inverted rate structure. When more than a set amount of water is consumed, the rate goes up for the next increment of water used. More could be charged during the summer dry season when water is not as available.

12. *Conservation coordinator.* Designate a water conservation coordinator responsible for preparing the conservation plan, managing its implementation, and evaluating the results.

13. *Wastewater prohibition.* Prohibit gutter flooding, sales of automatic water softeners, single-pass cooling systems in new connections, nonrecirculating systems in all new conveyer car wash and commercial laundry systems, and nonrecycling decorative water fountains.

14. *Residential ULFT replacement programs.* When homes are sold, require replacement of old inefficient toilets that used anywhere from 3.5 to 7.0 gallons per flush with 1.6-gallon-flush toilets (ultralow-flow toilets).

Only two best management practices are required by law in California. (1) no new toilets with more than 1.6 gallons per flush can be sold in the state (since 1980), and (2) local jurisdictions must either adopt their own or implement the state's landscape ordinance for large properties or greenways that are built by developers. This second law went into effect in January 1993. Local jurisdictions can adopt more stringent ordinances, as the City of Los Angeles has. Caltrans is required to use reclaimed water for landscape irrigation wherever available and must plant drought-tolerant landscape materials.

A Landscape Task Force, authorized by the legislature, has reinforced the need to reduce landscape water use, to improve irrigation efficiency, to encourage the use of low-water-use plants, and to apply conservation rate structures to send appropriate pricing signals. Adopting a landscape ethic is also considered a part of watershed management. The task force recommendations are posted at http://www.cuwcc.org/ab2717_landscape_task_force.lasso.

Wholesale agencies are required to comply with only the following best management practices: system water audits, leak detection and repair, public information programs, school education programs, conservation pricing, local agency assistance, and a conservation coordinator. The requirement to provide local agency assistance is taken quite seriously by most wholesale agencies. Their support results in the sum total of what conservation programs exist in much of the area outside of a few progressive cities.

CUWCC is exploring the following additional BMPs.

- *Implement rate structures and other economic incentives and disincentives to encourage water conservation.* Many local agencies have adopted inclining block rates. After a basic amount of water is served to consumers at a low rate, the next increment of water used is charged at a higher rate. Over half the water agencies in California apply a flat rate, charging the same rate no matter how much is used, or a declining block rate, where less money is charged for each additional block of water.

- *Implement efficiency standards* for water-using appliances, such as both dish and clothes washing machines and irrigation devices.

- *Replace existing water-using appliances and irrigation devices* (except toilets and showerheads, whose replacements are already BMPs). As more efficient washing machines are developed, some power companies and water agencies are willing to provide rebates because these machines save both energy and water. Front-loading clothes washers, also called horizontal-axis machines, are both energy and water efficient and are easier on the clothes washed.

- *Retrofit existing car washes* to recirculate some of the water used.

- *Allow gray water use.* Gray water is water that comes from showers, sinks, and washing machines. It has been approved for landscape irrigation in closed underground systems by the state, the City of Los Angeles, and some other jurisdictions.

- *Regulate distribution system pressure.* Water pressure varies throughout systems, depending on how far the user is from the pumps or from the reservoir if the water is distributed by gravity. When pressure is high and the tap is turned on, the water gushes wastefully. Water can be saved by installing pressure regulators that will produce a more moderate and consistent rate of flow.

- *Break down water-billing records by customer class.* The more information people have on their bills, the more intelligently they can behave.

- *Implement swimming pool and spa conservation,* such as covers to reduce evaporation.

- *Restrictions or prohibitions on devices that rely on evaporation to cool exterior spaces.* Evaporative coolers are an energy-efficient way to cool large spaces, but they consume lots of water. They should not be used outside.

- *Install point-of-use water heaters,* which heat the water just as it is about to be used. Recirculating hot water systems and insulation of hot water pipes save the water that is run to get hot water when desired. The City of Oceanside has mandated that all new homes be built with hot water circulation systems.

- *Implement efficiency standards for new industrial and commercial processes.* A rebate program offered by MWD to encourage industrial and commercial efficiencies was oversubscribed almost immediately in 2001.

- *Install irrigation devices.* Since on average 50% of the water in a single-family home is used outside, as much as 70% in the summer and in drier areas, the savings potential from efficient irrigation devices is enormous. The Irvine Ranch Water District (IRWD), in Orange County, has installed a programmable computer-operated irrigation controller, also called an ET controller, in 114 homes. These irrigation controllers are programmed to match the evapotranspiration, or ET, of plant materials already growing in the front yard and backyard of each home. The ET is the amount of water each plant uses. These irrigation controllers are connected by radio to the state weather station, which signals relative humidity and precipitation. With both ET and the weather plugged in, the amount of irrigation water can be programmed to provide the optimum required for healthy landscaping. Along with the education needed to understand this system, residents were given soil moisture probes. The volume of urban runoff, nutrients, herbicides and pesticides, and bacteria in the runoff from five different groups of homes were monitored. Each group shares a single storm drain. One group was educated only; the second group was educated and 114 out of 300 homes in the drainage area had the irrigation controller installed (participants self-selected because they were interested in conserving water). The other three groups were controls. The study tested the value of public education and the impact on urban dry-weather runoff. The typical savings was 10% of total household use and a 50% reduction in dry-weather runoff, with no increase in runoff pollution. Large landscapes saved even more. Education alone produced a 6% savings. And the landscaping is healthier because it is not over-watered (www.irwd.com/conservation/R3).

- *Include graphic information and more information on water bills.* Other agencies in southern California have changed their water bills to include graphic information about water usage, comparing customer's use against the previous year's use and against the agency average. Bills often also include tips on how to conserve. Using graphics instead of words has generated much more interest in water conservation than words alone.

Those Reporting on BMP Compliance

All but one of the wholesale municipal water agencies in the Los Angeles Area, the San Gabriel Valley Municipal Water District, have signed onto the MOU and have reported that they are doing all of the BMPs. Few of the retail agencies have signed the MOU. Table 7 presents a list of the other wholesale agencies and those retail agencies in the Los Angeles Area that have signed on to the CUWCC conservation MOU and their compliance as self-reported to the CUWCC website. Please note how many have signed the agreement and, by their own admission, are not implementing the BMPs to which they agreed. However, when contacted directly, most

TABLE 7. Compliance with CUWCC BMPs

	In 2003	In 2004
Cities		
Beverly Hills	none	none
Burbank	all	all
Compton	none	none
Covina	none	none
Garden Grove	all	all
Glendale	all	all
La Verne	none	none
Long Beach	all	all
Los Angeles DWP	all	all
Pasadena	all	all
San Fernando	none	none
Santa Monica	all	all
Torrance	none	none
West Covina	none	none
Other Wholesale Agencies		
Covina Irrigating Co.	none	none
Foothill Municipal Water District	none	none
Other Retail Agencies		
American Water Co.	all	all
Bellflower-Somerset Mutual Water Co.	none	none
California Water Service Co.	all	all
California-American Water Co	none	none
Crestline Village Water District	none	all
Dominguez Water Corp.	none	none
Lincoln Avenue Water Co.	none	none
Los Angeles County Waterworks Districts	all	all
Rowland Water District	all	all

SOURCE: From www.cuwcc.org.

were actually doing quite a bit, due to the requirement that each produce an Urban Water Management Plan in which their need for water during the next 20 years is projected as well as how they will meet this need, even in multiple dry years. (See the "Planning Processes" section of Chapter 5.)

Agricultural Conservation

Since there is so little agriculture left in the Los Angeles Area as defined, growing mostly nursery stock under the high-tension power lines, the formation of an agricultural conservation organization is addressed in Chapter 5.

California Urban Water Agencies (CUWA)

The California Urban Water Agencies (CUWA) is an association of the 10 largest urban agencies in the state. In September 2004, they completed a study called *Water Conservation and Demand Management.* The study concluded with four recommendations as a response to the various planning processes in the state: to promote collaborative actions among agencies; to promote better communications with stakeholders; to encourage follow-up research; and to reinforce the need for state and federal roles in supporting conservation (in other words, they don't want to have to pay for it).

They have not come very far from conclusions reached by their previous study, *The Urban Water Conservation Potential,* in 2001, when they took a cursory look at some of the CUWCC BMPs and concluded that for the south coast region, essentially the MWD service territory, the cost-effective net savings by 2020 could be only 581,000 acre-feet per year (afy). Statewide the cost-effective net savings by 2020 could be 972,000 afy.

Net savings takes into account the savings that would naturally occur as plumbing was changed as a result of home sales, etc. *Cost effective* refers to those that were cost effective at the time the study was written. These estimates are even more conservative than the old conservative estimates made by the state Department of Water Resources (DWR). DWR's early estimates had been roundly criticized by the environmental community as not being realistic, as being far lower than what can be easily accomplished. As conservative as the old CUWA's estimates were, they still add up to the equivalent of MWD's paper water from the State Water Project (www.cuwa.org/publications.html#conservation).

Association of California Water Agencies (ACWA)

This big association of all water agencies (and the most conservative group) adopted a plan called *No Time to Waste: A Blueprint for California Water.* The report supports the construction of additional surface water and groundwater storage and conveyance, relaxing of the Endangered Species Act and other regulatory constraints, and expedited water transfers as well as conservation, reuse, and regional planning. It also calls for a reevaluation of the problems in the delta (www.acwa.com).

Pacific Institute Study

The prestigious Pacific Institute for Studies in Development, Environment and Security has completed a massive study entitled *Waste Not, Want Not: The Potential for Urban Water Conservation in California,* dated November 2003. Its analysis suggests that vast quantities of water can be made available for other uses by replacing old technologies and practices with those that permit us to accomplish the same desired goals with less water. Well-known examples include low-flush toilets and water-efficient washers. Existing conservation measures reduced California's indoor residential water use by more than 700,000 acre-feet a year from what it would otherwise have been in the year 2000. If used efficiently, this conserved water could meet the indoor residential needs of 17 million people annually. Savings could more than double if all reasonable potential conservation could be captured. They conclude that managing demand by increasing efficiency offers a cheaper and lower-impact way of augmenting supply.

Their best estimate "is that existing technologies and policies can reduce current urban water use by another 2.3 maf, where at least 2 maf of these savings are cost effective. If current water use in California becomes as efficient as readily available technology permits, total urban use will drop from 7 maf to around 4.7 maf—a savings of 33%. This will reduce California's urban water use from around 185 gallons per capita per day to around 123 gallons per capita per day." Outdoor residential savings, more difficult to measure, could easily produce cost-effective savings of at least 32.5% relatively quickly with improved management and available irrigation technology.

The collecting of the data needed for this analysis from each water agency, each using different methodologies, has proven difficult. They recommend that agencies use the same words and the same methods of data collection to facilitate the adoption of reasonable policies. Besides data on usage, the economic, social, and environmental characteristics of water use in each region must also be considered. Because of this lack of coherent information, the state has never had a serious discussion of demand management, causing many economically viable options to be overlooked. The Pacific Institute points out the additional savings to be had by conserving water by reducing the energy needed to heat less water for bathing or for washing machines, by reducing the flow to wastewater treatment plants (and therefore the amount of wastewater that needs treatment), and, through outdoor conservation, improved water quality from reduced urban runoff.

The institute also calls for the phaseout of water subsidies to agriculture (www.pacinst.org).

Other Community Benefits

Retrofitting toilets in private homes is a big and difficult job. Some local agencies, led by the Los Angeles Department of Water and Power (LADWP), have seen fit to employ community-based organizations to help with this task. They can aid the agencies' conservation goals of replacing old toilets while benefiting themselves and their own communities at the same time. These community-based groups contact local residents and apartment owners, distribute new toilets and showerheads locally, and receive $15 to $35 from the agency for each old toilet turned in. Some are trained to install the new toilets. This creates jobs, and the money earned is plowed back into the community in the form of college scholarships or to help fund extras at local high schools or other programs.

Mothers of East Los Angeles, one of the first to participate, is the community group that established the methodology. Others that have led successful programs include the Asian American Drug Abuse Program in South Central Los Angeles, the Korean Youth and Community Center, the Calvary Baptist Homes, Inc., in the San Fernando Valley, and many high schools that participate in weekend events. Replacing toilets has become big business for nonprofits. LADWP is planning on using community-based organizations to help install other conserving devices.

Local Programs in Place

The two largest water supply agencies in the Los Angeles Area are the Metropolitan Water District of Southern California and the Los Angeles

Department of Water and Power. Because of their dominance, their programs deserve a special look. Some other agencies' efficiency programs are mentioned in Chapter 2.

Metropolitan Water District (MWD)

The Metropolitan Water District serves about half the population of the state. Because it is the importer and distributor of water from the Colorado River and the State Water Project and the de facto water planning agency for most of southern California, whatever the MWD does has great significance. It is an active participant in CCUWC and sets the pace in many ways for all of southern California by means of various incentive programs. They can offer only carrots; they have no sticks.

MWD updated its Integrated Planning Process in 2004 to address the reliability and affordability of water for the next 20 years and to target the preferred resource mix for cost effectiveness and environmental protection. This process has clearly identified the benefits of increasing dependence on local supplies, and MWD will continue to provide for 100% reliability through 2025. The target for conservation has been increased from 882,000 to 1,028,000 acre-feet a year by 2020, and the target for combined recycling, groundwater recovery, and desalination has grown from 500,000 to 750,000 acre-feet, with a 250,000-acre-feet buffer.

To reach these targets, MWD offers a Conservation Credits Program that consists of rebates to its member agencies of $154 for each acre-foot saved or one-half the cost of implementing the best management practice (BMP). It offers $250 an acre-foot for groundwater recovery programs and reuse and for desalination of ocean water. Since 1990, MWD has encouraged the installation of ultralow-flow toilets (ULFTs) by offering rebates to its member agencies ($80 for a dual-flush toilet, $60 for high-efficiency washing machines), and it is exploring other efficiency devices, such as irrigation controllers. Over 2 million ULFTs have been installed, and some agencies claim to be reaching saturation. Rebates have been given on 93,062 high-efficiency washers, and almost 3 million low-flow showerheads have been distributed.

MWD has adopted a competitive grant program for commercial, industrial, and institutional retrofits that is proving to be extremely popular with its member agencies. And it has unbundled its rate structure, instituting a tiered rate system to encourage the development of local resources.

As an active participant in CCUWC, MWD has been working with others to establish a uniform and simpler water use efficiency survey program and is researching better ways to automate sprinkler irrigation programs, especially for large landscaped areas managed by professional gardeners. Training programs have been established, and model drought-tolerant gardens have been built by some of its member agencies. It has also mounted a major Heritage Gardens and California program for home gardeners. MWD has built a huge website to promote native plants and to teach how to plant and care for them, has persuaded some nurseries to stock natives, and is providing additional learning opportunities, especially for landscape professionals (www.bewaterwise.com).

The conservation goals and programs are spelled out in its Regional Urban Water Management Plan, from which the numbers in Table 8 are taken (www.mwdh2o.com/mwdh2o/pages/yourwater/ywater01.htm).

City of Los Angeles Department of Water and Power

The Los Angeles Department of Water and Power (LADWP) is committed to implementing all of the CUWCC BMPs. It helped to develop the BMPs and promotes the council. As a result, residents of the City of Los Angeles had installed 1.24 million ultralow-flush toilets by 2005, and they have started a program of making ULFT toilets, installed, free to city residents. Free showerheads are also available for the asking. This program teaches the public that they can save money on their water bill without sacrificing the usefulness of their appliances. As a result, despite increases in population, water use has remained stable.

LADWP offers rebates for the purchase of high-efficiency washing machines of $150 per machine, plus the $35 rebate offered by MWD. As of 2005, 32,000 high-efficiency washing machines had been rebated, reducing annual water use by as much as 5,200 gallons per machine (total of 82 acre-feet saved per year). Southern California Edison has been offering a rebate because of the energy savings of $50 to $100 per machine, plus the MWD rebate. In 2007, these machines will become the state standard.

LADWP is also committed to reusing its wastewater. In 1990, the City Council adopted a goal to recycle 40% of its wastewater by 2010. The Integrated Resource Planning Process, under way as this is being written, presents three alternative ways to meet the city's future water needs. Reuse goals outlined in the EIR range from 42,000 acre-feet a year to as much

TABLE 8. Conservation Achievements in Metropolitan's Service Area

BMP Number	BMP Name	Metropolitan Program Description	Device/Activity Description	Number Implemented	Metropolitan Expenditures
RESERVOIRS					
1	Residential Water Surveys	Financial support for surveys, retrofits	Surveys	69,901	$1,960,538
			Toilets distributed	1,132,765	$1,311,740
			Residential R&D projects	8	$299,799
2	Residential Plumbing Retrofits	Financial support for retrofits and distributions	Low-flow showerheads distributed	2,968,576	$12,413,187
			Faucet aerators distributed	225,239	$244,073
6	High-Efficiency Washing Machines	Financial support for rebates	Residential high-efficiency washers rebated	92,062	$6,022,786
14	Residential ULFT Replacement	Financial incentives for toilet retrofits	Some agencies are reaching saturation	2,134,839	$133,501,638
RESIDENTIAL SECTOR TOTAL				6,624,390	$155,733,761
5	Large Landscape	Financial support for retrofit surveys	Audits conducted	2,173	$845,035
			Central controller	7	$703,175

#	Category	Description	Item	Count	Amount
			Protector del Agua graduates	30,747	$1,935,205
			Landscape R&D (projects)	11	$473,868
LARGE LANDSCAPE SECTOR TOTAL				32,938	$3,957,283
9	Commercial, Industrial, Institutional	Financial support for retrofit surveys, research, & development	ULFT	58,511	$3,777,731
			Urinals	2,146	$168,587
			Flush valve kits	755	$18,723
			Cooling tower retrofits	640	$311,615
			Clothes washer rebates	19,705	$4,258,134
			Industrial process improvements	3	$172,157
			Prerinse spray valves	12,675	$842,623
			Other device rebates	1,704	$429,576
			Workshops on commercial retrofits	7	$7,000
			CII R&D projects	11	$336,403
CII SECTOR TOTAL				96,157	$10,322,549
3	System Water Audits, Leak Detection	Distribution system audits/leak detection	MWD surveys own pipes and aqueducts		$3,850,000
4	Metering and Commodity Rates	All connections metered	Yes		
7	Public Information	Materials and programs provided	Launched multimedia regional message		$15,344,641
8	School Education	Full range of school curricula			$8,990,293

(continued)

TABLE 8. (continued)

BMP Number	BMP Name	Metropolitan Program Description	Device/Activity Description	Number Implemented	Metropolitan Expenditures
10	Wholesale Agency Assistance	Technical and financial support for BMPS 1, 2, 5, 6, 7, 8, 9, 11, 14	Regional water efficiency media campaign, some programs managed for MWD's service area		
11	Conservation Pricing	Commodity rate structure in place			$13,282,690
12	Conservation Coordination	Staff of 10 people			
13	Water Waste Prohibition	Exempt			$0
	Various	Programs no longer offered		1,719	$1,569,070
MISCELLANEOUS PROGRAMS TOTAL				1,719	$43,036,694
CUMULATIVE TOTAL SPENT BY METROPOLITAN WATER DISTRICT THROUGH FY 2004					$213,050,287

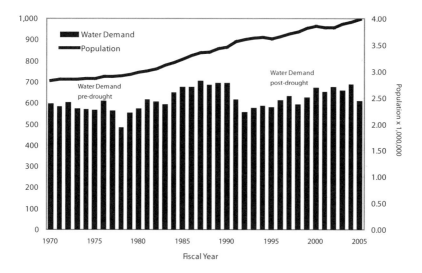

Figure 29. City of Los Angeles water supply and population growth. (SOURCE: LADWP.)

as 79,900 acre-feet a year. The East Valley Project, which is built and ready to go, is designed to recharge 10,000 acre-feet of reclaimed water a year, increasing to 35,000 acre-feet by 2020.

The city has adopted a more stringent landscape ordinance than the state's that applies to large landscaped areas or those installed by a developer. It has adopted an inverted rate structure, increasing the cost per unit of water used beyond an established baseline. The city further increases the cost of those additional units in the summertime to discourage profligacy. The city adopted a gray water ordinance in 1994, permitting the use of wastewater from showers, sinks, and washing machines for irrigation if distributed through an underground irrigation system. DWP makes loans available to help cover the costs of installing efficiencies, including loans to other city departments. It is studying the cost/benefits of replacing leaking flapper valves on old existing toilets and is researching landscape irrigation efficiencies that can come from installing computer-driven irrigation controllers connected to the state weather station.

A Technical Assistance Program for commercial and industrial water users offers a subsidy of $315 an acre-foot saved, which has been saving about a million acre-feet a year. Two hundred and fifty medical x-ray machine recirculation systems were installed with Proposition 13 money. These will soon be replaced with digital systems. Industrial cooling towers are being studied, and public agency retrofits are being encouraged (www.ladwp.com/ladwp/cons).

Per capita use peaked during the 1980s at over 180 gallons per capita per day (pcd). During the drought of the early 1990s, it fell to 145 gallons pcd; in 2005 it stabilized at 155 pcd. The daily water use per person is lower in Los Angeles than in other major cities in California.

Conclusion

The effectiveness of many kinds of conservation is difficult if not impossible to measure. A wide range of actions has been identified, both potential and current in the residential sector, and a wide range of compliance is noted, with about a third of the area doing little if anything to implement the BMPs that have already been agreed. Many others have not even signed onto the list of BMPs. The Pacific Institute has reached the conclusion that statewide about 33% of the urban water now used indoors could be saved cost effectively with existing technologies. There is the potential of saving an additional 10% with irrigation controllers that reduce overwatering, with much more savings available with the adoption of a landscape ethic that involves planting California natives and California-friendly landscape materials.

Other savings include less energy used to pump the water over mountain ranges and to its end use, less wastewater to be treated, and less polluted urban runoff.

The California Urban Water Agencies, among the most conservative of all those studying conservation, have identified about a million acre-feet of water that can be saved statewide. This is the equivalent of the MWD State Water Project shortfall, what the State Water Project promised to deliver to MWD and cannot.

RECLAMATION AND REUSE

Water reclamation is the process of treating wastewater to acceptable health levels for reuse. USEPA and the State Department of Health Services, both careful and slow-moving agencies, regulate the treatment standards closely, depending on how the reclaimed water is to be used. By law,

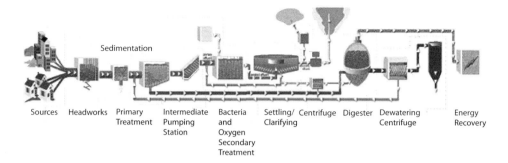

Sedimentation

Sources   Headworks   Primary   Intermediate   Bacteria   Settling/   Centrifuge   Digester   Dewatering   Energy
                      Treatment   Pumping   and   Clarifying   Centrifuge   Recovery
                           Station   Oxygen
                                     Secondary
                                     Treatment

Figure 30. Diagram of the wastewater treatment process. (SOURCE: LA Bureau of Sanitation.)

wastewater must be treated to secondary standards before discharge to the ocean. The Regional Water Quality Control Board requires treatment to tertiary standards before discharge to rivers and streams. These basic requirements must be met even if the water is not reused. It is a waste of public resources to spend the money necessary to clean up all the wastewater to almost-potable standards, only to throw it away. It makes much more sense to find healthful, safe ways to reuse what is daily becoming a more precious resource. It can be considered a new supply that is reliably always there.

The Los Angeles region is among the leaders in the state in wastewater reuse. Reuse has increased over the years and will continue to be a critical source of local water in the future. The use of reclaimed water in the County Sanitation Districts' service area (which includes most of the county not served by the City of Los Angeles) started as far back as 1927. In fiscal year 2002–2003 it reused 44.5% of its tertiary treated wastewater for landscape irrigation, agricultural irrigation, industrial process water, recreational impoundments, wildlife habitat maintenance, and groundwater replenishment. Its goal is to maximize the amount of treated wastewater reused.

The wastewater treatment process is a relatively simple one. Primary treatment consists of screening the wastewater as it enters into the wastewater treatment plant and passing it slowly through sedimentation tanks to allow the heavier material to settle out, with occasional chemical addition to aid in settling. Secondary treatment is a biological process where bacteria are added and air is bubbled up through the effluent. These good bacteria, or bugs, gobble up the organic materials and help to settle out more of the suspended solids. Heavy metals and other impurities attach themselves to the suspended solids, so removing them also removes much of the pollutants of concern. After chlorination and dechlorination, this water is then clean enough for discharge to the ocean.

Tertiary treatment includes more costly filtration to remove any remaining suspended solids, bacteria, and viruses. Advanced tertiary treatment, sometimes needed depending on the end use of the treated wastewater, can also include microfiltration, ultraviolet treatment, ozonation, and/or reverse osmosis.

Ultraviolet light kills many types of bacteria. Ozone is a highly reactive form of oxygen that combines with anything organic, killing bacteria and viruses. Reverse osmosis is a process whereby water is forced thru a special membrane that is so fine that nothing but water or the smallest of particles can make it through. This process is used to desalinate seawater.

Nonpotable Reuse

The water that is recycled is not used directly for potable purposes, such as drinking and cooking. To prevent any accidental use of reclaimed water for potable purposes, it is always carried in purple pipes. Some nonpotable purposes follow.

- *Industrial processes.* Many industries use reclaimed water for cooling and other process water purposes, such as paper making and fabric dying. Oil refineries are big users of reclaimed water in their operations. For example, refineries in El Segundo and Torrance currently consume about 8,000 acre-feet per year of recycled water.
- *Landscape irrigation.* Some of the golf courses, parks, cemeteries, and highway greenbelts use reclaimed water for landscape irrigation. This is now the most frequent reuse. Currently, about 86,000 acre-feet per year of recycled water are used for irrigation in southern California. Caltrans must use reclaimed water for freeway landscape irrigation if it is available.
- *Recreation.* Some artificial lakes and ponds, such as those found at golf courses, are supplied with reclaimed water. Lake Balboa and the wildlife lake in the Sepulveda Basin are filled with reclaimed water.

- *Environmental.* Certain aquatic habitats, such as wetlands and rivers, are maintained with reclaimed water.
- *Toilet flushing.* Some new buildings with access to reclaimed water have been double plumbed. An extra set of pipes has been installed to use reclaimed water to flush toilets and urinals. The Water Gardens complex of office buildings in Santa Monica has its own treatment plant and uses reclaimed water for toilet flushing. New construction in downtown Los Angeles and new high-rises in Glendale must also be double plumbed, anticipating the time when the pipes will be installed in the streets to make reclaimed water available.

Various qualities of water are often identified by color.

- *Gray water* is water that has been used in showers, sinks, and washing machines. It has been approved for irrigation purposes in the City of Los Angeles if it is distributed through underground irrigation methods.
- *Black water* is water from toilets and other highly contaminated sources and must be treated in a sewage treatment plant.
- *Purple* is the color of pipes that carry reclaimed water for reuse, for irrigation, and for numerous industrial purposes. This water is not fit to drink.

Groundwater Recharge, or Indirect Potable Reuse

The process of using reclaimed water for groundwater recharge or for seawater-intrusion barriers is sometimes called indirect potable reuse. The approval process for this kind of reuse is complicated, rigorous, and designed to ensure public safety. It is heavily regulated, as is all reuse. Indirect potable reuse is the most cost-effective way of reusing highly treated reclaimed water.

The biggest cost in making reclaimed water accessible for any reuse is building the system needed to carry the water to potential customers. The costs of digging up the street to install the necessary pipelines can be prohibitive. These costs can be minimized by installing one large pipeline, or by using existing streambeds, to connect the source of supply to where large quantities of water can be used. This also lessens the chance of cross contamination—of purple reclaimed water pipes being inadvertently connected to the potable water supply. Spreading grounds and seawater-intrusion barriers can soak up large quantities of water.

Soil Aquifer Treatment

Many believe that the most efficient and cost-effective way to reuse reclaimed water is for groundwater recharge, to add indirectly to our drinking water supply. After receiving tertiary treatment, the water is conveyed to spreading grounds, where it percolates into the soil along with diverted surface water, stormwater, and imported water. Eventually, after being naturally purified by moving slowly through the ground, it seeps into groundwater basins, commingling with existing groundwater. The bioreactions underground remove much more of any remaining contaminants, providing a natural form of water quality treatment in addition to the tertiary treatment. It may take anywhere from six months to decades and go through 500 feet to as much as dozens of miles of earth before it reaches the existing wells and the existing distribution system connected to those wells. It is then pumped up as part of our regular drinking water supply. It is chlorinated before distribution. This process, known as soil aquifer treatment, provides another level of protection on top of advanced tertiary treatment to guarantee safe and healthful drinking water.

Seawater-Intrusion Barriers

Reclaimed water, after being subjected to reverse osmosis (rigorous treatment), is injected into the ground at certain points along the coast to form a freshwater barrier between intruding seawater and the fresh groundwater supply. As groundwater basins are depleted, saltwater from the ocean can intrude to fill the void, causing the groundwater to no longer be potable. See Chapter 4, on drinking water quality, for more details.

Permits Designed to Safeguard Pubic Health

All uses of reclaimed water are subject to regulatory oversight and permitting. The Regional Water Quality Control Board is responsible for permitting projects, while the Department of Health Services establishes health standards and issues recommendations on the acceptability of reuse projects. The combination of water quality and health concerns by these two regulatory agencies leads to stringent goals and standards for recycled water and the rigorous permitting process that is needed to instill public confidence.

Permits require, among other things, a monitoring program. Water quality is monitored at four different locations on its journey from the reclamation plant to the spreading grounds to the groundwater basin to the customer. Sufficient levels of dilution are guaranteed by mixing it with other sources at three different locations. Upon entry into the spreading grounds, the reclaimed water is mixed with local runoff and imported water. As the reclaimed water travels through the ground, it mixes with the groundwater. And as the pumped groundwater enters the distribution system, it is mixed with other waters, which can be local and/or imported water. The minimum retention time is six months underground, and the minimum lateral distance to the nearest potable well is 500 feet. In reality, these minimums are far exceeded.

Title 22 of the California Administrative Code provides detailed guidelines for the treatment levels and use of all reclaimed water. Indirect potable reuse is slowly gaining public acceptance, thanks in part to extensive public education campaigns by water recycling agencies. They have explained the importance of this comparatively inexpensive and drought-proof source of water. They also explain that water is constantly being recycled by Mother Nature. The water in many of our rivers, including the Colorado River and the water pumped out of the Sacramento–San Joaquin Delta, has been reused many times by both cities and agriculture. They return their waste streams to the rivers from which the water was originally taken. The cities of Las Vegas, Laughlin, Sacramento, and Stockton are a few examples of cities that both draw water from and return their treated wastewater to sources of drinking water for southern California.

Studies such as the one by UCLA's School of Public Health in the 1970s show no adverse health effects from the consumption of water reused in this way. County San's *Health Effects Study*, published in 1984, concluded that "the recharge of reclaimed water into the groundwater drinking supply of the Central Basin did not adversely affect in a statistically significant way the health of people ingesting up to 30% reclaimed water over a 15-year period in regards to gastrointestinal disease and cancers or birth defects. It also determined that recharge with reclaimed water was not adversely affecting the groundwater quality of the Central Basin."

There have been two recent RAND epidemiological studies, dated 1996 and 1999, that confirmed the results of this study. They again showed that there are no statistical differences regarding certain cancers, gastrointestinal disease, or birth outcomes from drinking reclaimed water that has been blended with potable water underground, as required by the regulatory agencies. These studies examined the health of those served reclaimed water after it was recharged into spreading grounds near the Whittier Narrows as compared to a control group of similar people in a neighboring community. There were no statistical differences found in the health of these two groups.

Even so, some people continue to question the effectiveness of all the safeguards and resist this economical way to drought-proof our region. Some specific examples of using reclaimed water for groundwater recharge and seawater-intrusion barriers include the spreading of highly treated wastewater in the Montebello Forebay near Whittier Narrows by the Water Replenishment District of Southern California. This tertiary treated water was purchased from the County Sanitation Districts and spread since 1962 with no apparent ill effects.

There are plans to convey reclaimed water to the Upper San Gabriel Municipal Water District to spread into the Main San Gabriel Valley groundwater basin.

The Los Angeles Department of Water and Power has completed the East Valley Water Recycling Project to convey tertiary treated wastewater from its Tillman Water Reclamation Plant in the Sepulveda Basin to the spreading grounds below Hansen Dam to augment the city's water supply. It is about 6,000 feet from the Hansen Spreading Grounds to the nearest well, and the minimum retention time is approximately five years. This project is on hold, for political reasons.

After receiving advanced tertiary treatment, water is injected to create a seawater barrier in the West Coast Basin and at Dominguez Gap. There are plans to extend this use of reclaimed water to the Alamitos seawater barrier from the Terminal Island Treatment Plant.

U.S. Bureau of Reclamation's Southern
California Reclamation and Reuse Study

The U.S. Bureau of Reclamation, together with eight other cost-sharing agencies, performed a far-reaching, seminal study called the *Southern*

California Comprehensive Water Reclamation and Reuse Study. This six-year study cost $6 million and examined the feasibility of one large regional comprehensive water reuse system for the entire region, defined as Ventura to the Mexican border, essentially the MWD service area. The study states: "One of the most dependable, abundant, and underutilized supplies of water in southern California is reclaimed water."

Its goals were to provide an area-wide regional analysis of the political, institutional, and technical aspects of integrating existing freshwater and reclaimed water management crossing watersheds and hydrologic basins; to span agency jurisdictions and address economies of scale; to investigate innovative and cost-effective methods of reclaiming and transporting water; to optimize reuse and identify constraints in the regional context; and to develop both short-term and long-term implementation plans.

The study examined the feasibility of regional water reclamation, with the goal of identifying opportunities and constraints for maximizing water reuse. Phase I developed a database of all existing and potential reuse, including demand, supply, land use, environmental assets, and local plans, with the assistance of the cooperating agencies. In Phase IB, data management mapping systems and distribution models were developed to evaluate all of the regional projects. Phase II incorporated the tools developed to identify both short-term and long-term projects and includes, for the first time, along with the economic benefits, such additional benefits as environmental protection and quality of life. Phase II also acknowledged that one regional solution for such a large and varied area would never work, so they broke the area into four subgroups, for which short-term plans were developed.

By getting folks together by subregion to explore each of their needs and abilities, they learned to share information and began to think much more cooperatively than they had before. Thirty-four projects were identified, 15 of which were regional in scope.

As the results of this study were disseminated and 25% cost share for planning purposes was made available, interest in joining this effort grew. The eight original cost share partners quickly grew to 11, who identified 15 regional projects and 19 stand-alone projects that would reuse 450,000 acre-feet of water. Now there are 23 entities that have joined this initiative, and the amount of water that makes economic sense to reuse has blossomed to 760,000 acre-feet. Regional projects once thought impossible because

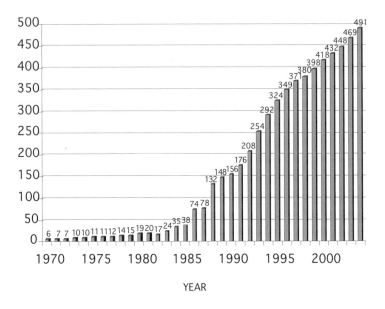

Figure 31. Increase in the number of reuse sites from 1970 to 2004.
(SOURCES: County Sanitation Districts.)

they cross jurisdictional lines are being actively planned, such as a project
to reuse wastewater from Los Angeles County San across county boundaries in Orange County. A number of these projects are now under construction or in the planning stage.

The major problem that has been identified is salinity, the amount of
salts in the reclaimed water. There are limits on how much salt can be
in the reclaimed water without destroying its usefulness. The excess salt
must be removed, and discussions now center on the need for a brine line
to carry the salt to the sea for disposal (www.sawpa.org/projects/planning/
socal-recyc.htm).

The U.S. Bureau of Reclamation is now considering a follow-up study
to see how many of the projects identified have actually been implemented.

A similar study has been performed by the Bureau of Reclamation for the
San Francisco Bay Area, published in December 1999. This study was
driven by the need of the wastewater managers to dispose of their effluent
responsibly, in contrast to the southern California study, which was driven

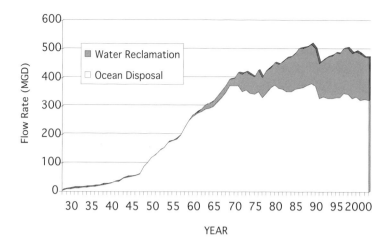

Figure 32. Graph showing how reuse has grown over time. (SOURCES: County Sanitation Districts.)

by the need to reduce demand on their imported water supplies. Because there are 33 wastewater treatment plants in the Bay Area, with overlapping geography and jurisdictions, it will be much more difficult to overcome the institutional barriers needed to work cooperatively for a common benefit.

Water Reclamation Efforts by Wastewater Treatment Agencies

What follows is a profile of the reclamation agencies that perform most of the reclamation in the Los Angeles Area.

THE SANITATION DISTRICTS OF LOS ANGELES COUNTY (COUNTY SAN). County San has adopted the goal "of maximizing the beneficial reuse of the highly treated effluents produced by its water reclamation plants." They work with a number of local, regional, and state agencies and other entities in an effort to develop reclaimed water more fully as a local water supply to supplement the area's limited groundwater and imported water supplies. County San has five upstream tertiary treatment plants and one small secondary treatment plant in the Los Angeles Area as defined. All the biosolids from these facilities are returned to the sewer system for further processing at their Joint Water Pollution Control Plant in Carson, where the wastewater is given

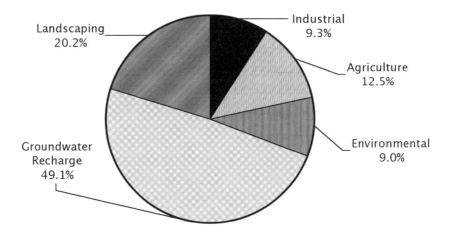

Figure 33. Reuse by end use: Pie chart showing the distribution of reclaimed water use in fiscal year 2003–04. (SOURCES: County Sanitation Districts.)

full secondary treatment before discharge to the ocean and where all solids are removed.

The biosolids are then taken to seven reuse sites in five counties, where they are composted, applied to land as a soil amendment, used as landfill cover, and fed as fuel to a cement kiln, where the ammonia helps to lessen the air pollution that would normally be generated by the kiln. They are partnering with the Inland Empire Utility Agency on an enclosed compost-ing facility and with a farmer in Kern County to cocompost the biosolids with green waste from their farming operation to use as a soil amendment.

County San publishes an *Annual Status Report on Reclaimed Water Use* that contains a history of their reuse activities starting in 1927, a descrip-tion of each reclamation facility, its inflow, outflow, water quality, and reuse projects. The 2002–2003 report states, "Of the 513.87 million gallons a day (mgd) of treated effluent produced by the Districts, 188.54 mgd (36.7%) was treated to a suitable level for reuse, with 85.17mgd (16.6%) actually being reused at 469 individual sites in 27 cities for numerous diverse applications (with the majority of reuse, 62.7%, being for groundwater replenishment)." Water discharged from the Whittier Narrows facility has been spread in the Montebello Forebay since 1962. The effluent from its Pomona facility is all reused during part of the year.

TABLE 9. LA County Reclaimed Water Use

Treatment Plant	Treated AF	Reused AF	% Reused
La Cañada	114	114	100.0%
Long Beach	20,160	5,324	26.4%
Los Coyotes	35,982	5,505	15.3%
Pomona	10,637	8,812	82.8%
San Jose Creek	94,124	53,482	56.8%
Whittier Narrows	8,728	7,281	83.4%

SOURCE: Figures are taken from FY2002–2003 LA County Sanitation District's Annual Status Report on Reclaimed Water Use.

The amount of reclaimed water used for replenishment of the underground water supply can vary greatly from year to year, depending on the amount and timing of rainfall runoff and by maintenance activities in the spreading grounds. Over half of the effluent reused is generally for groundwater recharge. The reclamation plants discharge to creeks or rivers that act both as recharge facilities themselves and as conveyance facilities to take the water to spreading grounds located conveniently near rivers. In fiscal year 2002–2003, 62.4% was used for groundwater recharge; 13.6% for landscape irrigation; 8.4% for agriculture; 7.2% for industrial process water that included two paper factories, a carpet dyer, two concrete batch plants, two power plants' cooling towers, oil field injection, and dust control at two landfills; and 8.3% to enhance wildlife habitat in the Mojave Desert.

The remaining effluent is discharged to the ocean from County San's Joint Water Pollution Control Plant in the City of Carson. County San has made continual efforts since 1962 to divert new wastewater flows to the upstream water reclamation plants for eventual reuse and away from the Joint Plant and ocean disposal. While flows to the Carson facility have been increasing, effluent flow to the ocean has held steady, even declining during the drought.

County San has determined that they generate about 190 million gallons a day that could be reused, and they are now reusing about one-third of this at over 500 sites. Their goal is to reuse it all when they find the customers. They have one staff person whose sole job is to market this water. They are also experimenting with using ultraviolet light to reduce the

TABLE 10. Water, Energy, Chemical, and Air Pollutant
Savings from Reclaimed Water Usage, Fiscal Year 2003–04

Category	Units	Savings
Water supply	acre-feet	72,972
Water supply	number of people	364,860
Energy	kilowatt-hours	218,916,000
Energy	megawatts	25.0
Energy	barrels of oil	118,632
Electricity	dollars	28,459,080
Petroleum	dollars	5,021,677
WRP chemicals	dollars	134,670
Nitrogen oxide	tons	125.9
Carbon monoxide	tons	21.9
Sulfur oxides	tons	13.1
Particulates	tons	4.4
Reactive organic gases	tons	1.1
Carbon dioxide	tons	164,187

SOURCES: County Sanitation Districts.

amount of chlorine needed to disinfect the water, and they are experimenting with a new process that would combine full secondary and full tertiary treatment together. There are many additional savings to be made from
wastewater reuse (www.lacsd).

CITY OF LOS ANGELES BUREAU OF SANITATION   The LA Bureau of Sanitation operates three tertiary or water reclamation plants and one full secondary
treatment plant. The Hyperion Sewage Treatment Plant, located just
south of Los Angeles International Airport (LAX), gives full secondary treatment to 365 mgd of influent and sells 34,000 acre-feet per year of its
effluent to the West Basin Municipal Water District before discharging the
rest to the ocean. West Basin has built a tertiary plant nearby and is marketing this additionally treated water. About 350 afy comes back to the city
to irrigate the landscaping around LAX and at the Playa Vista development.
The city is looking to capture both wet- and dry-weather runoff for
recharge by participating in the Los Angeles & San Gabriel Rivers Water-

Figure 34. Aerial photograph of Hyperion Wastewater Treatment Plant. (SOURCE: Los Angeles Bureau of Sanitation.)

shed Council's Water Augmentation Study and in the retrofit of the Sun Valley subwatershed. The 700 wet tons a day of biosolids removed during sewage treatment has received awards from the industry for the quality produced. The biosolids are taken to a city-owned farm in Kern County for use as a fertilizer and soil amendment. The three reclaimed-water plants are as follows.

- *The Tillman Reclamation Plant,* located in the Sepulveda Basin, San Fernando Valley, is providing reclaimed water to irrigate the golf courses in the Sepulveda Basin and for use in Lake Balboa and the wildlife refuge. It discharges the balance to the Los Angeles River. Tillman has the capacity to treat 64 mgd, but actually treated about 52 mgd in 2005 and reused about 16,300 afy. Because of the high nutrient level in Tillman's effluent, the city is planning a constructed wetland in the Sepulveda Basin to treat the effluent further, and to provide habitat and educational benefits for those who live nearby and use the basin for recreation. The city has built a pipeline to deliver reclaimed water at a rate of 10,000 acre-feet per year to the Hansen Spreading Grounds, just below Hansen Dam, for groundwater recharge and for such nonpotable purposes as irrigation and industrial uses throughout the San Fernando Valley, with the ultimate goal of recharging 35,000 acre-feet a year. It is building a nitrogen removal facility. The city has determined that the Los Angeles River needs a minimum of 27 mgd of water to support the established habitat.

- *The Los Angeles–Glendale Reclamation Plant* is operated in cooperation with the City of Glendale. It has the capacity to treat 20 mgd, is treating about 17 mgd, and currently provides irrigation water to Griffith Park and to Forest Lawn and Mount Sinai cemeteries. It plans to deliver an additional 2,100 acre-feet per year of reclaimed water to Elysian Park and the central city by 2010 for landscape and industrial purposes. A nitrogen removal facility is under construction as well. New buildings in the central city and high-rises in Glendale must now be double plumbed so that reclaimed water can be used to flush toilets and urinals.

- *The Terminal Island Water Reclamation Plant* has been rebuilt by the City Sanitation Department's Bureau of Engineering in a cooperative effort with LADWP. It has the capacity to treat 30 mgd, actually treats about 16 mgd with advanced tertiary treatment consisting of microfiltration and reverse osmosis, and reuses about 5 mgd. . This water will be used in the Dominguez Gap Seawater Barrier project for injection into the groundwater. As customers are found for more of this water and regulatory hurdles overcome, more will be given advanced tertiary treatment and marketed.

WEST BASIN WATER RECYCLING FACILITY The West Basin Water Recycling Facility purchases secondary treated effluent from the Los Angeles City Hyperion Wastewater Treatment Plant, located next to LAX. It persuaded its citizens to incur debt and to assess a standby charge to build this facility in order to reduce the amount of imported water needed to meet local needs. It has just expanded this facility to process 26,000 acre-feet per year. It is all reused for irrigation and industrial purposes. A nearby Chevron oil refinery is using all of the additional 4,000 acre-feet per year of the expansion. West Basin is producing five different qualities of reclaimed water, designed to meet specific customer requirements—designer water. West Basin has the largest

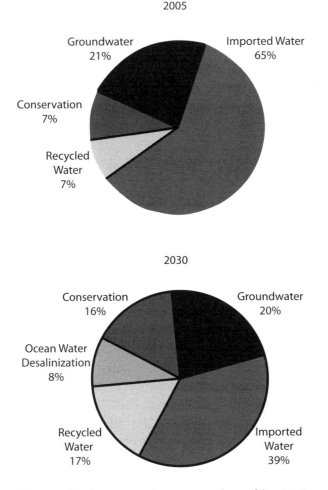

2005

Groundwater
21%

Imported Water
65%

Conservation
7%

Recycled
Water
7%

2030

Conservation
16%

Groundwater
20%

Ocean Water
Desalinization
8%

Recycled
Water
17%

Imported
Water
39%

Figure 35. Pie charts comparing water supply portfolios in West Basin, 2005 vs. 2030. (SOURCE: West Coast Basin MWD.)

plant of its type in the United States and is recognized as one of six national cities for water treatment technology. It has adopted a goal of lowering its need for imported water by 50%, reducing the treated wastewater discharge to Santa Monica Bay by 25%, and preventing seawater intrusion by injecting highly treated wastewater into the ground. In 2005, it sold 13,065 acre-feet for industrial and energy purposes, 3,800 af for injection into the West Coast Barrier, 7,000 af to Torrance, and 283 af back to the City of

Los Angeles. It is also researching the use of reverse osmosis and microfiltration for ocean desalination (www.westbasin.org/).

BURBANK WASTEWATER RECLAMATION PLANT The Burbank Wastewater Reclamation Plant has the capacity to treat 9 million gallons a day to tertiary treatment standards. The rest of its wastewater is discharged into the City of Los Angeles' sewage system for treatment. About 330,000 million gallons per day is reused, 50% at the Burbank Steam Plant, which generates electricity for the city, 30% for landscape irrigation at a local golf course, 10% at its own local landfill, and 10% for other purposes. New developments under its redevelopment agency are required to accommodate reclaimed water for landscape irrigation, and they are watchful for additional opportunities to reuse more (www.burbankwaterandpower.com).

LAS VIRGENES MUNICIPAL WATER DISTRICT'S TAPIA TREATMENT PLANT This plant can process up to 16 million gallons per day of wastewater but currently averages about 9 million. It is used to irrigate highway medians, golf courses, school grounds, and other public and commercial landscapes. About 20% of its water sales are for reclaimed water. Its winter effluent is discharged to Malibu Creek. Because of the ocean pollution at the mouth of Malibu Creek and concerns about mimicking Mother Nature, no effluent can be discharged between April 15 and November 15 during the late spring, dry summer, and early fall. Las Virgenes is not meeting the Regional Water Quality Control Board limits on pollutants and nutrients discharged to Malibu Creek. As this is written, an appeal has been filed with the Regional Board. Las Virgenes has no problem meeting this ruling during the summer. During the shoulder months, it encourages overirrigation, which has been running into the creek creating algae blooms. The Regional Board requires that any water not reused must be discharged down a tributary to the Los Angeles River.

Local groundwater, which is not potable, is pumped to the Tapia Treatment Plant, processed, and made available as reclaimed water (www.lvmwd .dst.ca.us/).

LONG BEACH Because a County San treatment facility is located in the city, which has first rights to all reclaimed water, Long Beach has been experimenting with recycling water since the 1980s. It has its own health department, its own groundwater treatment facility, its own water quality lab, and its own energy department. It has more than doubled its reuse capacity from 4,000 afy to 9,000 afy, with the goal of meeting 12% of the city's water demand. It now serves large irrigation customers and is sending reclaimed water to repressure the oil fields in the harbor, to recharge groundwater, and to inject in seawater-intrusion barriers. The next phase will bring reclaimed water to two local power plants for cooling water and to industrial users in the Port of Long Beach. It has created a network, a circle of purple pipe throughout the city, available to tap into.

It is now experimenting with pushing seawater through the nanofilters it uses to treat its groundwater. By pushing seawater through multiple times at much lower pressure than reverse osmosis, it claims that it can save at least 20% of the cost over the more traditional reverse osmosis technology (www.lbwater.org/projects/water_reuse.html).

Barriers to Expanding Water Reuse

Despite the promise of reclaimed water to increase local water supplies, there are always barriers to overcome. In October 2001, the governor signed into law AB 331, which directs the establishment of a task force to promote reuse. The task force issued its final report in June 2003, concentrating on the reuse of treated municipal wastewater, and concluded that then statewide reuse of 0.5 maf per year could be increased to 1.5 maf by 2030. The obstacles identified are the need to build the infrastructure to distribute the treated wastewater and the costs associated with that; the need for additional public education and outreach; research into emerging contaminants; and continued concern about public health issues (http://www.owue.water.ca .gov/recycle/taskforce/taskforce.cfm).

The financial obstacles are serious. Low-interest loans and planning grants are available from the State Water Resources Control Board, through Proposition 13, and the Water Reuse Financing Authority. End usage can require more stringent water quality standards, which can drive up the cost of treatment. The report by the Reuse Task Force suggests the need for nearly $11 billion dollars, or about $400 million a year, to build the infrastructure.

Delays in the regulatory process can hold up the construction of the separate systems needed to distribute reclaimed water to where it can be used. And the variability in demand and slow start-up as a user base is developed can act as a barrier to reuse and may increase the cost of the recycled water in the early years of operation.

As long as the cost of new water supplies is blended into the costs of old supplies, where facilities were paid for years ago, it will be difficult for reclaimed water to compete. Only when the marginal cost of new supplies is considered (what the next increment of fresh water will cost, such as the next dam and reservoir) does reclaimed water make economic sense.

The development of a water reclamation project may require cooperation and negotiation among several different districts or agencies. One agency may only be in the wastewater treatment business; another may clean up water in one location and sell it to a different agency in a totally different location. Agencies usually responsible for the treatment and disposal of wastewater may enter into the role of distributors of reclaimed water, which require adjustments in policy and management. For example, the Service Duplication Law of the Public Utilities Code prevents County San from substituting reclaimed water for potable water if the local retail agency objects or if the local agency is not compensated for lost income due to the substitution of recycled water for potable water. County San would like to use reclaimed water for dust control on its own landfill sites but cannot get permission from the city in which it is located. The City of Los Angeles' Department of Water and Power has the sole authority to sell water in the city. The city's Bureau of Sanitation runs the sewer and sewage treatment facilities. Which agency owns/sells the reclaimed water?

Because reclaimed water is a relatively new concept and not well understood by the public, the most difficult barrier, especially for groundwater recharge, is dealing with the public's concerns regarding water quality. Most water districts seeking to develop reclamation projects simultaneously engage in extensive public education programs on the safe and beneficial use of reclaimed water. Yet bad press, often triggered by cries of "toilet to tap," have led some to believe that there are health concerns, despite scientific studies indicating the contrary.

Most irrigation is performed at night, when parks, schools, golf courses, and other facilities receive little public use and less of the applied water will evaporate. However, that is when there is little flow in the system. Storing the day's reclaimed water for later use at night has been considered, but this option requires the construction of massive holding tanks or reservoirs, which are expensive and consume valuable real estate.

The recipients of the reclaimed water must be in relatively close proximity to the reclamation plant, due to the high cost of constructing a distribution system and the costs of the energy needed for pumping.

The construction of distribution systems and dual plumbing systems in an already-built environment is costly when compared to installing them during initial construction. The Irvine Ranch Water District, in a planned community, was able to install a dual system for landscape irrigation and other uses while the rest of the infrastructure, such as streets and water mains, was being built in this community.

New regulations being proposed by the Department of Health Services are exceedingly stringent, and water agencies are fearful of the costs of treatment and monitoring to meet the new regulatory standards.

Conclusion

The only comprehensive studies of the potential for wastewater reuse are those led by the Bureau of Reclamation. It has identified 760,000 acre-feet of additional reuse capability in what is essentially the MWD service area. Considering the ambitious plans and the aggressive history of County San, West Basin, and others, there is great promise that this will all be put to good use.

CONJUNCTIVE USE

Groundwater is our most reliable supply, especially during droughts. We have enormous aquifers underground that can store millions of acre-feet of water—water that can be available in the event that an earthquake destroys an aqueduct or some other catastrophe happens. It does not evaporate. The amount of underground storage capacity for southern California has been equated with that contained in eight Diamond Valley reservoirs. This storage capacity is not being used as well as it might be to maximize the effectiveness of both surface water and groundwater, a process called *conjunctive use.*

Conjunctive use is the use of surface water in conjunction with groundwater. In other words, it involves putting surface water underground when it rains, and therefore is in abundance, so that it can be pumped up or withdrawn later, when it is needed. Conjunctive use is now done routinely as a way of storing winter and spring surpluses against summer and fall need. MWD initiated a seasonal storage program in 1989 in which both direct and in-lieu recharge and storage (using MWD surface supplies directly in the winter and spring while local rain water is recharged) are encouraged. In addition, MWD offers financial incentives to its member agencies to take extra water during the winter and spring to be stored underground for summer and fall use. All these programs are voluntary on the part of member agencies.

There are many advantages to storing water underground rather than in above-ground reservoirs. The land under the reservoir is not lost for other purposes, such as agriculture, open space, and habitat, or for development. There are no evaporative losses when water is stored underground. Existing wells and infrastructure can be used to extract and distribute the water.

The constraints or challenges include the following.

- *Water quality problems can be exacerbated.* When water from different sources is put underground, contamination may be spread from one source to another. Surface contamination can spread to groundwater should the water table come up too high in areas where there are brownfields (where the soil has become contaminated due to some industrial use or from leaking underground storage tanks), with the danger that the groundwater would also become contaminated.

- *Liability issues must be reduced.* Who assumes the risks when water from one basin spills into another, either water quality risks or water supply risks?

- *Agencies don't have existing agreements.* Who decides when it is best to take water from underground, and under what circumstances, in nonadjudicated basins? The institutional barrier of who is in charge and has control is very difficult to overcome. Agencies also must have or build sufficient spreading and extraction capacities to take advantage of conjunctive use programs.

Water agencies are beginning to explore how they might capture wet-year surpluses to put underground against dry-year need. With just this goal in mind, MWD is negotiating with several owners of land located over aquifers that have storage capacity in the Central Valley and the Coachella Valley and near the Colorado River, both in California and in Arizona. Many if not all of these basins have not been adjudicated. Despite the local potential, MWD has also recently completed a huge new reservoir in Diamond Valley near Hemet in which 800,000 acre-feet of water can be stored. The reservoir is also designed to store water temporarily before it is put underground and to provide insurance against drought and against any act of God, such as an earthquake, that might disrupt the aqueduct systems.

Association of Groundwater Agencies (AGWA)

This association of the major groundwater management agencies on the coastal plain of southern California was formed in 1994 because of growing realization that they needed to talk to each other and to work cooperatively in order to advance the ability to store water underground. In October 2000, they completed a study of the major groundwater basins in southern California called *Groundwater and Surface Water in Southern California.* The association's goal was to identify how each of the groundwater basins is being used, the safe yield of each, the operational yield, and how much storage capacity remains in each. This information is needed to determine how much more surface water can safely be stored underground in wet years. By determining the safe yield of each groundwater basin, by putting hard numbers on the tremendous capacity that is just waiting to be taken advantage of, this study has identified how much more can be done. It also identified the following pluses and minuses.

The benefits of conjunctive use include water supply reliability, greater water conservation, decreased dependence on imported supplies during dry years and emergencies, less need for additional surface storage, fewer storm drain improvements needed due to better stormwater management, the absence of evaporation from underground storage, improved power load and pumping plant use factors, better control of timing of water distribution, and less required water treatment in some cases.

The possible disadvantages include the fact that more energy is needed to pump water up than just to take it from a surface reservoir, more management and monitoring are required than with just taking deliveries of imported water, and land subsidence can be caused by overpumping. If groundwater is too high, liquefaction of the land may occur. Saltwater intrusion may require management efforts. Contaminants in the soil may move into the aquifer. And increased diversion and/or conveyance of surface water may be required during wet years.

Following are the results of this study, by groundwater basin, in just the Los Angeles Area.

- *The San Fernando Basin* (Upper Los Angeles River Area, ULARA) has a surface area of about 175 square miles. The freshwater storage capacity ranges from 0 to 550,000 acre-feet, as determined by the ULARA Watermaster. The annual natural recharge averages 44,000 acre-feet per year, while artificial recharge averages 61,000 acre-feet per year. The present operational safe yield is about 100,000 acre-feet a year of water for Burbank, Glendale, and Los Angeles. Through conjunctive use, these cities have stored about 356,000 acre-feet and the operational yield has been increased by 43,700 acre-feet per year. There is the potential to store up to 150,000 acre-feet of water for dry-year use and a potential increase in basin operational yield of 27,300 acre-feet per year.

- *The Raymond Basin,* which lies mostly under Pasadena and Altadena, has a surface area of about 40 square miles. The freshwater storage capacity is a minimum of 250,000 acre-feet. As of June 1999, about 56,000 acre-feet were stored by various parties and approximately 194,000 acre-feet of unused storage was available. Recently, MWD stored 75,000 acre-feet of water for dry-year use. The present operational safe yield is 30,622 acre-feet per year, but actual annual production varies between 35,000 and 40,000 acre-feet per year, depending on local storm runoff. The AGWA survey indicates the potential to store an additional 144,000 acre-feet for use during dry years.

- *The Main San Gabriel Basin* has a surface area of approximately 167 square miles. The freshwater storage capacity of the basin is estimated to be about 8.6 million acre-feet. Only about 400,000 acre-feet is usable for water supply. Storage is dependent on the water surface elevation at the Baldwin Park key well. When that elevation exceeds 250 feet, neither imported nor reclaimed water can be placed in storage, except in the eastern portion of the basin, because of the high water table. Therefore, the amount of storage generally available varies from nothing to approximately 400,000 acre-feet. To date only 170,000 acre-feet of storage space has been committed for cyclical storage. The operational safe yield has ranged from 140,000 to

230,000 acre-feet per year. Existing conjunctive use programs have increased the basin operational yield by 76,000 acre-feet per year. There is the potential to store up to 400,000 acre-feet for use in dry years and potential increase in basin operational yield of 187,000 acre-feet per year.

- *The Los Angeles Coastal Plain Basins* includes the Central, West, Santa Monica, and Hollywood basins, totaling a surface area of 512 square miles. Existing conjunctive use programs have increased the basin operational yield by 54,000 acre-feet per year, with the potential to store up to 1,089,000 acre-feet for use in dry years and a potential increase in basin operational yield of 54,300 acre-feet per year.

- *Chino Basin.* Just east of the Los Angeles Area, under parts of Riverside and San Bernardino counties, lies the Chino Groundwater Basin. A recent study concluded that there is about 2 million acre-feet of potential storage in the Chino Basin that could serve the entire MWD service territory very well indeed, including the Los Angeles Area.

Conclusion

In summary, there is tremendous potential for expanding the use of our local groundwater basins. We have the capacity to store an additional 1.78 million acre-feet of wet-year surpluses for dry-year use just in the Los Angeles Area. The California Department of Water Resources has published a lot of information on groundwater management at www.groundwater .ca.gov/dwr_publications/.

WATERSHED MANAGEMENT

As the need to manage our water resources more efficiently has grown, so has our view of how to manage our watersheds in a much more sophisticated way. County Public Works has the dual challenge of providing flood protection and water conservation. The Army Corps of Engineers has flood control as its chief function, but it is also involved in water conservation, habitat restoration, and recreation. Both agencies have responded by building dams, concrete channels, and storm drains, primarily for flood management. Stormwater is detained behind the dams for later release and diversion into spreading basins, where the water can infiltrate the ground and replenish the groundwater. Though these agencies have prevented devastating floods from occurring, their facilities could be better managed to serve additional public needs, including habitat restoration and recreation.

Watershed management has come to mean much more than stormwater management in all its facets, providing open space and recreation, and restoring habitat. It really means providing a safe place for the multitude of agencies that manage these resources to work cooperatively with the community to plan how best to meet multiple objectives with multipurpose projects, projects that can address many needs and tap into multiple funding sources. And it means the adoption of a landscape ethic.

Stormwater Management

Interest is growing in adding to our drinking water supply by capturing more stormwater where it falls and infiltrating it into the ground. A study performed by the Los Angeles & San Gabriel Rivers Watershed Council showed how the amount of runoff has increased as the city has grown and become paved over with buildings, streets, parking lots, patios, etc. In the 1920s, 95% of the rain either infiltrated the soil or evaporated, and only 5% ran off. Today, only about half of the rain infiltrates the soil naturally (it cannot soak into paved or roofed-over areas), and 50% runs off. The Watershed Council is leading a 10-agency study to determine just how much can be added to our drinking water supply and where it is safe or makes sense to install infiltration devices, grassy swales, combination park/detention grounds, or other means to infiltrate water into the ground. The study is also examining what obstacles might be discovered that could interfere with retrofitting the region and to determine the economic benefits of such a retrofit.

The first concern was to protect groundwater quality from the witch's brew that is urban runoff and from the pollutants that wash out of the air when it rains. The study has now concluded that groundwater quality is no longer a concern (www.lasgrwc.org/).

Changes to local laws are needed, such as the requirement that roofs must drain to the street. They should drain instead to a landscaped area that is depressed so as to retain stormwater long enough for it to infiltrate the ground. Parking lot designs should be changed to direct the sheet flow off the paved areas into the planters, instead of building concrete curbs

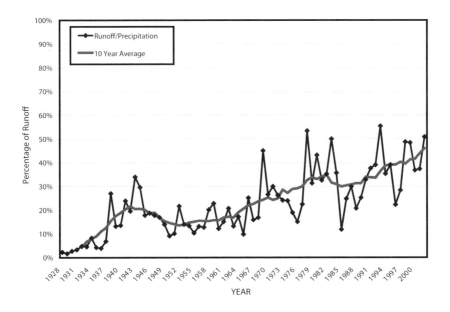

Figure 36. Graph showing average rainfall and runoff from 1928 to the present. (SOURCE: Los Angeles & San Gabriel Rivers Watershed Council, used with permission.)

around the planters to keep the water out. Placing some gravel under the plant materials' roots will help provide some temporary storage while the water infiltrates. Large perforated pipes can be placed under a paved area or elsewhere underground to store drainage temporarily until it has time to infiltrate. The large-scale use of permeable paving materials should be encouraged.

For really large storms, a combination park/detention basin works very well indeed. During those rare times when very large storms occur, the park can be closed and converted into a detention basin, to store water for recharge or to drain when the storm is over. Both the Sepulveda Basin, in the San Fernando Valley, and the Whittier Narrows are operated in this way. Pan Pacific Park, in the mid-Wilshire district near Park La Brea, was purposely built to accomplish this dual purpose.

The Regional Water Quality Control Board has ruled that all three-quarter-inch storms within a 24-hour period must be infiltrated on site or, minimally, filtered before release to the storm drains. This rule was made specifically to improve water quality, but it will also help with water supply. On average, over 500,000 acre-feet of runoff flow to the ocean from the Los Angeles County basin each year was identified by the Los Angeles & San Gabriel Rivers Watershed Council in its *Water Augmentation Study, Phase II Final Report*, August 2005. If some portion of this water can be captured for reuse, it will moderate the pressure from supplies in northern and central California.

There are many potential advantages to infiltrating stormwater on site where it falls. The drinking water supply stored in existing groundwater basins would be increased. It would relieve the constant pressure to expand the storm drain system as our cities continue to grow and pave over. Water quality would be improved by reducing urban runoff and by diluting the buildup of salts in our groundwater. The natural hydrology, the moisture in the soil, would be restored so that the many habitat restorations planned can grow naturally and be sustained. Water quality would be improved in areas where restored riparian habitat and/or wetlands increase infiltration. Riparian and wetland plants and animals provide water quality benefits. Restored habitat also improves the quality of life of those who live nearby and increases local property values.

The potential disadvantages are also many. Infiltration will not work in areas where clay layers exist between the surface and the groundwater, preventing infiltration to groundwater. Saturation of soils would increase the danger of liquefaction in areas with sandy soils during an earthquake. Infiltrating stormwater through contaminated soils, such as found on some industrial sites, may contaminate the underlying groundwater. Unmapped abandoned landfills may also contaminate the groundwater. Additional water would increase flooding in areas where the water table is already high. Moving funds from well-established methodologies in order to fund new stormwater retention projects may not be readily accepted. And there is the potential for misuse or improper maintenance of proposed water retention facilities.

In November of 2004, the residents of the City of Los Angeles overwhelmingly approved a half billion dollar bond act, Proposition O, to improve water quality and to provide many of the multiple benefits just listed. A citizen advisory committee was formed to establish criteria for project funding.

Sediment Management Behind Dams

The Los Angeles County Department of Public Works and the U.S. Army Corps of Engineers operate a series of dams that control the flow of water in the rivers of the county. These dams are used both for flood control and for water conservation. They are located in and below the San Gabriel Mountains and in the San Fernando Valley. The San Gabriel Mountains are among the youngest mountains in the world, are very steeply inclined, and erode easily, especially after many days of rainfall, when the ground is already saturated, and it rains again. Then massive amounts of debris erode off the mountains and collect behind the dams. As the rain is captured, the sediment carried with it settles out, slowly filling up the water storage space behind the dams.

One of the largest management issues facing the county is what to do with the debris, silt, and sediment that collect in the reservoirs, limiting the amount of storage available during storms. The county had been clearing sediment from behind the dams in the San Gabriel Mountains and stuffing it into nearby canyons. These are almost full, and doing so is no longer acceptable, so they are exploring other options. They did have permission to truck the sediment to the beach for sand replenishment, where it would have gone naturally before the dams were built, but the Coastal Commission now prohibits this. They can sell some as building materials and for landfill cover and are working to be able to dump the excess material into some played-out sand and gravel pits near the river. Trucking it long distances is not an environmentally or economically responsible response. How best to deal with the sediment from behind the dams remains a serious issue and the subject of intense study.

Reservoir Management for Conservation

Managing the dams is a balancing act between water conservation, flood control, and habitat needs. The Army Corps recently reviewed water conservation opportunities at their Santa Fe Dam and Whittier Narrows Dam. Santa Fe Reservoir did not originally have an authorized water conservation pool, a pool of water behind the dam saved for recharge. It has a 4,351-acre-foot debris pool. The Army Corps allows storing more water in this basin when weather forecasts and downstream conditions are favorable. This water can then be released to downstream spreading basins.

Whittier Narrows Reservoir is a flood control facility, with authority for water conservation as well. A conservation pool of 2,500 acre-feet behind the dam allows releases from the dam equal to the capacity of downstream spreading basins. The Army Corps' 1994 report suggested that the water conservation pool behind Santa Fe Dam could be increased to add an additional 1,680 acre-feet per year of local recharge. The capacity of the conservation pool behind Whittier Narrows Dam could be increased from 2,500 to 6,005 acre-feet. This would increase the amount of water that could be spread and add to our water supply.

Managing Spreading Basins

Spreading basins are established in those places where water can percolate or infiltrate quickly and easily into the soil. Established spreading grounds are located near the San Gabriel River and the Rio Hondo and at the mouth of the Tujunga Wash, in the San Fernando Valley. These places are ideal because they are located on alluvial fans where the sand, gravel, and boulders have eroded off the mountains over the millennia. In some places in the San Gabriel Valley the sediment is up to 20,000 feet deep. Because of the geology, these areas are also ideal places to mine sand and gravel for use in construction, for making concrete, and for many other purposes.

Some of the spreading basins are old sand and gravel quarries that have been dug deep down into the alluvial sediment. Other spreading basins are made up of a large number of interconnected shallow basins with earthen levees. County Public Works manages 28 spreading basins in the county, spreading water from three sources: captured storm and surface water, imported water, and reclaimed water. In order to maximize the effectiveness of its spreading operations, County Public Works has installed rubber dams in various soft-bottom places in the rivers to divert water into spreading basins or to hold water in the river to enhance percolation. These rubber dams can be deflated during storms.

Spreading basins have a tendency to silt up with very fine sediments from uncontrolled local flows in the creeks and rivers that are not dammed. Basins are scraped periodically to remove the fine silt layers and enhance percolation, but there is no exact science to the timing of the scraping. Nor is there agreement as to the optimal depth of water in spreading basins. In order to control algae and mosquitoes, the basins are periodically allowed to dry out. Because of the need to scrape and dry the basins, they can look

TABLE 11. Ten-Year Water Balance Chart

Water Year	% of Normal Rainfall	Local Storm Water Conserved (acre-feet)	Imported Water Conserved (acre-feet)	Reclaimed Water Conserved (acre-feet)	Reclaimed Water Injected Through Seawater Barriers (acre-feet)	Total Water Injected Through Seawater Barriers (acre-feet)
1994–1995	74%	401,218	43,033	33,300	67	24,767
1995–1996	75%	177,080	84,954	53,867	4,569	26,888
1996–1997	88%	179,966	65,543	49,960	5,062	28,947
1997–1998	211%	365,567	40,530	37,510	8,355	27,421
1998–1999	51%	95,166	28,588	48,233	7,076	24,964
1999–2000	73%	112,307	95,990	43,180	7,539	30,408
2000–2001	97%	144,599	58,448	46,343	6,753	30,970
2001–2002	32%	73,804	106,736	60,596	7,569	31,912
2002–2003	100%	134,611	81,129	42,640	7,841	29,413
2003–2004	55%	99,717	81,532	44,924	8,311	30,011
2004–2005	240%	570,618	36,814	23,547	4,234	24,876

SOURCE: County Public Works.

like a moonscape. County Public Works is planting the embankments with native plants to provide habitat and to improve the aesthetics of its spreading basins as funding is available.

During the wet season, when local rain/runoff is also available, MWD provides an economic incentive for member agencies to buy imported water (October 15 to April 15). This is the season of low demand, when MWD has surplus water available and when the county does most of its spreading. It is MWD's way of encouraging more use of imported water in the winter and spring and of encouraging the use of local groundwater during the summer and fall months. This makes supplemental imported water available cheaply at the same time that local water is available for free. During wet years, more low-cost imported water and free local water could be spread if more spreading facilities were available, especially near the Los Angeles River and in the eastern end of the San Gabriel Valley.

County Public Works continues to explore ways to optimize the rate of percolation in order to increase efficiency. The maintenance issues are how often and when to remove silt from spreading basins to encourage infiltration, how best to configure the basins to provide the correct balance between depth of the basin and amount of fine sediment buildup in the bottom of the basins, how best to deal with a clay lens about 15 feet under the Rio Hondo spreading ground that interferes with percolation (dig it up, perforate it, or replace it with gravel), other ways to optimize mosquito control, especially in the summer months (basins are dried out every two weeks in order to eliminate mosquitoes and to allow percolation rates to recover), continue to develop and implement its master plan improvements for existing spreading grounds and to create new basins. A number of inactive or nearly played-out sand and gravel quarries in the San Gabriel Valley could be converted.

Other potential sites should be explored. There are not many opportunities along the Los Angeles River because of heavy, claylike soils and clay layers underground in some places that interfere with percolation rates.

Landscape Ethic

Gardening in the Los Angeles Area and statewide has historically been a race to see who could grow the most exotic plants from all parts of the world most successfully. This competition has been possible because of our sunny climate and the seemingly endless supply of water. It has transformed our semiarid landscape into lush lawns, parks, and gardens, mimicking English country gardens and lush tropical gardens. Since almost anything will grow in this area with enough water, why not grow it?

Bringing plant materials from all over the world carries a price. Not all growing plants are created equal. Some exotic plants, those that are not native to our region, gulp vast quantities of water and deprive local wildlife (animals, birds, and butterflies) of the habitat needed to survive. They can also multiply and take over our local ecosystems, replacing native plants. A few of these exotics, such as *Arundo donax*, a bamboolike reed, create hazards as well. It is brittle, breaks in the wind and rain easily, and piles up on the beach and by bridges or any other obstacle in our waterways. It also requires about four times as much water as natives. Therefore a landscape ethic must eliminate noxious exotics such as Arundo and put much more emphasis on native or noninvasive Mediterranean plant materials to landscape our homes and businesses. These require much less water, none or very little in the summer, to survive and look good.

Currently, between 40% and 70% of a single-family home's water is used outside, depending on the microclimate (whether folks live near the beach or in an inland valley that gets very hot in the summer) and how big the lot is. With an increasing population and a decreasing water supply, inappropriate landscaping becomes increasingly problematic. New landscaping for large installations is now regulated by the state and by the City of Los Angeles in attempts at encouraging natives and Mediterranean plants that use less water. All jurisdictions must follow the state's landscape law unless they pass a more stringent law. Butterfly gardens are being planted in many schools in the area. By planting natives, habitat is provided that will attract, besides butterflies, hummingbirds and other birds.

The MWD is promoting heritage gardens in its service area and is developing materials to help people learn what is possible and how to plant and care for native and California-friendly plants. In conjunction with its member agencies it is maintaining a website on sample gardens, with information about how to plant, the water needs of different plant materials, etc., and with links to nurseries where plants can be purchased and links to local nonprofits active in the field. Some water agencies have constructed drought-tolerant gardens and there is an increasing number of educational initiatives to demonstrate that beautiful landscaping can be created with plant materials that consume much less water. Professional landscapers and homeowners can receive free training in water efficiency practices from such agencies. MWD claims that the average homeowner waters current landscapes twice as much as necessary (www.bewaterwise.org).

Interest is growing slowly. Few local nurseries carry native plants for sale. Plants lack labels indicating their water needs. Landscape architecture classes at local universities rarely teach about native plant materials; if they do, they are not promoted. Landscape maintenance firms have little if any experience planting and maintaining low-water-use landscaping. Very few people understand how to care for native gardens. Yet native plantings can look great. There are plants that flower just about all year round.

Because native plants are not carried by most nurseries and therefore are hard to find, a list of special organizations and nurseries where they can be purchased and information about their care and maintenance are provided following the Glossary at the end of this book.

Overwatering existing landscapes seems to be the norm. Water supply agencies are realizing the enormous waste of irrigation water that also unnecessarily waters sidewalks and streets, only to run in the gutter when local gardens are overwatered. Controlling irrigation practices with existing landscaping can also reduce urban runoff and the contaminants carried with it. A few of these agencies are now teaming up to subsidize ET-computerized sprinkler controllers.

The study by the Irvine Ranch Water District in Orange County has shown that with ET controllers, 10% of total water use can be saved. Education alone can save 6%. The legislature established a Landscape Task Force. Its recommendations can be found at .zwww.cuwcc.org/ab2717/landscape_task_force.lasso.

OCEAN DESALINATION

Using the desalinization process or reverse osmosis (RO) to remove the salt from brackish groundwater basins that are now unusable is certainly a viable option to be promoted. West Basin Municipal Water District has built a desalter to restore the usefulness of some groundwater that has become contaminated by seawater intrusion. Poor-quality groundwater such as that found in the Hollywood aquifer can benefit from desalting technology. It makes economic sense to do so.

Reverse osmosis is now being promoted to desalt seawater for potable use. Seawater is a life force, containing a rich mix of bacteria, viruses, and decaying organic matter in addition to eggs, larvae, plankton, nutrients, fine sediments, and, of course, larger marine plants and animals. It is this soup of dissolved and particulate material that supports the large fisheries and amazing biodiversity of our coastal oceans. Yet this is the source water that is under consideration.

Desalting seawater is not only environmentally destructive, it is very expensive. It takes a lot of energy to push water through membranes to filter out all the salts and other constituents in seawater that are undesirable, to clean it up so that it meets all potable standards. And chemicals that are not healthful for the ocean are used to prevent the membranes from clogging during the reverse osmosis process.

If this energy-intensive technology is to be employed, it makes much more sense to apply it to the stream of almost-potable cleaned-up wastewater we are now throwing away, year-round, into the ocean. Wastewater must by law be cleaned up to almost-potable standards. It will take little more effort to make it totally potable, and wastewater treatment plants are already located inland near existing distribution systems. Ocean disposal of treated wastewater is a freshwater river that flows year-round into the sea, not a normal occurrence in southern California.

Yet, as this is written, 31 seawater desalinization plants are proposed for the California coast. Membrane technology is improving and the costs are coming down. MWD is providing an incentive of $250 an acre-foot to those who can develop cost-effective desalting technology. Coastal power plants are aging and being retrofitted and modernized, so, it is argued, it makes sense to add desalting capability during the retrofit process. Desalination facilities can utilize the existing cooling water intakes and discharge pipes and use energy off-peak (although water usage peaks at nearly the same time as energy does). However, USEPA is concerned about the use of seawater in once-through cooling systems because of impacts to ocean ecosystems, and the agency has now outlawed once-through cooling as licenses come up for renegotiation. Some power plants had hoped to avoid having to build alternate cooling systems by using the intakes for a water supply as well.

Desalination of seawater will never be able to meet a large part of our water needs because of the way our water delivery system is sized, even when the cost comes down. The big pipes are located inland, getting smaller close to the ocean. The water produced by desalting seawater will have to be pumped inland before it can be put into the current distribution system, and pumping water uphill is also expensive. But the lure of a free water source, the ocean, has some engineering companies anxious to build desalination plants all along the coast of the state, most in conjunction with an existing power plant. For more on desalination, visit www.desalresponsegroup.org.

CONCLUSION

CONSERVATION Conservation is gaining in importance because CALFED and many other planning processes have adopted it as one of their primary goals. Ways to certify those agencies that are implementing the best management practices (BMPs) adopted by the California Urban Water Conservation Council (CUWCC) are being explored. There is mixed compliance at this time, as reflected on the CUWCC website, especially when, statewide, the vast number of agencies have yet to sign on. Conservation is voluntary, except for ultralow-flow toilets, which must be installed when property changes ownership, and the law that requires large landscape installations to be drought tolerant. The most conservative estimate in the state, made by the California Urban Water Agencies, is that a million acre-feet of water can be saved statewide.

The Pacific Institute's November 2003 study of indoor urban water use, *Waste Not Want Not: The Potential for Urban Water Conservation in California*, concludes: "Our best estimate is that one-third of California's current urban water use—more than 2.3 million acre-feet (AF)—can be saved with existing technology. At least 85% of this (more than 2 million AF) can be saved at costs below what it would cost to tap into new sources of supply and without the many social, environmental, and economic consequences that any major water project will bring."

RECLAMATION AND REUSE Reclamation and reuse for nonpotable purposes is now a common and growing practice. It is criminal to spend so much money, time, and effort to clean wastewater, only to throw it away. Using reclaimed water for groundwater recharge, though this has been practiced for over 40 years with epidemiological studies to prove it safe, can still

TABLE 12. Summary of Efficiency Potentials

Conservation[a]	Between 1 and 2 maf statewide, (up to 35% urban water use)
Reclamation[b]	760,000 af in MWD service territory
	400,000 af in Los Angeles Area
Conjunctive use[c]	Storage capacity in Los Angeles Area for an additional 1.78 maf; much more nearby
Watershed management	Mostly not yet studied
Landscape[d] irrigation	20% of outdoor use, 10% of total residential use
Native plant gardens	More than 50% of outdoor water use, where installed
Desalination of treated wastewater	Has tremendous potential
Desalination of seawater	Being studied; still too expensive and environmentally destructive; big money lies in retrofitting aging power plants located on the beach for desalination

NOTE: Efficiency potentials are not additive.

become a political football. All water is constantly being recycled and reused. Using the earth as a final treatment is the most economical way to reuse treated wastewater because it travels underground and can then be pumped up into the existing distribution infrastructure. Advanced tertiary treatment with reverse osmosis, microfiltration, UV, and ozonation, though expensive, can produce water so clean that it is injected into the ground to protect drinking water aquifers against seawater intrusion and so clean that minerals must be added to prevent the pipes from corroding. Applying reverse osmosis to make potable water from our wastewater stream makes much more sense than using the sea as source water.

The Bureau of Reclamation study has identified 400,000 additional acre-feet of water that could be potentially reused just in the Los Angeles Area.

CONJUNCTIVE USE Conjunctive use is finally coming into its own with the formation of the Association of Ground Water Agencies (AGWA). AGWA

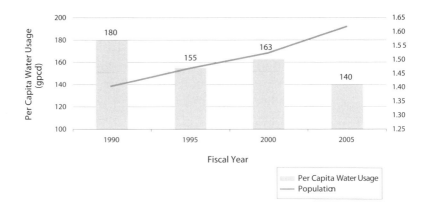

Figure 37. Per capita water usage decreases as population increases. (SOURCE: Central Basin MWD water use database and MWD demographic data, 2005.)

has studied the safe yield and storage capacity of southern California's groundwater basins and has concluded that there is over 1.73 million acre-feet of storage capacity in the Los Angeles Area. Underground storage does not evaporate or interfere with the land use above, and it uses existing distribution infrastructure. MWD is contracting with others to store water underground in the Central Valley, in Arizona, and near its Colorado River Aqueduct. Local groundwater managers have been reluctant to store MWD water. The Chino Basin, next door to the Los Angeles Area as defined, has about 2 million acre-feet of storage capacity.

WATERSHED MANAGEMENT Watershed management is now being studied for the first time, with the potential of saving more stormwater runoff for groundwater recharge, especially if captured and infiltrated where it falls. Additional huge watershed management savings can come from the adoption of a landscape ethic and creating excitement about planting native materials in our gardens to attract butterflies and birds. A 20% savings in landscape irrigation has already been achieved in Orange County by means of computerized irrigation controllers without any landscape changes, or about 10% of total urban water use. These irrigation controllers also reduce the amount of urban runoff and the water quality problems associated with runoff.

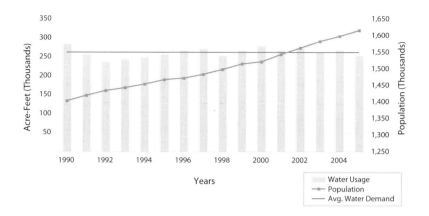

Figure 38. Population grew but total use remained flat. (SOURCE: Central Basin MWD water use database and MWD demographic data, 2005.)

DESALINATION Desalination is the only option for creating more. It makes both economic and environmental sense to apply the technology to groundwater that is high in TDS or has other problems that are readily fixable. It does not make economic or environmental sense to desalinate the ocean. It is energy intensive and very expensive at this time and creates its own environmental problems. The best alternative is to learn to live with what we have, conserve, reuse, better manage our surface and groundwater supplies conjunctively, adopt a landscape ethic to reflect the climate in which we live, and clean up what we have contaminated. All of these are cheaper, and the potential is enormous.

PER CAPITA WATER USE Per capita water use can actually decline, despite projections of real population growth. Several agencies are maximizing the use of their own local resources and are demonstrating that water use can remain flat as population grows. One example is the Central Basin Water District.

Maintaining and managing an adequate supply of water for its growing population is not the only water challenge facing the Los Angeles Area. Ensuring the quality of water in such a highly urbanized region is itself a formidable task. Many of the industrial, commercial, and private activities associated with a large city can easily contaminate local surface water and groundwater, causing adverse health effects and a reduction in supply. Large areas of groundwater in the Los Angeles Area are contaminated —from both natural sources and man-made causes. Some of these areas are so seriously contaminated that they have been designated as federal Superfund sites. Local surface supplies and imported water supplies, especially the Colorado River, are threatened as well. Hundreds of millions of dollars are being spent to clean up contaminated groundwater, restore surface water, and treat water to drinking water standards.

The sources of pollutants in an urban setting include industrial solvents and other chemicals from factories or leaking storage tanks, animal and human waste, pesticides, fertilizers, motor oil, and aerial fallout. Local surface water is impounded before it reaches the highly urbanized areas, where it would be impacted by urban pollutants, and is preserved for drinking water use by being slowly infiltrated in spreading grounds into groundwater basins.

Therefore, most of our drinking water comes from groundwater basins or is imported (brought in aqueducts from other parts of the state).

Drinking water quality is highly regulated by the federal Safe Drinking Water Act as well as state and local ordinances. In California, the United States Environmental Protection Agency (USEPA) and the State Department of Health Services are responsible for implementing the federal Safe Drinking Water Act. Federal and state drinking water regulations ensure that water served to customers meets standards. Water system operators are responsible for testing drinking water quality. System operators test their wells or surface water outlets on a regular basis, and more frequent testing is required of water within the drinking water distribution system. Water system operators are required to submit their water quality data to the State Department of Health Services. For the years 1996–2001, 172 of 372 public water systems in Los Angeles County had some level of a water quality problem in their drinking water sources. Drinking water served at the tap, however, met stringent standards, thanks to advanced treatment technologies.

In this chapter, we discuss the drinking water regulatory system (the laws and agencies that administer them), drinking water standards and monitoring, treatment processes, the status of the quality of surface water, imported water, and groundwater, and progress on cleanup of the major Superfund sites.

DRINKING WATER REGULATORY OVERVIEW

Federal Laws

SAFE DRINKING WATER ACT   The federal Safe Drinking Water Act was passed in 1974 and amended in 1986 and 1996. This law applies to all waters actually or potentially designated for drinking use, from either above-ground or below-ground sources. The law sets up a structure to regulate public water supplies in order to protect human health. It does not directly regulate private wells that serve fewer than 25 persons.

Most states, including California, have taken over direct responsibility for oversight and enforcement of water safety under a state drinking water program. USEPA has authorized California to implement the Safe Drinking Water Act within the state. In addition to implementation of the primary, human health–oriented drinking water standards, California added regulations for *secondary* drinking water standards that are based on aesthetic qualities, such as odors and taste (www.epa.gov/safewater/).

THE CLEAN WATER ACT The Federal Water Pollution Control Act, commonly known as the Clean Water Act, was put in place in 1972, "to restore and maintain the chemical, physical, and biological integrity of the nation's waters." The law focuses primarily on surface water. Groundwater is included indirectly through regulations that cover the interaction between surface water and groundwater and through requirements in the act for groundwater protection strategies. The act requires USEPA and those states with delegated authority to regulate industrial and other discharges of wastewater to rivers, streams, and the ocean, determine allowable levels of contaminants in discharges, and develop surface water quality criteria or standards.

One of the primary actions that states take is the establishment of desired beneficial uses for waterways, such as fishing, swimming, boating, wildlife habitat, agriculture, and drinking water supply.

An important element of the Clean Water Act is Section 404. The U.S. Army Corps of Engineers issues permits for discharge of dredge and fill materials into waterways, including wetlands. These materials often can have an effect on recharge to groundwater areas, which may, in urbanized areas such as Los Angeles, be used more often directly as drinking water sources than the surface waters, such as rivers, lakes, and estuaries. States are required to review proposed 404 permits to ensure that wetlands and waterways are protected (www.epa.gov/region5/water/cwa.htm).

RESOURCE CONSERVATION AND RECOVERY ACT (RCRA) Congress passed the Resource Conservation and Recovery Act in 1976 to address the management of huge volumes of solid hazardous wastes found in toxic sites throughout the United States. RCRA regulates the generation, transportation, treatment, and disposal of solid and hazardous waste, basically controlling hazardous material as it goes from "cradle to grave." The direct impact of this act on drinking water is that wastes that meet RCRA's definition of *hazardous* must be disposed of in an approved manner. Improper disposal of hazardous wastes has been one of the biggest problems in Los Angeles, leading to the designation of a large number of Superfund sites, as described later. In the amendments of 1984, land disposal of most hazardous wastes was banned

unless they had prior treatment. The 1984 amendments also added regulations for leaking underground tanks, another major source of groundwater pollution in Los Angeles County and across the country. The new
regulations mandated improved standards for tanks (requiring them to be
double walled), spill protection, and corrosion protection systems.

SUPERFUND (CERCLA) ACT Four years after the passage of RCRA, Congress
passed a companion statute, the Superfund Act, or officially the Comprehensive Environmental Response, Compensation and Liability Act of
1980 (CERCLA). This act provides a regulatory framework for the cleanup
of sites that have been created by dumping toxic wastes on land, in the
ground, and into surface waters. Often these sites are related to facilities
that are no longer operating, as opposed to RCRA, which focuses on pre-
vention and cleanup of pollution from active facilities. CERCLA was
added to by SARA, the Superfund Amendment and Reauthorization Act
of 1986, which created the Emergency Planning and Community Right to
Know program, by which major industries are required to report releases,
transfers, and recycling of toxic chemicals to USEPA as part of the Toxics
Release Inventory Program.

   CERCLA authorized a program for taxing the chemical and petroleum
industries and gave USEPA the power to respond directly to releases or
threatened releases of hazardous substances. There are short-term and
long-term processes under Superfund. Short-term actions occur in response
to acute situations where emergency action is taken. Long-term actions,
which are not immediately life-threatening, are placed on the USEPA's
National Priorities List, which designates Superfund sites (www.Yosemite
.epa.gov.r9/sfund/overview.nsf).

California Laws

CALIFORNIA SAFE DRINKING WATER ACT The State of California passed a Safe
Drinking Water Act in 1977, with the intent to "improve laws governing
drinking water quality, to improve upon the minimum requirements of the
federal Safe Drinking Water Act, to establish primary drinking water
standards that are at least as stringent as those established under federal law,
and to establish a program that is more protective of public health than
the minimum federal requirements." The California Safe Drinking Water

Act of 1989 built further on the federal Safe Drinking Water Act provisions. It was the first law in the country to require that water purveyors provide annual water quality reports for their consumers. The 1996 amendments established the first public drinking water *right to know* requirements, which led USEPA to adopt a requirement of national "consumer confidence reports" (www.dhs.cahwnet.gov/ps/ddwem/).

The amendments also established the Office of Environmental Health and Hazard Assessment, which provides technical research on the health effects of drinking water contaminants (www.oehha.ca.gov/water.html).

CALIFORNIA PORTER–COLOGNE WATER QUALITY CONTROL ACT   The California Porter–Cologne Water Quality Control Act, often referred to simply as Porter–Cologne and one of the first important water quality laws in the country, was enacted in 1969. The act authorized the state and regional water quality control boards to adopt policies and regulations to protect and clean up surface water and groundwater in California. The water boards also create Water Quality Control Plans, or water planning documents, which include the designated uses of waters, water quality standards that match the use, and protection strategies (www.swrcb.ca.gov).

HAZARDOUS WASTE CONTROL ACT   The Hazardous Waste Control Act of 1972 and the subsequent emergency regulations of 1973 established the California Hazardous Waste Control Program within the state Department of Health Services. This was the beginning of a hazardous waste control program in California and initiated definitions of hazardous waste, a tracking system, and a technical assistance center. The program developed into the Department of Toxic Substances Control (DTSC). The department grew in the 1970s and 1980s during a period of much new legislation. In 1991, legislation established the California Environmental Protection Agency and transferred the DTSC from the Department of Health Services to this new agency (www.calepa.ca.gov/About/History01/dtsc.htm).

HAZARDOUS SUBSTANCES CLEANUP BOND ACT OF 1984   A ballot measure approved by the citizens created the Hazardous Substances Cleanup Bond Act of 1984, also known as the California Superfund Act. This act provided $100 million to investigate and clean up abandoned toxic waste sites. Subsequent funding was provided by the state and has been administered by the Department of Toxic Substances for cleanup of hazardous waste sites.

SAFE DRINKING WATER AND TOXIC ENFORCEMENT ACT (PROPOSITION 65) In 1986, Californians voted in favor of Proposition 65, which created the Safe Drinking Water and Toxic Enforcement Act. This act requires the state to publish annually a list of chemicals known by the State of California to cause cancer, birth defects, or other reproductive harm. Over 700 chemicals have been listed to date. The act also prescribes that controls be placed on toxic substances in order to protect drinking water sources. The lead agency for implementing the act is the Office of Environmental Health Hazard Assessment, which works with the state Department of Health Services to develop regulations for water safety.

Drinking Water Regulatory Agencies

UNITED STATES ENVIRONMENTAL PROTECTION AGENCY The Safe Drinking Water Act, the Clean Water Act, and other federal environmental laws are administered by the United States Environmental Protection Agency (USEPA). It has 10 regional offices. Region IX includes California. Its main offices are located in San Francisco. Much of the day-to-day implementation of federal laws has been delegated to individual states, while USEPA retains oversight responsibility. On a practical level, this means that USEPA distributes money and grants to California, helps direct state information into national databases and geographical information systems (GIS), provides final review and approval for permits and other required documents, and compiles state information into national reports that are presented to Congress. USEPA is responsible for administering Superfund cleanups, and locally the regional board plays an oversight role (http://www.epa.gov).

STATE WATER RESOURCES CONTROL BOARD AND REGIONAL WATER QUALITY CONTROL BOARDS These state agencies are responsible for protecting water quality in California. The state Water Resources Control Board in Sacramento is both a sister and an oversight agency to the nine local regional water quality control boards. The state board allocates water rights, adjudicates water right disputes, administers grants and other funds, compiles regional information into state databases and reports, and acts as the appeal agency for disputes and regulatory actions at the regional level. The regional board for Region 4 covers most of Los Angeles and Ventura counties. The regional boards regulate residential, industrial, commercial, agricultural, recreational, and other activities to keep pollutants from entering water supplies; if sources become contaminated, they oversee cleanup and treatment efforts. Some of the most important jobs of the regional boards are to regulate wastewater discharges to surface water and ground water, to establish beneficial uses and water quality standards for local water bodies, and to provide public education on local issues. The regional boards do not keep records about specific groundwater drinking wells—the agencies assess water quality on a basinwide or sitewide basis. They are a part of CalEPA (http://www.swrcb.ca.gov/rwqcb4/).

CALIFORNIA DEPARTMENT OF WATER RESOURCES The Department of Water Resources (DWR) also operates as an arm of the state Water Resources Control Board. The agency directs water policy for the state and also has responsibilities in the areas of dams, flood control, and environmental impacts. Every five years DWR produces the *California Water Plan* (Bulletin 160), a comprehensive state water supply status report. In addition, the department designed, constructed and now operates the State Water Project, the aqueduct system that brings water from the Sacramento–San Joaquin Delta area to the San Joaquin Valley and to southern California. DWR is a lead agency in the implementation of CALFED, a program to protect and enhance water supply and quality in the Sacramento–San Joaquin Delta and to restore delta habitat. It is a part of CalEPA (http://www.dwr.wate .ca.gov/).

CALIFORNIA DEPARTMENT OF TOXIC SUBSTANCES CONTROL The Department of Toxic Substances Control (DTSC) protects against human health exposures to hazardous wastes. DTSC operates programs to enforce hazardous waste laws, oversees site cleanups of improperly managed hazardous wastes, ensures emergency planning, and regulates the generation, transportation, storage, and disposal of wastes. DTSC is also responsible for finding ways to reduce the hazardous waste produced in California (http://www.dtsc.ca.gov/).

CALIFORNIA DEPARTMENT OF HEALTH SERVICES The California Department of Health Services (DHS) regulates the quality of drinking water in public water systems and enforces state and federal safe drinking water acts. The Department of Health Services also reviews proposed recycled-water projects and issues advisory letters to the regional boards regarding public health implications. The regional board will not issue reuse permits without Health Department approval.

California has nearly 16,000 active drinking water sources and several thousand standby and inactive sources. These drinking water sources—groundwater wells or surface sources—are used to provide water to systems that convey water to individual users.

The California Department of Health Services maintains an extensive database of active wells for which drinking water monitoring is required or those actively used for public drinking water systems. The department, however, does not have a complete record of all of the wells in the county. In addition, the department has no record of how many wells have been shut down due to contamination or wells taken out of service or put on standby status for a variety of reasons (http://www.dhs.ca.gov/).

The Department of Health Services is responsible for the inspection and regulatory oversight of approximately 8,500 public water systems to ensure delivery of safe drinking water to all California consumers. Activities involved in this oversight include issuing permits, performing inspections of existing facilities, reviewing plans for new facilities, issuing administrative orders and citations for violations against systems in noncompliance with laws and regulations, and ensuring that water quality monitoring is conducted in accordance with the law.

It is also responsible for providing oversight, assistance, and training to the 34 county health departments, which have been delegated responsibility for regulating small water systems, maintaining the statewide databases for all water systems in the state, and providing assistance to local health departments, regional water quality control boards, and the Department of Toxic Substances Control on water quality issues

The numerous demands made on the Department of Health Services Office of Drinking Water has resulted in delays—often for over a year—to process permits for the use of contaminated groundwater that has been treated for beneficial use. This agency works in a slow and careful way to guarantee public health and safety. Several treatment facilities have been completed in areas where groundwater cleanups have been initiated (Superfund sites) that produce water of potable quality. The startup of the facilities is often delayed due to regulatory reviews and approvals or delays in the issuance of the final permits. This slows the pace of groundwater cleanup efforts as well as costing ratepayers more because larger amounts of water must be imported in the interim period. This agency is also extremely cautious in approving the use of tertiary treated wastewater for groundwater recharge.

DHS CALIFORNIA DRINKING WATER SOURCES ASSESSMENT AND PROTECTION PROGRAM (DWSAP)   In 1986, amendments to the federal Safe Drinking Water Act required that each state develop a wellhead protection program. California did not implement this program. Then, in 1996, additional amendments to the Safe Drinking Water Act required states to develop source water assessment programs to assess and protect sources of drinking water, including surface water sources, to ensure that drinking water quality is maintained. California has now started a program that satisfies both the 1986 and the 1996 requirements. The Department of Health Services runs the program, called the *California Drinking Water Sources Assessment and Protection Program (DWSAP)*, which protects both surface water and groundwater.

The key elements of the DWSAP program is the requirement that public water systems or the Department of Health Services perform assessments of water sources that include a delineation and description of the area that drains into or contributes water to a water supply, an inventory of activities that might contribute contaminants, and a vulnerability analysis showing potential pollutant threats. For surface waters, these assessments have been previously required under California law and are called *Watershed Sanitary Surveys*. Sanitary Surveys are conducted every five years (www .dhs.ca.gov/ps/ddwem/).

LOS ANGELES COUNTY HEALTH DEPARTMENT   Thirty-five county health departments, including one in Los Angeles County, have been delegated authority by the state to regulate small water systems. Small water systems are defined as those with fewer than 200 service connections, including community and noncommunity systems. Community water systems serve at least 15 connections used by yearlong residents or regularly serve at least 25 yearlong residents. Noncommunity systems include schools, businesses, and churches.

Recent amendments to the federal Safe Drinking Water Act call attention to the fact that many small public water systems lack the technical or financial ability to ensure a pure, safe, and adequate water supply. The state has, as of 1997, established a revolving loan fund to provide technical and financial assistance to operators of small systems and is prohibiting the establishment of any new public water systems or change in ownership that cannot demonstrate its ability to supply safe, reliable drinking water on a long-term basis.

As the immediate oversight agencies, state and county health departments conduct inspections, issue operating permits, review water quality monitoring reports, take enforcement actions in cases of violations, manage the State Revolving Fund Program, and conduct a Source Water Assessment Program that identifies and eliminates potential contamination sources.

The Los Angeles County Health Department keeps paper records of well installations and well destructions on an annual basis (by city) but does not maintain a database of active or inactive wells. There are approximately 184 small water systems in the county that draw water from about 230 wells. The county maintains "well construction records" for these wells, including community wells and some private wells. The total number of private wells in the county is unknown because they are not subject to monitoring requirements. There are a large number of private wells in the less developed areas of the county. In the Santa Monica Mountains, for example, west of Kanan Dume Road to the Ventura County line, there are 200–300 private wells (www.dhs.co.la.ca.us/).

OFFICE OF ENVIRONMENTAL HEALTH HAZARD ASSESSMENT The state Office of Environmental Health Hazard Assessment (OEHHA) implements the Safe Drinking Water and Toxic Enforcement Act (Proposition 65). The agency is primarily a research organization and performs major risk assessment and hazard evaluation of chemical contaminants in drinking water. OEHHA develops public health goals and recommended action levels for chemical substances in drinking water.

DRINKING WATER STANDARDS
AND MONITORING REQUIREMENTS

Drinking Water Standards

Under the federal Safe Drinking Water Act, USEPA is required to establish national drinking water standards. In California the State Department of Health Services enforces these national standards and has put into place additional drinking water standards, particularly in the area of secondary standards.

MAXIMUM CONTAMINANT LEVELS   Under the Safe Drinking Water Act, USEPA has established federal drinking water standards, known as *maximum contaminant levels (MCLs)*, for different natural and man-made contaminants potentially found in water supplies. USEPA prioritizes which contaminants to regulate based on human health risks and frequency of occurrence in drinking water supplies. First a health goal, called a *maximum contaminant level goal (MCLG)*, is set for a particular contaminant, and, after further study, either a legal limit or a required treatment technique is determined. USEPA takes cost–benefit analysis and public comments into account when establishing these legal standards. MCLs are enforceable.

In California, under the state Safe Drinking Water Act, the Department of Health Services establishes MCLs. Most of these are the same as the federal standards, but occasionally more strict standards are established. These MCLs are listed in Title 22 of the California Code of Regulations.

There are 84 primary MCLs in place in California to protect human health. Primary MCLs include metals such as arsenic and mercury, radioactive contaminants, and other constituents, such as solvents and pesticides. California has established 17 secondary MCLs for nuisance conditions, such as taste, odor or appearance of drinking water, color.

MCLs are established based on known or potential human health effects, the current technological ability to remove the contaminant, and the effectiveness and cost of treatment. For most contaminants, low-level, short-term exposure poses little health risk, so the MCLs are based on lifetime exposure, which assumes that an average adult drinks two liters of water each day throughout a 70-year life span.

Under California law, drinking water can contain low levels of contaminants and not be considered "out of compliance" with MCLs. MCLs are usually required to be met on an annual basis, and small exceedences will not trigger a violation if the water source can meet the MCL for the year on an average basis. When there are small exceedences, the water system will be under DHS oversight and on a time schedule to bring the system into compliance. On the other hand, if a contaminant exceeds its MCL tenfold, then the water source must be immediately taken out of service.

ACTION LEVELS AND PUBLIC HEALTH RECOMMENDATIONS/GOALS   In addition to MCLs, two lower, nonregulatory, levels of standards are set by California. Action levels (ALs) are health-based advisory levels that are established when an MCL is not in place and either a chemical is found in a proposed drinking water source or a chemical is in proximity to a drinking water source. An action level is the level of a contaminant in drinking water considered not to pose a significant health risk to people ingesting that water on a daily basis.

Chemicals that are guided by action levels may later be upgraded to MCLs, depending on contamination and risk to human health. Although action levels are not enforceable, drinking water system managers are required to notify governing agencies whenever an action level is exceeded and are encouraged to notify their customers. If a contaminant is found in a drinking water supply at a level 100 times (for a cancer risk contaminant) or 10 times (for noncarcinogenic risks) the action level, then the Department of Health Services recommends removing the water from service. For example, the action level for bromide is one part per million (ppm); a source with more than 10 ppm bromide would be removed from service.

Public health goals (PHGs) or recommended levels are established by the Cal/EPA Office of Environmental Health Hazard Assessment (OEHHA) for pollutants or chemicals for which more research is being conducted and an MCL might be revised or established. Public health goal water quality standards are set so that levels of contaminants in drinking water would not be expected to pose significant health risks to individuals, along with an adequate margin of safety. The levels are based on health risk considerations, not costs or feasibility, and thus public water systems do not have to comply with these goals.

Public water systems are required to notify their customers when their water has contaminants above public health goals and to hold periodic hearings to inform the public about the cost of complying with the goals. Their customers can request a referendum on paying the additional costs of treating the water. There have been no instances in California where the public has held such a referendum. Chromium 6 is a current example of a chemical that is being studied and will have a public health goal set.

MCLs that are established by the Department of Health Services are set at levels close to, but often *higher* than, public health goals because technological and economic feasibility are also taken into account. The department is required to review MCLs for chemicals for which public health goals have been established. After extensive scientific assessment, cost–benefit analysis, and public review, MCLs may then be established or, if existing, revised. An example occurred in January 2001, when a monitoring requirement for chromium 6 (separate from total chromium) was ordered.

MONITORING OF UNREGULATED CHEMICALS   Certain contaminants for which MCLs have not been developed are given special consideration for monitoring. A list of unregulated contaminants must be monitored by large public water systems. The federal unregulated contaminants on the current list contain 11 chemicals, including methyl tertiary butyl ether (MTBE) and perchlorate, that have been found in groundwater in Los Angeles County. The State of California requires the monitoring of nine contaminants, including chromium 6 and perchlorate.

Monitoring Programs and Reporting Requirements

The federal Safe Drinking Water Act requires public water system operators to monitor drinking water sources for regulated contaminants on a regular basis. The frequency of monitoring depends on the type of contaminant and the size of the system. Coliform bacteria, for example, are an indicator that cross-contamination could be occurring from sewage lines and therefore are monitored on the most frequent basis. Usually a system operator must monitor for a newly regulated chemical repeatedly, such as once a month or once every three months, but if the contaminant is not found, then the frequency can be reduced to once every year. The monitoring of some constituents can be reduced significantly. For example, contaminants such as chromium and mercury must be tested once a year for a city that uses surface water as its supply. After three years, if these constituents do not pose a problem, the city can apply for a waiver to skip sampling of those contaminants for up to nine years.

Large systems that serve more than 10,000 persons are required to monitor their water for the presence of unregulated contaminants, such as bromide and chromium 6, which are included on a special list.

The California Department of Health Services compiles the data reports into a Water Quality Inventory (WQI) database and disseminates the information. The state produces an annual report on violations of primary drinking water regulations by public water systems and transmits this report to USEPA.

WATER TREATMENT PROCESSES

Water cannot be served to the public unless it meets state and federal standards. Basic water treatment, therefore, is often needed. How much treatment is given depends on the water's source and the level of impurities detected in that water. Pristine groundwater often needs little treatment because of the natural filtration that comes with the slow movement of water through the ground, often involving years of natural cleansing. Large water suppliers or purveyors, such as municipal systems, often use surface water sources primarily, whereas small systems depend mainly on groundwater. Some or all of the following treatment is given to drinking water before delivery to customers.

Groundwater Basic Treatment

Groundwater is usually of high quality and requires minimal filtration and disinfection. Water is filtered, if needed, by running it through an adsorbent material such as pulverized coal. Low-level chlorination or other disinfection treatment keeps bacteria from growing in water distribution pipelines.

Surface Water Basic Treatment

1. *Screening.* Water entering a treatment plant is first screened to remove larger objects, such as rocks, leaves, and paper.
2. *Flocculation/coagulation.* Water is then subjected to flocculation, which is the process by which small particles clump together to create larger particles that settle out of water as sediment. Chemicals called coagulants, such as alum, iron salts, and synthetic organic polymers, are added to cause clumping. Many contaminants cling to these coagulated particles and are also removed.
3. *Sedimentation.* Water enters a sedimentation basin, where particles and sediment settle to the bottom and are removed.

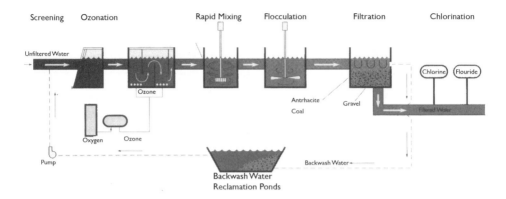

Figure 39. Drinking water treatment process. (SOURCE: LADPW.)

4.   *Filtration.* With the water free of large particles, it is passed through filter beds composed of pulverized coal and/or sand that remove smaller particles such as clay and silts, natural organic matter, bacteria, and some viruses. Filtration clarifies the water.

5.   *Adsorption.* If needed, certain organic chemicals and taste-, odor-, and color-causing constituents in the water are removed by granular or powder-activated carbon. Adsorption is the process whereby a constituent is attracted to the surface of an introduced particle. The adsorption process is not often considered necessary for public water supplies.

6.   *Disinfection.* Finally, chlorine is added to the water to ensure that it remains free of water-borne diseases, such as cholera and typhoid, as it travels from the plant to the tap. Other disinfection processes include treatment with ozone gas or ultraviolet light. Ozonation involves cooling liquid oxygen down to 300° below zero and then creating ozone (O3—very active oxygen) by means of a high-voltage chamber. Ozone is then bubbled through the water to kill viruses and bacteria. The ozonation process is more expensive than chlorination but does not leave disinfection by-products, unless the water is originally high in bromide.

The levels of disinfection are carefully controlled throughout the treatment and distribution process in order to provide the minimal amount of protection needed and to reduce the addition of unnecessary chemicals and chemical by-products.

Groundwater and Surface Water Cleanup Processes

When man-made contamination occurs in surface water and groundwater supplies in the state, state agencies require cleanup by the responsible party or parties. The regional boards usually order a site investigation to determine the source of contamination and then a specified process of assessment and cleanup under such programs as the Leaking Underground Tanks Program or the Site Investigation Program. The Department of Toxic Substances Control investigates and requires cleanup of sites where hazardous materials are involved. Both agencies launch specialized regional investigations when needed. Recently, the Los Angeles Regional Board initiated a survey of chromium 6 occurrences in the region. Local entities are delegated authority for less significant contamination problems. For large-scale and complicated contamination areas, USEPA provides assistance and sometimes initiates the Superfund process.

Contaminated Groundwater Cleanup Processes

Hundreds of production wells throughout the Los Angeles Area have been identified as contaminated. When water from a specific well exceeds acceptable contamination levels, one of three actions may ensue.

1. The site is analyzed and extensive remediation occurs, which involves pumping and treating the water before distribution and discharge to the storm drain system or back to groundwater recharge. Monitoring wells may be drilled in proximity to the contaminated production well to assess the extent of the contamination.

2. The water is pumped and blended with imported supplies until contaminant concentrations are reduced to safe levels.

3. The well is completely shut down pending further action, if any.

Cleanup of contaminated groundwater can involve one or more of several extensive and costly procedures. Aeration is a groundwater treatment process used in the Los Angeles Area to treat volatile organic compounds (VOCs). Groundwater is pumped into an aeration tower, where it falls as much as 50 feet through diffusers, packing material, and an upward flow of air. Contaminants in the water vaporize and enter the air stream, which flows through filters that trap them.

Ion exchange is used to remove any contaminant that has a strong electrical charge. Inorganic constituents that cannot be removed by standard filtration and sedimentation treatment processes are exchanged into less harmful constituents. The undesirable constituents are attracted to and exchange ions with a solid medium called the ion exchanger. Examples of constituents that can be treated by ion exchange include arsenic, nitrate, perchlorate, and chromium.

Ultraviolet light kills a wide range of microbes and also can break down a number of organic chemicals such as NDMA, an aerospace contaminant.

Biological treatment is used to treat a range of chemicals that can be broken down or biodegraded by microbes. Contaminants that can be removed include benzene, nitrate, perchlorate, and MTBE. The technique can be used in the ground or in a treatment facility after water has been extracted from the ground. Microbes and food and oxygen for the microbes are injected into or installed in a contaminated area, and the microbes eat the contaminants, forming harmless by-products. These systems usually work best when microbes that are native to the area are involved. Sometimes, the resident bacteria in the area are used, and only additional nutrients and oxygen are supplied to speed up the natural breakdown process. In above-ground systems, called fluidized-bed reactors, contaminated water is pumped over a bed of biological sludge that has been created on carbon. The bacteria in the sludge break down the contaminants. The resulting material, however, sometimes becomes so contaminated that it must be disposed of at a hazardous waste landfill.

Hydrogen peroxide and other strong oxidants break down a number of organic contaminants, including TCE, PCE, MTBE, taste and odor compounds, pesticides, and herbicides (breakdown products may be an issue).

Granular activated carbon or liquid-phase carbon is used to remove a wide range of organic chemicals such as PCE, TCE, MTBE, pesticides, herbicides, taste and odor compounds, trihalomethanes, and a range of naturally occurring organic chemicals. Contaminated water flows over a bed of specialized beads or of activated carbon or coal. Contaminants "stick," or absorb onto the carbon. The carbon or beads can be cleaned and reused.

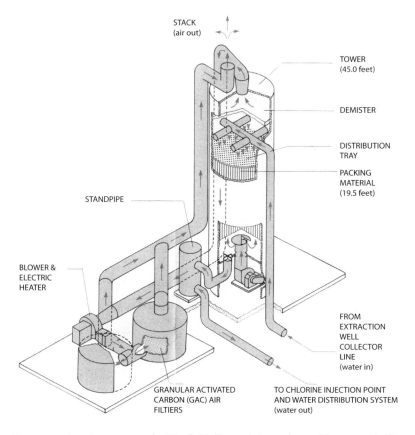

STACK
(air out)

TOWER
(45.0 feet)

DEMISTER

DISTRIBUTION
TRAY

PACKING
MATERIAL
(19.5 feet)

STANDPIPE

BLOWER &
ELECTRIC
HEATER

FROM
EXTRACTION
WELL
COLLECTOR
LINE
(water in)

GRANULAR ACTIVATED
CARBON (GAC) AIR
FILTIERS

TO CHLORINE INJECTION POINT
AND WATER DISTRIBUTION SYSTEM
(water out)

Figure 40. Aeration tower at the North Hollywood Groundwater Treatment Facility showing the groundwater treatment process. (SOURCE: LADWP.)

Air stripping is used to remove any chemical that evaporates easily, such as TCE, PCE, radon, or MTBE. Air bubbles are introduced into the water, which moves slowly through a column filled with a packing material (to slow the flow and maximize contact with the air). Contaminants migrate from the water into the air bubbles. The air bubbles are then passed over a bead of carbon to remove the contaminants.

Air sparging is a process in which air is injected directly into the groundwater and contaminants are volatilized in place and removed with the upward movement of the air bubbles.

Reverse osmosis membranes, or fine molecular sieves, remove nearly everything in water down to a small molecular size. The membranes can be used to remove almost all contaminants. This technique is one of the most expensive.

POTENTIAL TYPES OF CONTAMINANTS
IN DRINKING WATER SOURCES

Water is not delivered to the consumer's tap unless it meets stringent federal and state standards. Contaminants found in water before treatment may fall into any one of the six following categories.

MICROBIAL CONTAMINANTS These include viruses and bacteria. Microbes come from wastewater treatment plants, septic systems, and animal waste. These contaminants may cause gastroenteric infections, dysentery, hepatitis, typhoid fever, or cholera. Often coliform bacteria are used as an indicator that human or animal wastes have leaked into drinking water supplies.

INORGANIC CONTAMINANTS These include salts, metals, and nutrients and occur naturally or may result from human activities. Salts, or general minerals, include total dissolved solids (TDS), salinity, sulfates, and chlorides. Inorganic minerals occur naturally in Los Angeles County bedrock and over time get eroded into surface water and ground water. These salts, metals, and nutrients can be increased to unhealthful levels or unsavory levels by human activities related to sewage treatment, oil and gas production, and mining. In addition, nutrients such as nitrogen and phosphorus come from wastewater discharges or discharges from excessive fertilization of residential or agricultural areas. The presence of nitrates in infants under six months of age causes a serious condition called *blue baby syndrome* or *methemoglobinemia* due to a lowering of oxygen in the blood. High levels of sulfate cause diarrhea, which can be a large problem, particularly with infants. Elevated concentrations of minerals can have adverse impacts on agricultural and landscape irrigation.

HEAVY METALS This category of inorganic contaminants is considered to be more serious for human health effects. Examples are antimony, beryllium, cadmium, chromium, lead, and mercury. Heavy metals are found in various commercial and industrial manufacturing processes and leak into water systems through spills on the ground, damaged storage tanks and other direct routes to the ground, or, like lead, fallout from air pollution. Arsenic and chromium have been metals of particular interest in Los Angeles because of recent reviews of their drinking water standards. Metals may adversely affect the nervous system, kidneys, liver, and skeletal system.

OTHER MEASUREMENTS Other measurements of water quality that do not involve a specific contaminant but are generally related to inorganic contaminants include turbidity (cloudiness of the water) and pH (acidity of the water).

ORGANIC CONTAMINANTS Organic contaminants contain the element carbon. They may be naturally occurring, such as from rotting vegetation and animal feces, or synthetically manufactured. Synthetic organic chemicals were first created in the laboratory at the turn of the last century and are found today in a wide range of products, including pesticides, solvents, paints, and dyes. This group of contaminants has become a large problem in groundwater supplies in Los Angeles in the past 30 years. Since the 1940s, in manufacturing areas of the county, organic chemical wastes were disposed of in back lot pits due to a belief that they would not migrate into the drinking water supply. Many of these areas are now Superfund sites. A recently discovered contaminant, MTBE, an additive in gasoline designed to reduce air pollution, has been found in groundwater near leaking storage tanks at gasoline stations. Organic chemicals may affect the nervous system, kidneys, and liver. Some cause cancer.

RADIOLOGICAL CONTAMINANTS Man-made or natural elements that emit radiation may enter the water supply through the leaching of radioactive waste or the mining of phosphorous. Nuclear power plants and research facilities as well as some medical facilities all produce radioactive wastes. Radionuclides also occur naturally in water, including radon and uranium. Trace amounts of tritium have entered water supplies as a result of atmospheric nuclear testing prior to the nuclear test ban treaties of the 1960s. Radionuclides are considered to cause increased risk of cancer in humans. In addition, uranium may cause an increase in toxic effects to the kidney.

DISINFECTION BY-PRODUCTS Disinfection is an important part of the treatment process and has saved countless lives over the past 100 years. Disinfection, such as chlorination, is added at the end of a treatment process and is kept at the minimum needed to protect against any contamination that might occur in the distribution pipes. The reason that disinfection chemicals are kept at a minimum is to reduce the potential for the creation of new compounds, called *disinfection by-products,* due to interaction with organic matter. Groundwater or surface water that has passed through soil picks up small amounts of organic matter, such as humic and fulvic acids. This is especially true for waters coming from heavily forested areas and from areas such as the San Francisco Bay Area that are dominated by tule-peat. When chlorine or ozone is applied to disinfect this water as part of the drinking water treatment, the organic compounds can combine with the disinfectant to create disinfection by-products. These products, including trihalomethane, haloacetic acid, formaldehyde, and bromide compounds, are now regulated by the state and may be present in drinking water in only small amounts. Some disinfection by-products are carcinogenic and some have been linked to higher incidences of miscarriages.

"EMERGING CONTAMINANTS" This category refers to contaminants related to residential, industrial, and agricultural wastewaters that previously were not thought to be a problem in drinking water but have been identified in a United States Geological Survey study published in March 2002. Included in this study were human and veterinary pharmaceutical chemicals or drugs, such as antidepressants, ibuprofen, and birth-control hormones, that are designed to be stable in the human or animal body. Excess amounts are excreted. It turns out that these chemicals are hardy enough to make their way through treatment facilities to rivers and streams. In this study, researchers tested 139 streams in 30 states during 1999 and 2000. A wide range of sites was chosen, ranging from those near waste treatment facilities and those in more remote locations, but all were sites that were expected to have contamination. Eighty percent of the sites had at least one contaminant.

Scientists tested for 95 wastewater-related organic chemicals; 82 were found. The most common chemicals (discovered in more than 50% of the streams) were fecal steroid coprotanol (a natural part of human and animal waste), plant and animal steroid cholesterol (naturally occurring), the insect repellent *N-N*-diethyltoluamide (in 75% of the samples), caffeine (in 70% of the samples), triclosan (an antimicrobial disinfectant found in soaps), the fire retardant tri (2-chloroethyl) phosphate, and the detergent by-product 4-nonylphenol. These chemicals were found in low amounts, mostly below drinking water or aquatic health standards. Ten sites in California were tested and more follow-up studies are anticipated by the Geological Survey.

WATER QUALITY ISSUES, BY SOURCE

Most of our water supply is either pumped out of the ground locally or imported via aqueducts from hundreds of miles away. Just a small quantity of our water supply is taken directly from the mountains.

Local Surface Water

Because the majority of the Los Angeles Area is urbanized, little of its local surface supplies are introduced directly into the drinking water system. Most of the surface water bodies in Los Angeles, however, are designated as potential drinking water sources in case drought conditions or other crisis situations necessitate tapping the rivers for drinking water. A small portion of the runoff from the San Gabriel Mountains is used directly for local drinking water supply. Chlorination treatment is applied before distribution because the surface water may contain microbial and organic contaminants from wildlife in the area.

Local surface water, however, is used extensively for recharge of the local groundwater basins through spreading at spreading basins and through recharge within the river channels. In some areas the level of total dissolved minerals or solids (TDS) is of concern.

More information about the water quality of our local rivers can be found in *Beneficial Uses of the Los Angeles and San Gabriel River Watershed,* published by the Los Angeles & San Gabriel Rivers Watershed Council. In addition, the regional board's water quality assessment reports include detailed information about surface water contamination. Contamination in local surface waters includes such things as metals, bacteria, organic chemicals, nutrients, PCBs, and DDT (http://www.waterboards.ca.gov/losangeles/html/programs/programs.html).

Local Reservoirs

Water imported to the Los Angeles Area is often stored in surface water reservoirs prior to treatment and delivery to consumer's taps. The major reservoirs are Lake Mathews, Lake Perris, Castaic Lake, Pyramid Lake, and Diamond Valley Lake. Smaller reservoirs used by the Los Angeles Department of Water and Power (LADWP) include a series of reservoirs from Silver Lake west through the Hollywood Hills. The water quality in these reservoirs is protected by restrictions on boating and swimming. A new USEPA regulation called the Surface Water Treatment Rule requires that new reservoirs subject to urban runoff must either be covered (enclosed in tanks) or receive additional filtration before entering the drinking water system. The rule is designed to reduce the potential for *Cryptosporidium* problems. The LADWP recently replaced the Hollywood Reservoir, located near Griffith Park just below the Hollywood sign, with two 360-foot-diameter, 42-feet-high tanks buried underground. Each tank holds 30 million gallons of water. The Hollywood Reservoir itself remains as a standby water source to be used in case of emergencies. Other reservoirs are undergoing different adaptations to this rule, depending on input from local residents.

Imported Water

The water quality from the three aqueduct systems that serve the Los Angeles area vary greatly.

LOS ANGELES AQUEDUCTS   Water delivered to the City of Los Angeles from the Owens Valley has the highest quality of our imported water due to its source in the relatively undeveloped watersheds of the eastern Sierra Nevada Mountains. The water is essentially pure snowmelt. It possesses the lowest TDS, at an average of 210 parts per million (ppm), and therefore is the softest water from the three major aqueducts. Because minimal recreational activity occurs on any of the aqueduct's reservoirs, the water is virtually free of any human contamination. The water is treated at the terminus of the aqueduct, the Los Angeles Filtration Plant at the north end of the San Fernando Valley.

COLORADO RIVER AQUEDUCT   At its headwaters, the Colorado River has a salt concentration of 50 ppm. By the time the river reaches the intake of the

Colorado River Aqueduct at Parker Dam, its concentration has increased to 700 ppm. The Metropolitan Water District often reduces the high salinity of Colorado River water before delivery by blending it with less salty California Aqueduct water.

Several of MWD reservoirs are exposed to the by-products of recreation use, but these reservoirs are engineered with water system intakes located at various depths so that withdrawals can occur at depths having lower contaminant levels.

Besides TDS, other contaminants in the Colorado River system include perchlorate and radioactivity (alpha-emitting particles). Since 1997, perchlorate has been measured in Colorado River water in and near Lake Havasu at concentrations ranging up to 9 parts per billion (ppb). The sources have been identified as ammonium perchlorate manufacturing facilities in the Las Vegas/Henderson area that were discharging concentrations up to 1,000 ppb. In addition, low levels of radioactive particles, below current federal and state water quality standards, are increasing concentrations in the river. These particles may be coming from uranium mine tailings upstream of Lake Mead. The United States Department of Energy is overseeing a cleanup of an 11-story-high, 10.5-million-ton pile of uranium mill tailings near Moab, Utah. The heap, only 600 feet from the Colorado River, is estimated to release 28,000 gallons of radioactive waste, arsenic, lead, and ammonia, per day into the river.

CALIFORNIA AQUEDUCT The California Aqueduct, part of the State Water Project, brings water to Los Angeles from the Sacramento–San Joaquin Delta. The TDS level ranges between 247 and 410 ppm, somewhat higher than the Los Angeles Aqueduct water and significantly lower than Colorado River water. This variation reflects seasonal changes and tidal flow patterns as well as the source of the water. Both state and federal water quality standards have been established for the delta. Neither have been enforced. Yet there are many threatened or endangered species in this changing ecosystem. Water quality within the delta impacts both fisheries and people. A lawsuit has been filed to require that these standards be implemented.

Because the State Water Project source water is much less hard or salty than the Colorado River, MWD blends it with water from the Colorado River before delivering it to member agencies. The delta is composed to a

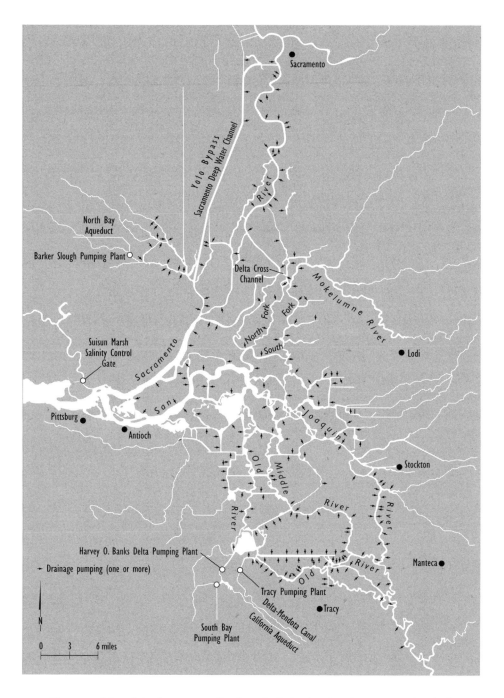

Figure 41. Map of the Sacramento–San Joaquin Delta showing the pumps and agricultural drains. (SOURCE: California Department of Water Resources.)

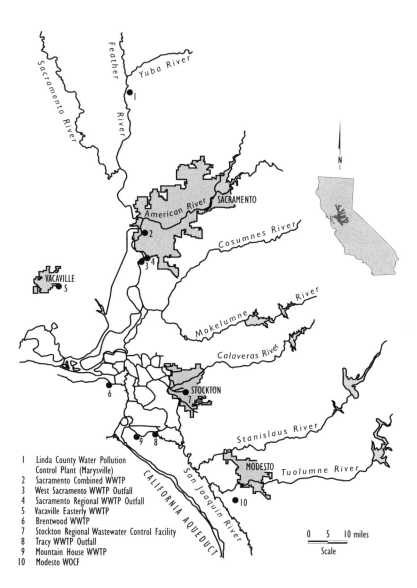

Figure 42. Map of sewage treatment plants in the Sacramento–San Joaquin Delta. (SOURCE: California Department of Water Resources.)

large extent of tulepeat, the organic remains of the tule swamp that was there before it was converted into a thousand miles of waterways and islands that are now farmed. Organic material in the water combines with chlorine. This process creates disinfection by-products known as trihalomethanes

(THMs), which have been found to be carcinogenic. Therefore, the preferred method of treatment is with a combination of chlorine and ammonia called chloramine, which is much healthier for people to drink but creates other problems for diabetic patients when they undergo kidney dialysis and for fish after used water is discharged back to surface waters.

As a result of increased development in the delta, additional sewage treatment plants are being built that discharge to the delta. The lower reaches of the San Joaquin River is composed mostly of agricultural runoff, with discharge points near the intake pumps of the aqueduct. Most agricultural chemicals now in use biodegrade before they reach the pumps. Some of these chemicals, however, degrade to by-products that are toxic.

Local Groundwater

Californians, southern Californians in particular, depend on groundwater for a significant amount of their drinking water supply. California leads the nation in use of groundwater, with an average of 14.5 billion gallons of groundwater extracted per day. The Los Angeles Area sits atop large, high-quality groundwater basins that were developed with deep wells in the twentieth century, helping to spur the growth of the region.

HISTORICAL CONTAMINATION OF GROUNDWATER IN LOS ANGELES   Unfortunately, in the Los Angeles Area we have slowly contaminated our groundwater supplies, primarily through negligence or accidents. Starting in the 1940s, industries such as defense and aerospace manufacturers developed in inexpensive farmland areas on the outskirts of our urban areas. These areas, such as the San Fernando Valley and the San Gabriel Valley, are now home to millions of people who depend on the groundwater for up to 60% of their water supply. From the 1940s through the 1960s it was a common practice to dump used solvents and other manufacturing-related chemicals out on the "back lot" or down a dry well. It was believed that chemicals would not travel far down into the ground and that if they did, groundwater moves slowly and so there would be no impact on drinking water wells. Government regulations were weak as a reflection of these beliefs. It has now been shown that these chemicals did indeed impact our groundwater.

The leading causes of problems were elevated levels of nitrogen, volatile organic compounds, minerals, and TDS. Other sources of contamination are associated with the recent introduction of new chemicals to the environment, whose solubility and density allow them to infiltrate easily and degrade groundwater supplies. Many of these contaminated areas are now Superfund sites and are in the process of being cleaned up.

Only small amounts of a contaminant are needed to pollute a large groundwater area. The standards are in the parts per million (ppm), or the equivalent of four drops of ink in a 55-gallon barrel of water, or in parts per billion (ppb), or the equivalent of one drop of ink in the largest gasoline tanker truck . The costs to clean up these chemicals is high, about $600 per acre-foot of water produced. The costs, however, are still lower than those of sewage treatment, making this water less expensive to produce than water reuse. However, reclaimed water is often sold for less. By replacing potable water, its cost should be compared to the cost of the next increment of replacement water, the cost of the next dam and reservoir.

Many wells that are contaminated have been taken out of service. There have been few violations of the Safe Drinking Water Act in the county that have necessitated corrective action.

Again, even though the City of Los Angeles had contaminated wells, it did not serve contaminated water to its customers. The city has been a leader in the development of treatment and cleanup programs.

Countywide Summary of Selected Contaminants

Following is a summary of some of the more widespread or recently highlighted contaminant problems.

TCE AND PCE   The solvents PCE and TCE are widespread in Los Angeles County groundwater and have triggered major Superfund investigations. In the upper Los Angeles River area groundwater basins, for example, 77 wells contain TCE and 35 wells exceed the 5-ppb standard. This represents, respectively, 59% and 27% of the total wells in the basins' 12 well fields. Most of these wells are now on inactive status or are being treated.

CHROMIUM 6   Water systems have only recently been required to sample for chromium 6, a heavy metal and a current chemical of concern in Los Angeles due to recent research indicating health concerns. Total chromium has been analyzed for years, and total chromium's MCL is 50 ppb; chromium

6 levels have not yet been assessed. Chromium 6 has been particularly prevalent in the San Fernando Groundwater Basin. It has been consistently detected in shallow and deep wells in the areas of North Hollywood, Glendale, Burbank, and Pollock at depths from 31 to 580 feet below the surface.

An interagency committee, the Chromium Task Force, has been meeting quarterly since 1998 to try to understand the sources and causes of the chromium 6 contamination in the San Fernando Valley Basin. In addition, USEPA gave a special grant to the regional board to fund the task of finding the sources of contamination and performing follow-up cleanup and, if necessary, enforcement actions. The regional board has identified over 210 chromium users in the area and is conducting follow-up investigations to determine specific sources. USEPA is creating an updated map of the chromium 6 contamination plume. The Office of Environmental Health Hazard Assessment expects to release a draft Public Health Goal for chromium 6 in the fall of 2005.

ARSENIC Arsenic, a heavy metal, another chemical of concern, was been detected at levels above the September 2001 MCL of 10 ppb at 26 water systems in the county. In one additional water system, the level of arsenic was detected above the former arsenic MCL of 50 ppb. USEPA lowered the arsenic standard in 2001 (effective 2006) to 10 ppb due to human health concerns. According to David Spath, chief administrator of the California Department of Health Services and chairman of the National Drinking Water Advisory Council, 500 public water systems in California will have to treat for arsenic to achieve the 10-ppb standard.

MTBE Another major source of groundwater contamination in Los Angeles County comes from leaks of MTBE leaks, a gasoline additive. Hundreds of leaking fuel storage tanks and fuel pipes have been the primary source of contamination in California. Most of these sources are currently under investigation or are being remediated; the gasoline, diesel fuel, and related contaminants are being removed from the soil to prevent further contamination of the groundwater. The Department of Health Services has required water systems to monitor for MTBE, as an "unregulated chemical," only since 1996, when it was beginning to be discovered in California groundwater supplies. It became a regulated chemical in May 2000, when the state defined a primary MCL of 13 ppb. It is also regulated under a secondary MCL (for taste and odor) of 5 ppb.

As of February 2002, 54 public drinking water wells and 31 surface water sources in California had been contaminated by MTBE, 21 of these at levels above the 13-ppb MCL. MTBE has been found in 19 water supply systems (14 groundwater and 5 surface water) in Los Angeles County. The largest number of contaminated wells statewide, 16, are in Los Angeles County, primarily in Santa Monica, Glendale, and Burbank.

PERCHLORATE Perchlorate, an organic chemical that is a constituent of rocket fuel, is also an "unregulated chemical" that has been detected more frequently in Los Angeles County than elsewhere in the state. In high doses it can interfere with the thyroid gland's ability to take up iodide. Thyroid function is associated with the growth and development of both pre- and postnatal babies and with normal metabolism and mental function in adults. It has been found in 34 systems in Los Angeles County and only in 35 other systems in California in the following eight counties: Orange, Riverside, Sacramento, San Bernardino, Imperial, Santa Clara, Sonoma, and Ventura. In those 34 water systems in Los Angeles, 104 surface water or groundwater sources have perchlorate above the action level of 4 ppb. It has also been found on lettuce and in commercial milk samples. No MCL has yet been determined by USEPA.

Water Quality in Each Groundwater Basin

The Los Angeles Area has essentially two levels of groundwater contamination. The shallow zones have small pockets of contamination from leaking underground storage tanks or other small-scale polluted sites. The deeper zones have large, slow-moving plumes of contamination that are caused by a single large contamination source or from coalesced smaller ones. The majority of the large contamination plumes are located in the San Gabriel and San Fernando valleys. In the first half of the 1900s, these valleys were used primarily for agriculture. During and after World War II, these inexpensive agricultural areas, far from urban centers, were quickly developed into large manufacturing areas. Before the creation of the USEPA and the implementation of environmental regulations in the early 1970s, little was done to regulate industries from discharging chemicals such

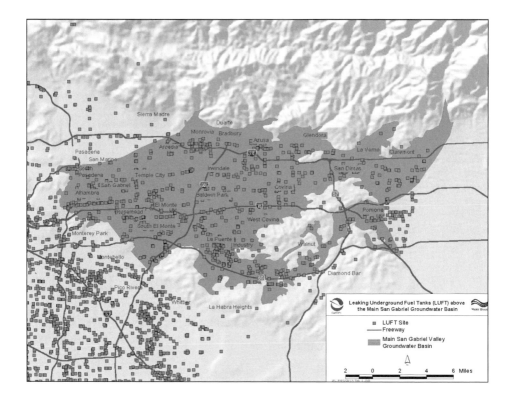

Figure 43. Leaking underground storage tank sites in the San Gabriel Valley. (SOURCE: Los Angeles Regional Water Quality Control Board.)

as PCE, TCE, other volatile organic compounds, and perchlorate, which eventually found their way into the groundwater supply.

Thousands of gasoline and diesel fuel storage tanks at service stations and industrial facilities were found to be leaking into underlying shallow soils and groundwater in the 1980s. The pollutants associated with gasoline and diesel fuel include a group of chemicals called BTEX, or benzene, toluene, ethanol, and xylene, as well as the more recently discovered additive MTBE. A large number of tanks have been investigated and have undergone cleanup in the past 10 years. In the upper Los Angeles River area alone 4,790 sites have been cleaned up, but the net effect is that the shallow aquifers in a large part of the region have been contaminated.

In addition to regional problems such as leaking underground tanks, leaking pipelines, and spills, each major basin has other contaminant problems,

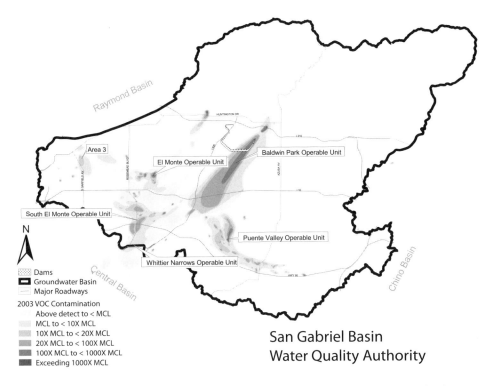

Figure 44. Plumes of contamination in the San Gabriel Basin. (SOURCE: San Gabriel Water Quality Authority.)

the most serious of which have become Superfund sites. For more information, visit http://www.epa.gov/region09/cleanup/California/html.

Main San Gabriel Valley Basin

This basin is the primary source of water for 1.4 million people. In addition, it is an important recharge area, in which stormwater and surface water are impounded and allowed to percolate into the ground to replenish drinking water both within the basin and the down-gradient Central Basin. The area has become host to major Superfund sites due to industrial contamination dating back to the 1940s. There are about 250 active wells in the basin, of which about 180 are public drinking water supply wells. Approximately an additional 60 wells are inactive or have been destroyed due to water quality problems.

Contamination in the basin was discovered in 1979; by 1984, four broad areas were placed on USEPA's National Priorities List as part of the San Gabriel Area site. Later, USEPA divided the contaminated areas into eight operable units covering nearly 30 square miles of contaminated groundwater in order to better define cleanup strategies. In 1986 and 1992, USEPA released reports that included a conceptual hydrologic model of the basin and data to provide the basis for remedial, or cleanup, investigations. The regional board, as a partner to USEPA, has focused on identifying potential contamination sources and overseeing soil and groundwater cleanups. The San Gabriel Valley Water Quality Authority was formed to push for the cleanup of the Superfund sites.

In the San Gabriel Valley nearly 200 potentially responsible industrial parties have been identified. In general, the contaminant sources are from solvents and other industrial chemicals that have leaked out of storage tanks, septic tanks and cesspools, pits and sumps, and floor drainpipes. The central area of the basin is the most porous and thus has been the location of the largest number of water wells. Unfortunately this area has also been most impacted by contaminants. A huge amount of effort has gone into cleanup of this basin. Each operable unit, categorized into four areas, is described next.

AREA 1: EL MONTE, SOUTH EL MONTE, WHITTIER NARROWS

This area is over 4 miles long and ½ mile wide and is contaminated, primarily by TCE and PCE. All but one of these areas has now signed a Record of Decision (ROD) detailing the responsible parties, the approved remedies, and the cleanup timeline.

EL MONTE OPERABLE UNIT   The groundwater contaminants in this 10-square-mile unit include PCE, TCE, 1,2-DCA, 1,1-DCE, cis-1,2-DCE, and 1,1-DCE, with highest concentrations in the shallow groundwater. In March 1995, an agreement to complete the investigation and cleanup was reached between USEPA and 15 potentially responsible parties. USEPA's plan was to install extraction wells strategically to keep the contamination from spreading farther. A cleanup plan was proposed in late 1998. An Interim Record of Decision was signed in June 1999. Because the responsible parties fought over cleanup plans, two different consent decrees were signed, for the east side and the west side of the area. Construction was scheduled to begin in 2006.

SOUTH EL MONTE OPERABLE UNIT   This eight-square-mile unit covers part of the Whittier Narrows Flood Control Basin and the entire City of El Monte. Volatile organic compounds were discovered in the intermediate zone of the western portion of the unit. The contaminants include PCE, TCE, 1,1-DCA, cis-1,2-DCE, and 1,1-DCE. The concentrations are highest in the shallow groundwater near industrial potential sources. Several wells have been shut down and others have been equipped with wellhead treatment facilities to reduce contaminant levels to drinking water standards. The contamination from this unit has migrated down to the Whittier Narrows Operable Unit. The selected treatment remedy is to contain the contamination by extracting and treating contaminated groundwater along the down-gradient edge of the contamination plume. In addition, a hot-spot cleanup effort is currently under way. An Interim Record of Decision was signed in September 2000. On July 3, 2002, the San Gabriel Basin Water Quality Authority announced that it and three water purveyors had reached a $4.7 million settlement with 13 parties responsible for the cleanup of groundwater contaminants in the South El Monte–Monterey Park area. Despite the fact that many facilities have already been built, no consent decree has yet been signed with USEPA.

WHITTIER NARROWS OPERABLE UNIT   The contamination plume in this area originates in the Main San Gabriel Basin and has recently begun to migrate down-gradient into the Central Basin. USEPA is taking the fiscal responsibility for the cleanup of this area because the responsible parties involved in the South El Monte Unit were fully taxed. USEPA saw that the concentrations in this unit were beginning to increase in 1996, and they decided to use federal funds. A local water purveyor was contracted to conduct the treatment operations. Extraction wells have been installed. Pipeline and treatment plant construction, using liquid-phase carbon tanks in series, was completed and is treating both shallow and intermediate zones. The system is designed to treat 12,000 gallons a minute and to last for 30 years.

AREA 2: BALDWIN PARK

BALDWIN PARK OPERABLE UNIT   This 7-mile-long, 1-mile-wide unit's contaminants include PCE, TCE, carbon tetrachloride, 1,4-dioxane, perchlorate, and NDMA. The maximum contamination of PCE found in the groundwater exceeds the MCL by 7,500 times. With the help of the Water Quality

Authority, the potentially responsible parties (PRPs) have agreed to spend about $250 million on four big cleanup projects. After cleanup, the water will be distributed to local water agencies for distribution.

Cleanup progress was stalled for at least a year until treatment processes could be developed and tested for additional contaminants: perchlorate in 1997 and NDMA in 1998. They are now able to reduce the levels of perchlorate from above 75 ppb to below 4 ppb. The treatment system is an elaborate "pump and treat" system, in which approximately 21,000 gallons per minute of contaminated water is treated via ion exchange, aeration and filtration, ultraviolet light and hydrogen peroxide, air stripping and off-gassing, granular activated carbon, and disinfection, in sequence. A big part of the effort has been to clean up the chlorinated solvents in the vadose zone (the shallow area between the surface of the land and the top of the groundwater) in order to reduce the migration of the contaminants to the groundwater itself.

The perchlorate pollution in the San Gabriel Basin was caused by Aerojet and 18 other aerospace companies. The construction costs are expected to be $80 million, and subsequent operation and maintenance costs will run up to $14 million per year. A milestone in the cleanup agreement was reached in March 2002, when Aerojet and seven other companies agreed to buy insurance for the $250 million cleanup effort; in April 2002 the same parties agreed to a cash settlement with USEPA. A pump-and-treat facility has been built and is operating, cleaning up the contamination.

AREA 3: ALHAMBRA

ALHAMBRA OPERABLE UNIT This unit is located in the cities of Alhambra, San Gabriel, San Marino South Pasadena, Rosemead, and Temple City. The groundwater is contaminated with low levels of TCE and PCE in concentrations of only up to three times the MCL. Six of the City of Alhambra's wells were impacted by contamination in the early 1990s. No potential responsible parties have been identified to date. A remedial investigation is in progress to evaluate cleanup alternatives. Almost 400 individual facilities have been found to have contaminated soils. Three additional monitoring wells were installed during the winter of 2004–2005.

RICHWOOD OPERABLE UNIT In 1992, USEPA installed a water treatment system to provide treated water to the water supplier. In 1993, responsibility for operating the plant was transferred to the California State Department of Toxic Substances. The remedial action for this water supply has been completed.

SUBURBAN OPERABLE UNIT This site is now cleaned up.

AREA 4: CITY OF INDUSTRY AND PUENTE VALLEY

PUENTE VALLEY OPERABLE UNIT The approximately 5-mile-long plume of contaminated groundwater is centered below San Jose Creek in La Puente and the City of Industry. Original contaminants discovered were TCE, PCE, 1,1-DCA, 1,1-DCE, 1,2-DCE, and 1,1,1-TCA. The remediation plan is to extract contaminated groundwater at shallow and intermediate depths at the mouth of Puente Valley and to treat the water to drinking water standards. La Puente Valley County Water District is also treating groundwater contaminated with perchlorate and NDMA. The Record of Decision (ROD) has been signed, as has a consent degree to clean up both the shallow and intermediate groundwater zones, and construction has begun. Treatment for the shallow zone should begin in 2006. Processes used include air stripping and adsorption to prevent the plume from migrating. The treated water is either discharged to the San Jose Creek or delivered to municipal water supply systems.

Nearly 400 individual sites have been identified with soil contamination. The state Water Resources Control Board is in charge of the cleanup.

OPERATING INDUSTRIES INC. LANDFILL SITE

Another distinct Superfund site in the Main San Gabriel Basin is the Operating Industries Inc. Landfill site, located along the Pomona Freeway in Monterrey Park. At this site extensive soil contamination is accompanied by lesser groundwater contamination along the perimeter of the landfill. The source is industrial waste liquids known as leachates, as well as hazardous wastes from the landfill. The landfill was closed in 1984. A leachate treatment facility was built to clean up the leachate and to prevent more material from leaking into the groundwater.

PUENTE BASIN

Puente Basin groundwater, located up-gradient of the Main San Gabriel Basin, has high total dissolved solids and is also contaminated by volatile organic compounds. The Rowland Water District developed groundwater from the Puente Basin and is working with a local industry to utilize the treated water from the cleanup project within the Puente Basin by adding it to their reclaimed-water system, which is used for irrigation.

Central Basin

Seawater intrusion occurred in the Central Basin prior to the 1920s, when salt water was drawn into the aquifer because fresh groundwater was over-pumped. Los Angeles County installed three large seawater-intrusion barriers from the 1950s to the 1970s. These barriers are made up of a series of groundwater wells along the edge of the groundwater basin in which freshwater is injected into the ground to form a barrier, or an underground dam, of freshwater to guard against inward movement of seawater. The Alamitos Barrier Project protects against seawater intrusion near the mouth of the San Gabriel River and includes 35 injection wells.

The Whittier Narrows Area, at the northern end of the basin, is also being monitored because of concern about the flow of contaminated groundwater from the Main San Gabriel Valley Superfund sites through the Whittier Narrows down to the Central Groundwater Basin. USEPA has recently installed several monitoring wells in the Narrows to monitor the migration of the contamination. The Water Replenishment District established a Wellhead Treatment Program in order to remove PCEs and TCEs. Air stripping or granular-activated carbon treatment is used at the wellheads to remove the contaminants and to continue to serve the water. In 1991, treatment facilities were installed at 19 well sites. More have been added since then. The program was expanded in 1996 to include treatment for additional contaminants, such as iron and manganese.

In 1973, the Water Replenishment District of Southern California and others initiated a Joint Agency Water Quality Monitoring Program for the Central Basin. Wells in the Montebello Forebay area were used to monitor the quality and quantity of water being recharged to the basin. This network of wells now totals 19 production wells and 6 monitoring wells that serve to assess water quality at varying depths, at a yearly cost of $500,000.

A Superfund site within the basin, Cooper Drum Co. in South Gate, is being cleaned up under the USEPA. The site was initially investigated because of contamination found on the adjacent Tweedy Elementary

School property. Also, this site may be tied to elevated volatile organic compounds (vinyl chloride, PCE, TCE, and benzene) in four municipal wells drawing water from the Silverado aquifer. These four wells were closed by the City of South Gate in 1987.

Another Superfund site, located in Whittier, is the Omega Chemical Corporation site. The groundwater below Omega Chemical Corporation is contaminated with PCE (at levels of 86,000 ppb in the mid-1990s), TCE, other chlorinated hydrocarbons, and Freon. This site was so contaminated that USEPA used an emergency Superfund Response to remove several thousand drums of hazardous materials and wastes in 1995. The groundwater contamination is limited to the upper aquifers at present, but these aquifers are hydrologically connected with deeper drinking water aquifers within two miles of the site. The drinking water wells most threatened by this site are those of the City of Santa Fe Springs. A consent decree was signed in February 2001 that paved the way for groundwater cleanup.

A third Superfund site in this basin is the Pemaco site, a former chemical mixing plant located in Maywood. Soil and groundwater contamination at this location includes PCE, TCE, TCA, DCA, and vinyl chloride. Soil cleanup is under way. Once cleaned up, the site is going to be made into a park by the City of Maywood as part of the Los Angeles River Greenway.

Finally, a fourth Superfund site, Waste Disposal Inc., City of Santa Fe Springs, is the location of an old buried concrete reservoir that was used to store petroleum products and wastes. In 1999, USEPA concluded that the site did not contribute contamination to groundwater but that the potential for the pollutants to migrate to groundwater exists and preventative actions are required.

West Coast Basin

The largest contamination problem in the West Coast Basin is seawater intrusion along the coast. A huge barrier project was initiated in the 1950s and now includes 153 wells between Los Angeles International Airport and the Palos Verdes Hills, installed to hold back the intrusion. A second barrier along San Pedro Bay, called the Dominguez Gap Barrier Project (41 injection wells), began operations in 1971.

Before the seawater barrier project was initiated, a large amount of seawater infiltrated into the West Coast Basin, rendering a number of wells as far inland as 2.5 miles too salty for use. This saline plume is being pulled inland because of pumping in the Carson/Dominguez area. In order to halt the movement of the plume, a Saline Plume Program has been initiated, which includes desalting plants in Torrance, in which chlorides are being removed by a reverse osmosis process, producing 2,400 acre-feet per year of potable water. In addition, four oil recovery and basin cleanup activities are under way. Oil companies are pumping up salty water from oilfield areas, treating it, and returning it to the basin.

There are many contaminated sites in the West Coast Basin area, but the largest is the combined Superfund sites of the Del Amo Facility and Montrose Co. (near the intersection of the 405 and 110 highways). The Del Amo Facility has significantly contaminated the groundwater beneath the site with benzene and toluene, polynuclear aromatic hydrocarbons (PAHs), and semivolatile organic compounds. The immediately adjacent Montrose Co. site also contaminated groundwater, with chlorobenzene, DDT, and other chemicals. The top few of six interconnected aquifers are impacted by this contamination, but these aquifers are not currently used for drinking water. Deeper drinking water aquifers have not been contaminated by these sites. A variety of soil and groundwater cleanup efforts are under way.

San Fernando Valley Study Area: Upper Los Angeles River Area
(San Fernando Basin, Sylmar Basin, Verdugo Basin, and Eagle Rock Basin)

The upper Los Angeles River area (ULARA) includes 122,800 acres of alluvial valley fill and 205,700 acres of hills and mountains, totaling 328,500 acres. ULARA is divided into four distinct basins—San Fernando, Sylmar, Verdugo, and Eagle Rock—that provide an important source of drinking water for the Cities of Los Angeles, Glendale, San Fernando, and La Crescenta. These basins are recharged by a combination of natural subsurface inflow from uphill areas, water from the eastern Sierra, and stormwater that is captured and spread at the various spreading basins to replenish groundwater. In general, because of variations in soil conditions, infiltration rates increase from west to east, and the depth to water ranges from 20 feet in the western end of the valley to 300 feet in the Glendale Narrows, an area with many drinking water wells. In addition, groundwater in the eastern valley is unconfined (there are no impermeable layers between the groundwater and the surface). This means that contamination at the surface can

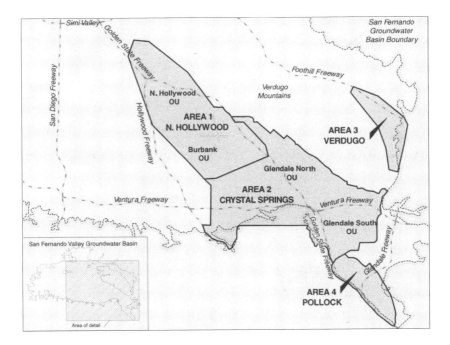

Figure 45. Map of Superfund sites in the San Fernando Valley. (SOURCE: LADWP.)

more easily and quickly make its way to the groundwater as compared to the western valley.

San Fernando Valley groundwater historically had high concentrations of nitrates due to past and present agricultural activities and due to the large number of septic tanks. Since the 1980s, contaminants such as industrial solvents TCE and PCE have been discovered. A large number of water supply wells (45% of the eastern valley wells) were impacted and many were taken out of service. Because this contamination is so widespread, much of the San Fernando Valley population now receives its drinking water from imported MWD and Owens Valley supplies instead. In 1984, four Superfund National Priorities List sites were delineated: North Hollywood, Crystal Springs, Pollock, and Verdugo. In 1987, USEPA and the Los Angeles Department of Water and Power signed a cooperative agreement providing federal funds to investigate and clean up groundwater contamination in the whole area. A separate agreement between USEPA and the regional board covers an investigation into potentially responsible parties. USEPA is conducting a Basinwide Monitoring Program that includes quarterly sampling of over 500 groundwater wells in the eastern valley area in addition to 87 specifically installed groundwater-monitoring wells. Distinct from this basinwide effort, the following four operable units are being handled separately for clean up.

AREA 1: NORTH HOLLYWOOD AND BURBANK OPERABLE UNIT

These two units have been joined together as Area 1 and are in the Interim Remedy Phase, all have records of decision. The contaminated groundwater in this area covers four square miles and previously provided water for over 800,000 residents, accounting for 10% of the Los Angeles Department of Water and Power's total water supply. This area is in the part of the San Fernando Groundwater Basin that has what are considered the best aquifer characteristics (i.e., most permeable, good water flow). In 1980, elevated concentrations of TCE (up to 1500 ppb) and PCE were discovered. Aerospace and defense manufacturers as well as dry cleaners, metal platers, and others used these solvents as far back as the 1940s in this area. Groundwater monitoring from 1981 to 1987 showed that over 50% of the water supply wells in the eastern San Fernando Valley were contaminated, including more than 60 wells within Area 1. These wells were shut down, and more expensive imported water was substituted or blended in. In 1991, USEPA signed an agreement with Lockheed Corporation, Weber Aircraft, and the City of Burbank to conduct cleanup activities. This agreement extends to 2018. Lockheed is currently operating a treatment system that removes the volatile organic compounds by using air stripping and a liquid-phase granular carbon filter. The treated water is then chlorinated and distributed to the City of Burbank public water supply. Some of the water has to be blended with imported MWD water because the treatment system does not reduce the high levels of nitrate contamination in the groundwater.

In North Hollywood, phase one of the treatment system began operations in 1989, and in Burbank a facility began phase-one operations in 1996. Both treat more than 15 million gallons of contaminated water per day. An update of the basin groundwater model was begun in 2002 to determine how the cleanup is working. It will be used as part of the feasibility study yet to be performed.

These units are in the Remedial Design Phase and combined cover an area of 6,680 acres near the Crystal Springs well field in Los Angeles and Glendale. In 1980, TCE and PCE were found in levels above the MCL standards and a large number of wells were shut down. USEPA released investigation, cleanup, and design reports for the area from 1992 through 1996 that called for the construction of a treatment facility. The facility treats 7 million gallons a day from four north unit wells and four south unit wells with air stripping and liquid-phase granulated activated carbon and blends the treated water with MWD water to reduce nitrates. It was completed in 2000 and will operate for at least 12 years. A consent decree was signed in August 2000 between the responsible parties and the City of Glendale, which is in charge of operation and maintenance of the facility.

This unit, not now considered an operable unit, covers about 4,400 acres in the Verdugo Basin. Wells in the basin were sampled in 1993, and some were contaminated with PCE at concentrations up to 52 ppb, especially the wells in the Glenwood Well Field. USEPA entered into a cooperative agreement with the City of Los Angeles Department of Water and Power, and a remedial investigation report was released in 1992. USEPA has monitored the groundwater wells on a regular basis since then. By 1997, the PCE concentrations had decreased to levels below MCLs except for one well in the Glenwood Well Field. Nitrate concentrations, however, are still detected at levels above MCLs (up to 101 ppm). Potential sources of nitrates in this historically agriculture-dominated area are excess fertilizer applications, confined animal wastes, and malfunctioning septic tanks. The City of Glendale blends the water to reduce nitrate concentrations in served water, and the Crescenta Valley Water District operates the Glenwood Nitrate Water Treatment Plant. A no-action-remedy ROD was signed in February 2004, and Verdugo was eliminated from the National Priority List in October 2004.

Area 4, not now considered an operable unit, covers 5,860 acres near the Pollock Well Field in the City of Los Angeles. TCE and PCE were found first, and USEPA completed an interim investigation in 1994. Because the Los Angeles Department of Water and Power planned to conduct a well-head treatment project, USEPA decided that the area did not need to be designated as an operable unit. The Pollock Treatment Facility is currently operating and producing water that is being served to DWP customers. Additional work is being done on contamination problems in the Taylor Yard site, which is part of the area.

OTHER AREAS OF THE SAN FERNANDO VALLEY

Other contaminant plumes are being investigated or cleaned up at other sites within the San Fernando Valley. These sites are described next.

POLLOCK WELLS The DWP 3,000 gallon-per-minute Pollock Wells Treatment Plant was completed in 1999. This liquid-phase granular activated-carbon treatment facility in the Glendale Narrows area allowed two Pollock production wells to come back into service. One goal of the project is to capture the contaminant plume and prevent migration of the contaminants into the Los Angeles River. The treated water is blended with MWD imported water to reduce high nitrate concentrations.

HOLCHEM, INC–PACOIMA AREA GROUNDWATER INVESTIGATION A groundwater plume of TCE, PCE, and 1,1,1-TCA contamination extends from near the intersection of the Simi Valley Freeway and San Fernando Road toward the Tujunga Well Fields. The Department of Toxic Substances Control is directing this investigation. Two monitoring wells were installed downgradient of the site by LADWP to monitor groundwater quality.

BOEING (ROCKWELL-ROCKETDYNE) Boeing pumps and treats contaminated groundwater from beneath their Santa Susana Field Lab, Rocketdyne Lab, near Simi Valley. This site was where rocket engines were designed and tested from the 1950s to the 1980s. Nuclear research was also conducted there from 1956 to 1989 under contract to the U.S. Department of Energy (DOE) and the Atomic Energy Commission. They currently have eight treatment facilities but are considering ways to make their treatment system more efficient. The groundwater in this area is contaminated with chemicals that were used as solvents to flush out rocket engines after testing:

1,1-DCE, TCE, PCE, TCA, and 1,1-DCA. Because the TDS of the treated groundwater is too high to discharge into the Los Angeles River, the water is used for irrigation on site. The DOE operates part of the site, and DOE is responsible for much of the cleanup.

TAYLOR YARD (NARROWS AREA) The state Department of Toxic Substances Control oversees the cleanup of a six-inch-thick plume of product perched at a depth of 30 feet over five acres. Installation of monitoring wells began in 1997, and vapor extraction will be used to remediate the site, which is now a state park and slated for development to include athletic fields and a restored wetland.

The Los Angeles Department of Water and Power is planning to build an air stripping treatment facility at their Headworks Spreading Grounds, located adjacent to the Los Angeles River. Groundwater, including water impacted by Superfund site contamination, will be pumped up, treated, and then used in part to create a wetland. This site is also being considered as the location to build large underground storage tanks to replace a nearby open reservoir.

Raymond Basin

Pockets of high fluoride levels (possibly naturally occurring) have been found in the foothill areas of the Raymond Basin, and high nitrate concentrations are found in the Monk Hill and Pasadena subareas. Volatile organic compounds occur in the Arroyo Seco area, and a wellhead treatment facility has been installed for removal of volatile organic compounds.

A contaminant plume, including trichloroethylene and carbon tetrachloride, was discovered in 1990 in Pasadena. The contaminants leaked from the Jet Propulsion Lab (NASA) through 35 seepage pits and other toxic material disposal sites. Four municipal wells and two Lincoln Avenue Water Company wells were closed down from 1987 to 1989 by the pollution. Treatment facilities were installed on these wells, and they are all operational at this time. USEPA, the regional board, and the California Department of Toxic Substance Control jointly oversee the cleanup of the groundwater contamination plume. The groundwater is also contaminated with recently discovered perchlorate. The site is being used as a research opportunity by Cal Tech, including a long-term soil vapor extraction pilot test. Soil vapor extraction is a treatment method in which volatile contaminants are allowed to out-gas, or blow off, into the atmosphere, through the drilling and installation of small wells and piping systems.

Santa Monica, Hollywood, and La Brea Basins

Santa Monica Basin groundwater has historically had problems with hardness and high iron concentrations. There are localized volatile organic compound problems, such as TCE and PCE. The Hollywood Basin also has hard water, with iron, manganese, odor, and color problems.

MTBE has been detected in hundreds of well sites in Los Angeles County. The City of Santa Monica, one of the cities most effected early on, discovered MTBE at its Charnock well field in 1995 and its Arcadia well field in 1996. These two well fields provided over 45% of the city's water supply. The Charnock well field had five operating municipal supply wells that were impacted by up to 600 parts per billion MTBE. A court-ordered settlement was agreed to in 2003 that requires the major oil companies to design and construct the facilities needed to clean up all the MBTE as well as the tri-butyl alcohol, or TBA, which is a daughter product of MTBE. The oil companies are also required to reimburse Santa Monica for the costs of replacement water purchased from the Metropolitan Water District until the groundwater is once again potable. A leaking underground storage tank at a Mobil Station was the source of contamination for the Arcadia well field, and Mobil has taken responsibility for cleanup costs. Treatment technologies were installed, and treated water is being served.

COORDINATED EFFORTS TO CLEAN UP DRINKING WATER IN THE LOS ANGELES AREA

One of the biggest complaints about the cleanup of drinking water in Los Angeles has been the slow pace and the lack of coordination among responsible organizations. This is an ongoing theme everywhere.

Watershed Approach

In the early 1990s, the regional water board, with support from USEPA, initiated a watershed approach to the management of water quality concerns in the Los Angeles Region. Surface water was the primary focus, but groundwater issues also were folded into some of the watershed planning.

Since then, a number of watershed groups have developed, including the Los Angeles & San Gabriel Rivers Watershed Council, the Rivers and Mountains Conservancy, the Arroyo Seco Foundation, and several groups in Ventura and Orange counties. These groups have provided a forum in which drinking water issues, especially the slow pace of cleanup, can be addressed and responsible agencies can respond.

San Gabriel Basin Water Quality Authority

The San Gabriel Basin Water Quality Authority was created by the California legislature in 1993 to help coordinate the cleanup of the Superfund sites in the San Gabriel Basin. They are authorized to obtain funds and to implement groundwater treatment programs. The seven-member board is composed of one member from each of the overlying municipal water districts, two cities, and an investor-owned utility water producer. This group has been instrumental in getting funding and settlements for the groundwater cleanups (www.wqa.com/).

MWD Groundwater Cleanup Programs

Over the past 20 years, the Metropolitan Water District has distributed a large number of grants directed at cutting-edge cleanup of groundwater in the Los Angeles Area. Some of these projects include removing nitrates (via ion exchange) from groundwater in the Crescenta Valley County Water District, removing TDS and VOCs from the Puente Groundwater Basins (via VOC removal), and reverse osmosis to treat TDS and chlorides in the West Coast Basin.

Total Maximum Daily Loads (TMDLs)

Due to pressures from environmental groups, USEPA and the regional board have begun to conduct total maximum daily load (TMDL) studies in the Los Angeles Area. A TMDL is a calculation of the maximum amount of a pollutant that a water body can receive and still meet water quality standards and an allocation of anything above that amount to the pollutant's sources (such as industrial dischargers and municipal treatment works). Each TMDL focuses on a specific contaminant within a specific watershed, such as nutrients within the Los Angeles River Watershed. This new focus on TMDLs has created an unprecedented opportunity for watershed coordination that can address both surface water and groundwater contamination together with a host of other issues. Although TMDLs are structured to deal with surface water beneficial uses, such as drinking water supply, aquatic life, and recreation, groundwater concerns play an important role. For example, in the Sepulveda Basin, treated sewage water from the City of Los Angeles' Tillman Facility may be diverted into a specially constructed wetland. This wetland will serve to clean up nutrients and other contaminants before the water flows into the Los Angeles River, but at the same time clean water will percolate into the ground, helping to recharge the groundwater basin. The wetland would also provide a piece of nature in a heavily populated part of town and a learning experience for children and others about the natural world.

CONCLUSION

Water served to the population of Los Angeles meets stringent water quality standards. California has traditionally led the country in cutting-edge legislation and technology for environmental issues, including clean water and safe drinking water. The major water systems have regularly implemented new requirements, such as covering reservoirs and putting in a new treatment technology in advance of regulatory deadlines. And the regulatory agencies are strict, enforcing stringent standards and monitoring schedules. Therefore people can be assured that their drinking water is safe.

Los Angeles, however, is an area that faces serious problems of contamination of the local groundwater supplies. A large amount of money is being spent to clean up contaminated groundwater sites. This money must be spent because of the need for an ever-greater reliance on local sources of water in place of imported sources. Unfortunately, starting in the 1940s, due to a lack of knowledge about how easily groundwater can be contaminated, industrial facilities disposed of hazardous wastes by dumping them in pits or down dry wells on their properties. These solvents and other organic chemicals migrated down to valuable water-bearing aquifers, creating contaminated groundwater plumes that are difficult to clean up. Many of these are now designated as Superfund sites. Los Angeles County has 16 of the active 113 California Superfund sites, second only to Santa Clara County (Silicon Valley), with 23 sites.

The Department of Health Services (DHS) has published a report that shows that Los Angeles has significantly more contamination problems in the areas of inorganic constituents and organic chemicals as compared to other counties. The inorganic minerals are probably due mostly to local geology, such as chloride-rich formations, but the organic chemicals are the result of local industrial activities. Hopefully the majority of groundwater contamination in the Los Angeles Area has been detected.

Statewide, DHS has shown that the number of cases of new contamination in drinking water supplies has declined, with the peaks having occurred in the 1980s and early 1990s. Measures are in place to try and prevent the further contamination of our precious groundwater resources. Unfortunately, with increasingly stringent water quality standards and improved technology to measure water quality, it is likely we will discover other contaminants.

Getting contamination out of groundwater, in contrast to surface water, is extremely difficult. The process of cleaning up groundwater in the Los Angeles Area has been painfully slow, and this delay has likely increased the ultimate cleanup costs. It took 22 years, for example, for the companies responsible for the San Gabriel Valley Baldwin Park (Area 2) Superfund site to agree to pay for the cleanup facilities. In the meantime, only one treatment facility (out of a needed six) was constructed, and the contaminated groundwater plume moved at a rate of up to four feet a day toward the Whittier Narrows, threatening pollution in another groundwater basin, the Central Basin.

Although coordination efforts have been initiated, more coordinated cleanup efforts are needed in order to manage the groundwater contamination situation in the Los Angeles Area. Each groundwater authority or entity tends to look only at the groundwater contamination in its own jurisdiction, with little coordination occurring among areas within groundwater basins or at the interface between basins. The lack of coordination is a statewide problem, not one experienced solely in Los Angeles.

Chapter 5 | STATE POLICY AND THE LOS ANGELES AREA

Water is far too important to human health and the health of our natural world to be placed entirely in the private sector.

PETER GLEICK, *Pacific Institute*

Water flows uphill, to money.

Anonymous

The wars of the next century will be about water.

The World Bank

In this final chapter, an attempt is made to integrate our regional issues into a broader statewide context. We face many uncertainties that must be examined, such as population growth, water use projections, and climate change. The projections made by various agencies to determine future water need are highly variable, depending on their assumptions and who is doing the forecasting.

Then, after a quick review of the shortfalls from each of our water sources, an examination of how the state is doing with all of the efficiencies described in Chapter 3 teaches us that the rest of the state has a lot of catching up to do.

Since agriculture uses about 80% of all the developed water in the state, a closer look at how agriculture is managing and how globalization impacts the business of farming is instructive. Almost half of the state's agricultural water is used to grow low-value and subsidized crops. Is this sustainable? Or will changes in subsidies brought about by the World Trade Organization and worldwide competition dramatically change cropping patterns and agriculture's use of water?

Before looking at water marketing, or the privatization of water, a quick overview of water rights and the public trust is required, as is an understanding of how water is priced.

Water marketing—transforming water into a commodity that can be bought and sold like soybeans or pork bellies—is being touted by many, especially by those who can profit from marketing, as the best way to reallocate a limited resource. They have been working to change the rules to promote or make easier the ability to transfer water. What are the costs and benefits? Who wins and who loses? How do you charge for the private use of publicly funded aqueduct systems? Many issues must be addressed if we are to privatize or deregulate our water resources.

And finally, a description and an analysis of the effectiveness of the planning processes now in place are examined and put into the context of our water future. Consensus has been building around two ideas or policies, especially among the larger agencies and more thoughtful policy makers in Sacramento: (1) We must learn to use our local resources much more effectively, and (2) we must begin to plan regionally and cooperatively. In order to accomplish both of these goals, a comprehensive statewide water policy seems in order, minimally a policy that establishes standards for data collection, respects the public trust and sound science, and involves all of the people of the state in determining our water future.

For far too long, water policy has been written behind closed doors to benefit those few in the room, no longer smoke filled. If we are to resolve these problems in an orderly way and in the public interest, policy options must be debated and discussed by all of the stakeholders in an open and constructive way. The Conclusion at the end of this chapter contains a first attempt at spelling out some of the elements of what a sustainable statewide water policy could look like so that the debate can begin.

STATEWIDE UNCERTAINTIES

Statewide, water shortages are being predicted by almost all water agencies. Their predictions differ only as their time frames' differ and according to how wet or dry the year is. Eleven major groundwater basins around the state are overdrafted, especially in the San Joaquin Valley. There are no new sources of imported water to replenish these aquifers as the aquifers in the Los Angeles Area are being replenished with imported water and, more recently, reclaimed water.

All four of the major aqueduct systems that move water around the state are unable to deliver as expected or planned. Each one's shortfall impacts everyone else because the state is almost totally plumbed, so shortages anywhere affect almost the entire state. Reductions in supply from the eastern Sierra to the City of Los Angeles mean that the city calls on the Metropolitan Water District of Southern California (MWD) and its supplies from the Colorado River and northern California to make up the difference, reducing the amount MWD can make available to others. When environmental or water quality concerns limit the amount of water the State Water Project or the Central Valley Project can deliver, everyone is affected.

These uncertainties are exacerbated by the vagaries of projecting such things as population growth (some are predicting that California will grow at a rate that creates a city the size of San Francisco every 15 months) and water consumption into the future, including agricultural consumption, aqueduct deliveries, and the impacts of climate change.

Population Growth Projections

Two factors go into projecting our future water needs: the number of people who will need to be served, and the amount of water per capita per day each person will demand. These two factors are multiplied together to determine our water future. How these numbers are arrived at depends on who makes the projections and the assumptions on which they are based. Projecting population growth and/or water demand per capita is not a science but an art, one that is quite subjective, causing projections and forecasts to diverge wildly.

In October 1999, the Public Policy Institute of California analyzed three government agencies' and two independent organizations' population projections and found that they diverged over time substantially. By 2025, the difference was 10 million people. By 2040, the difference between projections increased to over 16 million people, almost half the state's current size.

The Public Policy Institute, in another report, dated September 2001, raised additional issues about how accurate these agency forecasts are, despite the fact that they are treated as gospel. They are rough estimates at best, replete with errors no matter how good the forecaster. "Twenty-year projections of population growth made in the 1950s understated sub-

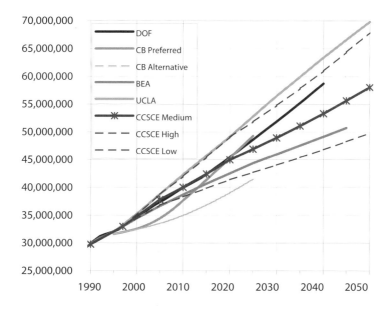

Figure 46. Population projections. (SOURCE: Public Policy Institute of California, "California Counts, How Many Californians," October 1999.)

sequent growth by 2.4 million people. Similar projections since 1970 overstated growth by 6 million people over a 20-year period. . . . [C]urrent plans tend to merely scale up estimates of demand along with growth. This approach assumes that behavior won't change significantly over decades, despite much historical evidence to the contrary." The report further states, "In light of these forecasting limitations, flexibility must be embedded into infrastructure plans at their inception" (www.PPIC.org).

The rates of births over deaths are among the most reliably forecast in the short term, but these rates are subject to change as immigrant cultural patterns change as immigrant women become better educated and choose to have smaller families. Migration patterns are much more difficult to forecast. The economic climate can change dramatically in unexpected ways, impacting migration patterns and rates and places of growth. Changes in these factors are difficult if not impossible to predict. In other words, despite all the best brains working to forecast population, many variables are difficult if not impossible to assess.

MWD has concluded that population projections are accurate for only about 10 years out. The farther out in time, the more variable researchers' and government agencies' projections are. Do we plan for ever-increasing immigration and an exponentially growing population on into the future? Or should we think about a future more like that of Japan or Europe, where populations are shrinking over time. Finally, there are those who are concerned about how many people can be sustainably maintained on spaceship earth. A petition candidate for the Sierra Club Governing Board, Ben Zuckerman, was elected in 2002 with the most votes of any in the election because of his strong stand against an ever-growing population, both in California and world wide. Yet two years later, a slate running on this same population platform was roundly defeated because of concern that the stand would be interpreted as immigrant bashing and therefore politically incorrect.

Interest is increasing in slowing or even preventing growth in many parts of the state. Ballot measures in every election, somewhere in the state, are designed to control or manage growth. Recognition is also increasing that resources are finite and that growth should somehow be tied to resource availability. State Senators Sheila Kuehl (SB610) and Jim Costa (SB221) both authored bills signed into law in January 2002 that require having an available water supply before development projects can be approved. The Kuehl bill requires that developers of 500 units or more be able to identify a reliable supply of water for the next 20 years, even in multiple dry years. The Costa bill requires that water supplies be included in urban water management plans and environmental impact reports.

Water agencies have long avoided responsibility for determining where growth can or cannot occur. They insist it is the job of land use planning agencies, city councils, and boards of supervisors to make these determinations, and they fought hard against these two laws.

One example of a water agency truly assessing its supply and therefore determining how many people it can serve is the East Bay Municipal Water District, which serves Oakland and Alameda County. This agency analyzed all of its water supplies and determined that it had enough water for the people within its service area, with a little left to accommodate some infill. It also looked at the almost 100 new towns planned for the state and wondered where all the water would come from to serve these new towns. It successfully fought off legislation that would have forced it to annex additional land slated for development and lobbied hard to pass the Kuehl and Costa bills just described.

Demand is usually based on the number of people projected times daily usage, and daily usage is usually based on the assumption that each person will continue to use the same amount of water, making no allowance for changing times. Therefore, demand numbers can quickly get very skewed. Different countries around the world use vastly different amounts of water per capita, showing just how variable water use per person can really be. The internationally accepted daily water requirement is 13.2 gallons per day (gpd) according to the U.N. Population Fund. In the United States, Los Angeles now uses 140 gpd, Oakland 160 gpd, Seattle 103 gpd, Salt Lake City 284 gpd, and Las Vegas 307 gpd. In the 1950s, experts forecast U.S. water consumption by the year 2000 at a level three times the actual rate.

Climate Change: Global Warming

There is no longer any doubt that the planet is warming, that levels of carbon dioxide in the atmosphere are increasing, and that the consequences can be as variable as our climate. As the data accumulate regarding global warming, scientists are attempting to predict the impacts of climate change on various parts of the world. The consensus now is that higher temperatures forecast for later in the century will reduce water flow in the Colorado River, which fluctuates by as much as 50% from year to year. As temperatures go up, particularly over the winter, more rain and less snow will fall. The mountain snowpacks will melt earlier in the season and more quickly, leading to greater flooding and potentially less stored water to meet summer demands.

A comprehensive multiagency assessment of climate change impacts on California's water resources was released in late 2000 through the U.S. Geological Survey. The report states that climate change is already being seen everywhere. California is experiencing earlier snowmelts, higher temperatures, earlier migrations of birds and butterflies, and plants blooming at different times. Peter Gleick, the lead author, predicts saltwater intrusion into the Sacramento–San Joaquin Delta over the next 50 years, changes in the timing of snowmelt and river runoff, the disappearance of San Francisco Bay shorelines under water, and more extreme floods and droughts. These changes will pose serious challenges for our water systems.

A UC Santa Cruz study modeling the impacts on California predicts the doubling in the atmosphere of carbon dioxide from before the Industrial

Revolution to as soon as 2050. The greatest increases in temperature will occur at the higher elevations in the Sierra Nevada and the Cascade Range—an increase in the average June temperature in the Sierra Nevada of 11°F. Rainfall will increase in northern California but will stay largely the same in southern California, while snow accumulation in the mountains will decrease dramatically. The height of the snowpack at the end of March will drop by 13 feet, and by the end of April it will be almost completely gone. Water demand will increase with warmer weather.

A Climate Action Team composed of professors from UC Berkeley and Scripps submitted a reported to the governor and the legislature dated March 2006 that predicted the snowmelt in the Sierras would occur 5–30 days earlier in the spring and that this would have a cascading affect on water supply, natural resources, and winter recreation. However, the models predict "no clear trend in precipitation projected for California over the next century." The loss of snowpack, our winter water storage system, will cause us to depend on reservoirs that are managed to capture early snowmelt without losing flood control capacity. This report also predicts sea level rise of 7.6 inches during the next 100 years, with extreme weather events especially exacerbating the problems in the delta (http://www.ucsusa .org/clean_california/ca-global-warming-impacts.html).

Others have predicted a sea level rise of 20 feet or more if and when the ice on Greenland and in the Artic and Antarctica melt.

The Pacific Institute study entitled *Climate Change and California's Water Resources: A Survey and Summary of the Literature,* dated July 2003, analyzed over 150 peer-reviewed studies. It concludes with the following recommendations: Follow a "no-regrets strategy," that is, one that has net societal benefits whether or not there really is climate change. Specific locations often do not have enough data, but none of the data from all of these many studies contradicts another. Communication and collaboration between and among agencies is a must. And research must continue to gather information on hydrology, water quality, demand management, and how to deal with the loss of supply (www.pacinst.org).

PROJECTED SHORTAGES AT EACH AQUEDUCT SYSTEM

Statewide, shortages of water are already being felt in dry years because none of the systems that have been put into place are able to deliver as planned.

The population continues to grow, the amount of land under irrigation has swelled, new towns are being planned all over the state, and the environmental movement is demanding that more habitats be restored (that more water be left in rivers and streams for the fish), that water quality be protected, and that groundwater be protected against seawater intrusion and subsidence.

Many groundwater basins around the state are overdrafted (mined), especially in the San Joaquin Valley, where the land has subsided as much as 75 feet. The land has sunk down, collapsed, to fill in the void created by overpumping. The storage capacity underground that once existed is now gone. There are no new sources of imported water to replenish these aquifers. When the State Water Project was on the ballot, we were told that state water would be used to replenish the overdrafted groundwater basins in the Central Valley, but it has been used to put more farmland under irrigation instead. The federal Central Valley Project was also supposed to replenish overdrafted groundwater basins. Yet additional demands continue to be made on both of these over subscribed systems.

Each of the four major delivery systems in the state has been treated in more depth earlier in the book. Here we provide a quick review of what was originally projected and what each can deliver.

LOS ANGELES AQUEDUCTS   The Los Angeles Aqueducts bring water from the Owens Valley and the Mono Lake Basin to the San Fernando Valley for use by the City of Los Angeles. Between a third and 40% of the water that historically was sent down the aqueducts is now being held to restore Mono Lake, to restore the Owens River and some of its adjacent wetlands, and to deal with the air quality problems at Owens Dry Lake and the overpumping of Owens Valley groundwater as ordered by the courts. The Los Angeles Department of Water and Power (LADWP) anticipates being able to take, on average, 321,000 acre-feet a year down its aqueducts instead of the almost 500,000 acre-feet a year it has taken historically. LADWP is counting on MWD to make up for any shortfall of water supply.

COLORADO RIVER   Most years, the Colorado River ends in a puddle in Mexico, rarely reaching the sea. The entire river is all used up. Before Arizona and Nevada built-out, as they both have in the last decade or two, the Secretary of the Interior designated their unused entitlement "surplus water" on the river. MWD used this surplus together with its own entitlement to keep its Colorado River aqueduct full. Now the days of surplus are over. The Secretary of the Interior has decreed that California must learn to live within its basic entitlement of 4.4 million acre-feet by the year 2015. This decree will leave MWD with an aqueduct capable of delivering 1.25 million acre-feet a year but with an entitlement of only 0.55 million acre-feet a year. It is working hard to find ways to keep the aqueduct full, persuading some farmers to fallow land in dry years or to store wet-year surpluses in groundwater basins near the aqueduct. Efforts to restore the Colorado River Estuary and the entire watershed will create additional demands on what is already a totally oversubscribed resource.

CALIFORNIA STATE WATER PROJECT The California State Water Project is only half built. It can deliver less than half of the water contracted for in an average water year. After passage of the bond act that authorized its construction, the state signed contracts to deliver 4.2 million acre-feet a year. The average delivered during the 10 years from 1991 to 2001 was only 1.86 million acre-feet. The contracts are not entitlements but service contracts that require the state to make its best efforts to deliver the contracted amount. The project will never be completed because no more dams will be built on the north coast wild and scenic rivers, and there is no agreement about how or if water should be directed around or through the Sacramento–San Joaquin Delta from the Sacramento River to the pumps. The threat of sea level rise due to global warming and the threat of major storms, or earthquakes that could cause liquefaction in the delta, are creating even more conflict between those who want to build more dams and conveyances and those who see demand management and restoration as a more benign and cheaper solution.

Environmental concerns were never part of the original planning process but are now a major factor in limiting deliveries. Water must be left in the rivers and be permitted to flush through the Sacramento–San Joaquin Delta for two reasons: to protect and sustain many endangered species that live some part of their lives in northern California rivers and in the largest and most important estuary on the west coasts of both American continents; and to protect drinking water quality from saltwater intrusion for all those who take their water supply from the delta.

CENTRAL VALLEY PROJECT The Central Valley Project (CVP) is a federally funded project authorized in the 1930s. The U.S. Bureau of Reclamation built dams on most of the rivers in the Sierra Nevada Mountains as well as Shasta Dam on the Sacramento River. It delivers water to agricultural irrigation districts to irrigate farms and to serve cities in the Great Central Valley. The project is operated in conjunction with the State Water Project and contributes to the massive decline of biological productivity that has occurred in the delta and in local rivers and streams. The CVP contractors have paid only about 10% of the capital costs of the project and no interest over the past 60 years. They have been paying $30 an acre-foot or less, while the market rate for agricultural water was $120 to $150 an acre-foot.

The San Joaquin River is now bone dry for as much as 70 miles of its length, and the delta ecosystem is in crisis, about to collapse. To help deal with these environmental problems, Congress passed the Central Valley Project Improvement Act in 1992. The act requires, among other things, that 800,000 acre-feet a year of water be reserved for the environment. As contracts with the farmers come up for renewal, implementation of conservation measures is required. Farmers are now supposed to pay the costs of operating and maintaining the project, not just capital costs, and the new contracts will be for a shorter period of time, 25 years instead of 40. However, contracts are being signed that will increase the amount of water delivered by 1.5 million acre-feet a year, further devastating the delta environment. The project will never be paid for. This act also permits farmers to sell their CVP-subsidized water on the open market, with some restrictions.

LAWSUITS TO CHANGE MANAGEMENT STRATEGIES Such lawsuits include one that was brought challenging the legality of Friant Dam, located on the San Joaquin River above Fresno. An old state law requires that when dams are built, enough water must be left in the river or stream to maintain the fishery below the dam. The suit was decided in favor of the river. A settlement is now being negotiated to rewater the San Joaquin River.

A judge, in a lawsuit challenging the environmental documentation of CALFED, has thrown out its EIR/EIS, citing three reasons: reducing pumping from the delta was not considered as an alternative required under the law; the water supply to fill proposed new dams and reservoirs was not

TABLE 13. Summary of Water Delivery
Shortfalls Statewide (in acre-feet)

Project	Designed to Deliver	Capable of Delivering	Shortfall
Central Valley Project	7,700,000	N/A	800,000
Los Angeles Aqueduct	500,000	320,000	180,000
Colorado River Aqueduct	1,250,000	550,000	800,000
State Water Project	4,200,000	1,860,000	2,340,000
Total			4,120,000

identified; and there needs to be an evaluation of the environmental water account established to provide water for fish and to sustain the ecosystems. This ruling, in the fall of 2005, requires that a new EIR/EIS be written, and that none of the projects planned by CALFED can be built until such time as a new EIR/EIS is certified. This decision will have huge repercussions on the entire management of both the State Water Project and the Central Valley Project. However, DWR and the federal government seem to be moving forward as if this ruling had never been issued.

SUMMARY In summary, the four systems together can deliver about 4 million acre-feet less each year statewide than was originally planned. How this shortfall is to be met is under continual debate in Sacramento and in Washington. The water industry wants more dams, bigger pumps, and a water market, while environmentalists want more efficient use of water by both the urban and agricultural sectors and the restoration of riparian habitat, fish and wildlife, and the delta. Lawsuits that challenged the water industry's way of doing business are being decided in favor of the environment. These two lawsuits will have enormous impact on how the state thinks about water policy in the future.

STATEWIDE EFFICIENCIES

As discussed in Chapter 3, there is a great deal of room for increasing the efficiency of how we use water within the Los Angeles Area. There are even more opportunities statewide.

Statewide, additional opportunities for water use efficiency are clear, beginning with the implementation of the CUWCC list of best management practices. As part of the CALFED process, ways to certify those implementing the best management practices are being debated. Both the State Water Resources Control Board and the Department of Health Services can give grants or loan money from revolving funds. These monies are being made available only to those who are implementing the BMPs. This policy can create pressure on water agencies to comply and even to compete with each other, depending on how it evolves. As one measure of how much still can be done, the Pacific Institute has stated that out of the 17 million toilets in the state, only about 7 million are now low flush.

Many within the state take their right to use water as they wish for granted. Several cities, such as Stockton, Sacramento, and Fresno, do not even have water meters. They charge a flat rate no matter how much water is used. The state legislature has finally passed a law requiring these and other cities that lack meters to install them by 2025 and to charge by volume used. This license to waste will end, eventually.

An Associated Press story (May 14, 2001) documented the 100 lush golf courses in the Palm Springs area, together with gardens fit for the tropics in the desert, and an average per capita water use of 375 gallons a day (twice the national norm) at a cost per household of half as much as cable TV. Other new developments around the state are featuring lakes, some big enough to water ski on, giant fountains, more golf courses, and other water features that are attractive but not sustainable in our semiarid climate.

RECLAMATION AND REUSE   The use of reclaimed water is strongly encouraged by the Bureau of Reclamation and the State of California and is gaining momentum in urban areas. Los Angeles County Sanitation Districts has long been a leader in wastewater reuse, and the City of Los Angeles has completed construction of the East Valley Water Recycling Project, though it has yet to be turned on. West Basin has incurred debt and assessed standby charges to build a tertiary advanced treatment plant near Hyperion and is marketing this water, and many agencies are exploring reverse osmosis technology that may someday bring the cost of treating wastewater and perhaps even seawater down to where it is competitive with the MWD wholesale cost of potable water. The U.S. Bureau of Reclamation, together

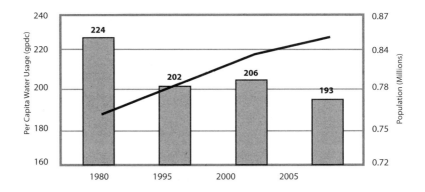

Figure 47. Per capita water usage in the West Coast Basin MWD. (SOURCE:
West Basin MWD water use database and WMD demographic data, 2005.)

with local water agencies, studied just how much of this treated wastewater
can be reused by customers in southern California and in the San Francisco Bay Area. It also identified substantial institutional barriers to reuse.

As the water supply crunch becomes more serious, many creative ways
of managing local resources so as to become less dependent on imported
supplies are surfacing. The Orange County Water District has long injected
highly treated wastewater into the ground as a seawater-intrusion barrier
at a facility called Water Factory 21. Los Angeles Area water agencies are following suit with the three seawater barriers now in place. Orange County
citizens have approved a $600 million reuse project in which highly treated
wastewater will be pumped 13 miles from Fountain Valley to percolation beds
in Anaheim. And San Diego is once again trying to develop community support for what they are calling "repurified water," which will be added to an
existing reservoir and held there for some length of time before reuse. They
are calling this "showers with flowers" (http://www.sdcwa.org/).

The Inland Empire Utility Agency, located over the Chino Groundwater Basin and in an area with 350,000 dairy cows, is using the cow manure's
methane gas to generate electricity to clean up the groundwater basin, which
has become contaminated with nutrients from the cow manure. By cleaning up the Chino Basin, enough wet-year surpluses can be stored there so
that this agency can manage without any imported water, even during three
consecutive years of drought. They also plan on reusing between 75% and
90% of their treated wastewater and putting it underground, with the goal

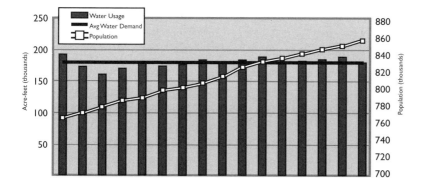

Figure 48. Historical retail demand and population in the West Coast Basin MWD. (SOURCE: West Basin MWD water use database and WMD demographic data, 2005.)

of not needing to buy any imported water. Its new headquarters building is a LEED-certified platinum building, and they have daylighted or restored a creek that dissects the property (www.ieua.org/).

The Santa Ana Watershed Project Authority, SAWPA, a joint powers authority composed of water agencies in the upper Santa Ana River Watershed in Riverside and San Bernardino counties, has also found its way to independence from imported water, even in multiple dry years. These creative responses are just beginning to surface, and almost all are in southern California (http://www.sawpa.org/).

Within the Los Angeles Area, the West Coast Basin has demonstrated how population can grow, per capita water use fall, and total water use remain flat, despite a growing population,

GROUNDWATER MANAGEMENT   Farmers are always concerned about maintaining local control over their resources and their lives. Yet they have mined, overdrafted, their groundwater resources in many places, especially in the San Joaquin Valley. As many as 35% of our aquifers have been depleted, drying up some rivers and lakes. Many efforts to pass legislation that would require groundwater management or require adjudication and the imposition of a Watermaster have been met with fierce opposition and have failed. Local governments, county supervisors, and water agencies are now permitted, encouraged, to divide the pumping rights among themselves and to find ways to prevent further subsidence. To compound the matter, there are no more external water supplies on which to draw to correct this major long-standing problem.

California and Texas, alone among all the western states, do not manage groundwater. A 1913 law prohibits the State Water Board from regulating "percolating groundwater" but allows the state to regulate subterranean streams flowing through "known and definite channels." This law was passed before the connection between surface water and groundwater was clearly understood and before the invention of high-powered electric pumps. It has been interpreted to mean that there can be no groundwater management. A new and controversial interpretation, written by the prestigious Berkeley law professor Joseph Sax, states that if groundwater pumping impacts a lake or stream, the State Board does have jurisdiction. Groundwater and surface water are inextricably one, totally connected. They cannot be managed separately. Without management we have a tragedy of the commons. The person with the deepest well and/or the most powerful pump wins.

The state has not performed a comprehensive study of groundwater overdraft since 1980. It publishes a Bulletin 118, last updated in 2003, that reports on groundwater by compiling the information given to it by groundwater pumpers. Since the adoption of AB 3030, the law that encourages groundwater management, some 200 agencies have adopted groundwater management plans. However, they are not required to submit them to the state, nor is there any way to evaluate their effectiveness. Information contained within the planning documents, about who pumps up how much, about water quality, about the geophysical properties of the various groundwater basins, etc., is not available to the state for planning purposes, for the next B-118 or for inclusion in the B-160 process. The state estimates overdraft at between 1 million and 2 million acre-feet a year (www .groundwater.water.ca.gov/bulletin118/).

CONJUNCTIVE USE   Conjunctive use can only be practiced in groundwater basins that are managed. The groundwater basin's storage capacity and safe yield must be determined, and a system must be in place to keep track of who uses how much water in the basin. Only then can water be stored underground and be accounted for. The groundwater basins in the Los Angeles Area have been adjudicated. The Association of Ground Water Agencies in southern California has undertaken a major study to quantify the safe yield and the storage capacity in local groundwater basins, specifically to encourage more effective conjunctive use. There are millions of acre-feet of storage capacity in southern California. Little similar activity is happening elsewhere in the state, even where groundwater basins are severely overdrafted, despite requirements in both the State Water Project and the Central Valley Project contracts that water be used for this purpose. The water industry, especially giant agribusinesses, continues to fight against any kind of groundwater management.

WATERSHED MANAGEMENT Capturing stormwater on site for infiltration into the ground can harvest much more water and improve water quality in our streams and rivers and in the ocean. Eliminating impervious paving, redesigning parking lots so that the sheet flow of water pours into planters, instead of planters being protected from the water with concrete berms, and directing downspouts from roofs into a grassy or planted area for infiltration are all ways to permit stormwater to percolate into the ground. Better operation of dams, reservoirs, and spreading grounds can also add to the supply.

We need a landscape ethic. Half of all water consumed in the residential sector, on average, is used outside. The really big conservation payoff will come from changing the plant materials around homes to natives or California-friendly plants and installing programmable irrigation controllers. Green lawns take about four times the amount of water as other ground covers or native plants. Native plants attract birds and butterflies and are adapted to our climate. Urban runoff will also be substantially reduced, improving water quality in the storm drain system and at the beach. Watershed groups also speak of the quality-of-life advantages that restored rivers and creeks bring and the increased property values nearby. Increased property values can lead to the redevelopment of our inner cities and the lessening of urban sprawl.

And best of all, watershed management means the process whereby all the stakeholders, government agencies, and community groups sit around the same table and work cooperatively together. They can develop multidisciplinary projects that can dip into multiple pots of money to fund projects that meet many goals when single-goal projects would not make economic sense.

NEW TECHNOLOGY   New waterless urinals, dry composting toilets, and new washing machines are now available that take much less water and energy. Reverse osmosis makes economic sense now to clean up brackish or colored groundwater and further clean already highly treated wastewater to put it underground as part of our drinking water supply. The price is coming down as membrane technology improves. The desalination of seawater via reverse osmosis is also being pushed as old power plants along the coast are modernized.* However, destroying the life force that is the ocean while dumping rivers of almost-potable treated wastewater into the sea just doesn't make economic or environmental sense. And we must be open to new discoveries that are not yet apparent.

The Agricultural Sector

Just as population projections have varied over the years, so has the amount of land to be irrigated. In DWR's Bulletin 3, the very first California Water Plan, it was projected that over 19 million acres would be irrigated by 2020. Today only about 9 million acres are actually irrigated.

About 80% of the developed water in the state is used by agriculture. Yet agriculture is so efficient that it was able to increase the tonnage harvested per acre-foot of applied water by 40% between 1980 and 2000. Agriculture is an obvious source of additional water for urban areas because cities are willing and able to pay more for water than farmers are.

AGRICULTURAL WATER MANAGEMENT COUNCIL   In direct response to the formation of the California Urban Water Conservation Council (CUWCC), the legislature passed AB 3616 in 1990 to set up a similar Agricultural Water Management Council, to develop efficient water management practices (EWMPs) and to implement them at the highest practical, feasible level. The irrigation districts that are signatory to this council agree to prepare a plan with its water suppliers; designate a conservation coordinator to implement the plan and report on progress; provide technical support services to their users and education to farmers, staff, and the public; improve communication and cooperation between and among suppliers, users, and others; and evaluate needs for changes in policies for more

*With the EPA's new ruling against once-through cooling at power plants, it is no longer possible to use the power plant's intake and discharge pipes to reduce costs.

flexibility in the delivery and storage of water. This program is also totally voluntary.

In 1996 a nonprofit group was formed, and funding was found by the end of 2001 in Proposition 50. Irrigation districts representing 3.5 million acres of irrigated farmland signed on in 2001. The acreage has grown to a total of 4.65 million acres in 2005, out of a total of 9 million acres of irrigated farmland in the state. However, no mechanism exists to measure how effective this program is (www.agwatercouncil.org).

Historically, some farmers have had an excellent record of using water efficiently, especially in those areas where water is costly. However, those with riparian or appropriative water rights (not those operating under contracts with the state and/or federal governments) operate under the rubric of "use it or lose it." In other words, if these farmers do not consume their full entitlement, the next farmer downstream can do so. To protect their water rights, it is in these farmers' self-interest to use all they can, especially since interest is growing in using a market in water as one way to reallocate water around the state.

CROPPING PATTERNS   California agriculture produces over half of all the fruits, nuts, and vegetables consumed by the entire nation. We are proud to be the number-one agricultural state in the nation, even though agriculture represents only about 3% of the state's economy. Almost half of all the agricultural water in the state is used to grow cotton, rice, alfalfa, and irrigated pasture. Two of these water-intensive low-value crops, rice and cotton, are also subsidized with price supports by the federal government. Alfalfa can be grown without irrigation east of the hundredth meridian, in the Midwest, where rainfall occurs naturally.

The Environmental Working Group, in a study called *California Water Subsidies: Large Agricultural Operations—Not Small Family Farmers—Are Reaping a Windfall from Taxpayer-Subsidized Cheap Water*, examined who gets the federal subsidies that were originally designed to help destitute farmers recover from the Great Depression. In 2002, the largest 10% of farmers got 67% of the water, with an average subsidy of $349,000 each at the market rate for replacement water. Twenty-seven of the largest farmers got a million dollars or more worth of water at replacement costs (www.ewg.org/reports/watersubsidies/).

We are beginning to learn that farmers, faced with increasing globalization and competition from around the world, are finding it difficult to compete on the world market without price supports. Some farmers with water rights are more interested in marketing their water than in growing crops.

If cattle were to be fattened in the Midwest, there could be a lot of water made available for other, more valuable crops in California, for cities, for habitat restoration, or for other uses.

The new farm realities were summarized by Lloyd Carter, president of the California Save Our Streams Council, August 3, 2001, in the *Fresno Bee*: "While the twentieth century was dominated by Valley agriculture's demand for more publicly funded water storage, a more realistic assessment indicates that oversupply—everything from grapes and raisins to cotton, tomatoes and almonds—has been the principal problem, not water shortages. . . . It now takes $750 worth of retail water to grow $150 worth of wholesale cotton." J. G. Boswell, the world's largest grower of cotton, has been quoted in the book *The King of California,* by Marc Arax and Rick Wartzman, "There probably won't be any cotton growing in California 10 years from now. What the hell you doing growing cotton? I mean, let the Chinese grow cotton." What will happen to the water now used to grow cotton once the World Trade Organization requires that the United States end its cotton subsidies?

LAND RETIREMENT   There are areas, especially on the west side of the San Joaquin Valley, where the soils naturally contain high levels of selenium or boron. When these soils are irrigated, the runoff is poisonous to wildlife and people. The implications of irrigating this land were well understood before a drop of irrigation water was applied. The Kesterson Wild Life Refuge, where this runoff has been directed, has produced many malformed and dead birds, and local wells have been poisoned. Since a drain is not practical, the best alternative is for government to purchase this land and to retire it from farming. This could save about 2 million acre-feet of water, and pollution would be greatly reduced.

Should this farmland be retired, who owns the water that irrigated it? The irrigation district and/or the landowners will want to retain title so that this water can be marketed. Or should it return to state control to be reallocated in the public interest? The water could be kept in the delta for fish and wildlife and to improve our ability to meet water quality standards and the impacts of sea level rise.

WATER RIGHTS AND COSTS

There is a long tradition in our state that we do not pay for water. We pay for the facilities needed to bring it to us, for the pipes, pumps, aqueducts, energy, and the costs of operating and maintaining the delivery systems. Water, in fact, belongs to all of us. Those with water rights have the privilege of using the water for beneficial purposes. There has never been a true public debate about who has the right to sell water and to profit from that sale. The debates, if any, have been held in Congress and in the state legislature, without much public knowledge. Over time, as a result, water rights have assumed some of the characteristics of property rights. The laws are slowly being changed to encourage water transfers.

There are different kinds of water rights. *Riparian* rights go with land ownership along a river, stream, pond, or lake. The landowner can use the water that flows by as long as she or he does no harm to downstream landowners. Use it or lose it. *Appropriative* rights holders can use water not taken by anyone else. This originated during gold rush days, when streams of water were utilized to wash down mountains in search of gold. First in time, first in right. *Prescriptive* rights can be achieved by unauthorized taking that can yield title if it continues longer than the five-year statute of limitations. This is the water commandeered by the state and federal governments to fill their aqueduct systems. There are also *contractual* rights in the state and federal contracts and Los Angeles' pueblo water rights.

Public Trust Doctrine

An important part of water rights law that applies to transfers is the Public Trust Doctrine, which dates back to ancient Rome, to the time of Justinian. It is a part of the English common law that has been adopted into our own legal structure. Water, the sea, and the rivers utilized for transportation belong to all of the people and must be used for the benefit of all the people. The public trust can supersede existing water rights, which can be reviewed in the light of new conditions by regulatory bodies and the courts. The state constitution declares that water is for public consumption, subject to the regulation and control of the state, and that water

TABLE 14. Wholesale Costs of Water (per acre-foot)

SWP contract water in 2003	
Near the Feather River	$37
Southern California	$277
Central Coast	$629
San Joaquin County	$74
CVP water	
Agriculture	$2–30
Urban sector	$9–64
Imperial Irrigation District	$12.50
Proposed sale to San Diego	$249 ($311 in 10 years)[a]
MWD	
Untreated water	$431
Treated water	$450
Reverse osmosis	$1,300 ($800 projected)
Los Angeles Aqueduct	$100–500 (in a dry year)
Pumping groundwater on average	$150
Market rate for agricultural water	$120-$150

[a]These costs do not include the costs of transporting the water from the Imperial Valley to San Diego or the cost of treatment.

must be used beneficially in the interests of the people and for the public welfare.

This doctrine was applied by the courts in the Mono Lake decision to require that the Los Angeles Department of Water and Power leave water in the Owens Valley and in the Mono Basin that it had been sending south. This doctrine could play an important role in helping to restore more of the state's desiccated habitat, its fish, and its wildlife.

Wholesale Costs of Water, 2005

It is also instructive to understand how water is priced at the wholesale level around the state. Because of subsidies, the way contracts have been written, how long ago they were written, distance from the source water, and political pressures, the price of water varies wildly. Table 14 presents some examples of the cost of water around the state.

Water has been transferred around the state for many decades. For years, farmers have been trading water within their own area, like borrowing a cup of sugar from a neighbor. All of our aqueduct systems transfer water from one part of the state to another. However, these transfers are not being made for direct private gain. They are made between government agencies to meet existing or anticipated needs—to provide water for a growing population or to irrigate additional agricultural land. Whatever profit is made comes to those who put the water to economic use, such as land developers and farmers, not to those who are engaged in the transfer. Transfers have also been employed by the state to purchase environmental water to mitigate some of the environmental damage done by moving water over great distances from places of seeming abundance to places of need. MWD made a deal with the Imperial Irrigation District in 1988 to line Imperial's irrigation ditches in exchange for the water saved—over 100,000 acre-feet of water.

Economists like the idea of using market forces to allocate resources. They believe that the marketplace will always put a resource to its highest and best use. Those who can pay will buy it. Those who can't afford it will just have to do without. Since agriculture consumes the overwhelming majority of the state's developed water and cities are willing to pay more for water, some believe that cities should buy water from those farmers who are willing to sell. But not all farmers have the water rights needed to make the sale. Nor does the thought of taking some farmland out of production sit well with those people who live in the areas that are farmed and who are dependent on the farm economy.

Developing a market for water, which would be dependent on water transfers, is a seemingly easy answer to the problems involved with meeting the needs of a burgeoning population and increasing competition. It is a politically expedient way to get around the questions raised by old, well-established water law that assigns responsibility to the state to see to it that all people have an affordable supply of water to meet their basic health and sanitation needs. It is a much simpler solution than conservation, reuse, conjunctive use, and watershed management. Its main attraction is that money can be made at public expense by exploiting the systems that were developed and built with public monies.

There is a long tradition in our state that we do not pay for water. We pay, instead, for the facilities needed to bring it to us, for the pipes, pumps, aqueducts, energy, operations, and maintenance. There also is a strong tradition in our country to let market forces work, to see competition as the best way to guarantee efficiency instead of relying on government. However, we have learned from the deregulation of energy that basic services such as water are by their very nature monopolies and must not be deregulated.

Privatized or deregulated water in times of drought would flow most often from field crops to trees and vines or to the urban sector. Such water transfers found their greatest use in 1991, near the end of the last drought, when a drought water bank was formed by the state to provide farmers growing trees and vines with the water needed to keep these permanent crops alive and growing and to provide water for the urban sector. Farmers, with access to groundwater, pumped and sold this water for a substantial profit, sometimes mining their groundwater supply.

There are dangers in subjecting water to a free market economy, where there are winners and losers. Water is too important a necessity for there to be any losers.

Impacts of Water Markets on Areas of Origin

Moving water from areas of plenty, especially from the Sacramento Valley watershed, to cities raises serious ethical issues, whether done by the state or federal government or through market mechanisms. Should not the area from which the water is drawn be protected from economic and environmental damage as water is transferred away? Solano County is asking for more water from the state so that three of the county's towns can grow: Vacaville, Fairfield, and Benicia. This demand is being made on the State Water Resources Control Board, the state agency that manages water rights as well as water quality. If granted, it will further diminish the amount of water available for export or transfer.

The concept of "do no injury to the areas of origin" dates back to 1850 but was not applied until the 1990s. The California Water Code was amended in 1980 to encourage transfers as long as they are beneficial to both parties to the deal and the transfer does no harm. The Central Valley Project Improvement Act (CVPIA) of 1992 specifically allows for the sale of federal water by its contractors but also requires that any contractor who sells more than 20% of his or her water must get special approval.

In 1982, DWR and others were encouraged to facilitate transfers outside the district as long as the use would be reasonable. In 1986, DWR began to list willing buyers and sellers and prohibited the denial of unused conveyance (space in the aqueduct system), but *unused conveyance* was not defined. The State Water Project agreements guarantee that area-of-origin communities will be protected. CALFED approves of transfers that protect water rights, the environment, and the economy of areas of origin. These concepts can be summed up by these three rules: There shall be no injury to other legal users, nor unreasonable effect on fish and wildlife, nor unreasonable economic impacts. Other laws passed by the state are making it easier to wheel water through the existing aqueduct system.

Local economies can suffer if the land is not farmed, local farm laborers do not have jobs, the fertilizer and farm machinery businesses languish, and the small towns wither away. More groundwater overdraft is a real possibility. Many groundwater basins statewide are already in severe overdraft. Yet pumping groundwater remains a source of water for sale. Moving large quantities of water damages the environment from which it is taken and promotes growth in those areas to which it is moved. And it is difficult to determine an equitable charge for wheeling or moving water in aqueducts built and paid for by others. Wheeling water, and the charges for doing so, will inevitably also raise the cost of water.

The Environmental Water Account (EWA) is operated by CALFED as a way to protect habitat and fish. It buys water from farmers to put back into the environment. An article about transfers written by Vic Pollard of the *Bakersfield Californian*, August 10, 2003, states, "When almonds and wine grapes started losing money, Blackwell Land Co. cut production of those crops and turned to another, potentially more lucrative, "crop" to shore up its bottom line—water. . . . Blackwell . . . is selling water it buys from the state for irrigation back to the government as part of a plan to protect endangered fish in the Sacramento–San Joaquin Delta, 250 miles to the north. . . . Taxpayer boondoggle? In fact, Kern County has lots of water to sell— at the right price, of course." The article further explains that Blackwell Land Co. was paid $1.36 million dollars at $170 an acre-foot, and it sure helped its bottom line. In 2001, a very dry year, EWA paid to another Kern County farmer $460 an acre-foot for EWA water. Price depends on supply and demand. Do the contracts for state water carry within them the right to sell the water that was purchased from the state for 10 times the original purchase price? How do we square the responsibility to the public with private use and private benefit?

Sources of Water to Be Transferred

Each of the following sources raises ethical issues about who really owns the water and can profit from its sale.

REDUCE AGRICULTURAL USE In order to live within its entitlement to 4.4 million acre-feet a year from the Colorado River, MWD has negotiated to pay farmers not to grow crops so that their water could go instead to urban areas during times of drought. In July 2001, a 35-year deal was announced that would immediately pay farmers in the Palo Verde Irrigation District, near Blythe in eastern Riverside County, $3,170 per acre if they agree to leave up to 29% of their land fallow in any year. For each acre left fallow, unplanted, a farmer will receive $550 a year. For a farmer who agrees to leave 1,000 acres fallow, the payment is nearly $3.2 million, with an annual payment of $550,000. In addition, MWD has paid $6 million to the Palo Verde Irrigation District for community projects. The maximum amount MWD will gain from this deal is 111,000 acre-feet of water for either immediate or storage purposes. Palo Verde is first in line to get Colorado River water, due to historical agreements. They staked their claim in 1877.

Previous similar proposals in other areas of the state have been rejected by farmers, who feared that it would enrich a few at the expense of others or that leaving land fallow will negatively impact their own communities. Other proposals by MWD have been negotiated and signed with water districts in the Central Valley, especially in Kern County, near the Colorado River Aqueduct, and in Arizona.

CONSERVATION PRACTICES As the agricultural community learns how to conserve, does the water saved by a farmer with riparian or appropriative rights belong to him or her for resale? Or does it just flow downstream to the next farmer, helping to maintain stream flow for fish and wildlife? Who owns the conserved water? Those who contract with the federal government are being given the "right" to resell their water. Is this in the best interests of the state? If agriculture could conserve as little as 15%, it could double the water available for cities.

RESERVOIR STORAGE Water released from reservoir storage can be sold by the state, and has been during recent droughts. The governor established a drought water bank during the drought of 1991, composed of water from willing sellers, usually from north of the Sacramento–San Joaquin Delta. This water was made available for sale to those, again usually farmers, who had permanent crops, like fruit trees or grape vines, that must be irrigated.

UNTAPPED GROUNDWATER SOURCES Most of the groundwater in the LA Area has been adjudicated. Many areas that have not been adjudicated have mined their groundwater, especially in the San Joaquin Valley. Should water from an already-overdrafted groundwater basin be sold outside of that groundwater basin? If the groundwater basin has not been adjudicated, who owns the groundwater that is for sale—those with the deepest wells and the most powerful pumps? For more on transfers, visit www.watertransfers .water.ca.gov.

The Monterey Amendments: When State Water Project Contracts Become Entitlements

As originally written, the State Water Project contracts were service contracts, a promise by the state to deliver the agreed amount of water if it could. In 1995, in a secret meeting in Monterey, amendments were agreed to by most of the State Water Project contractors and the Department of Water Resources that changed the service contract language to firm entitlements. This was accomplished by eliminating two provisions. One required the state, in case it could not deliver as promised, to divide what could be delivered among the contractors on a pro rata share. The other provision eliminated a requirement that agriculture take the first hit in times of drought. With those provisions eliminated, the agricultural contractors could call on the state to deliver all contracted water, whether available or not; and by not having to reduce their take in times of drought, they would have water to sell to the cities. If the state did not deliver, it could be taken to court and forced to deliver. The contracts, by not reflecting true water availability, would be turned into the equivalent of entitlements.

To clinch this deal, contractors were given the right to transfer water through the state aqueduct system. These and other amendments to the State Water Project contracts were the subject of legal challenges. The amendments were agreed to without public review or input, not all the contractors participated, and the environmental documentation, the environmental impact report, was declared inadequate by the court. The original EIR was written by a small water agency that is not even a contractor for state water. DWR, the appropriate lead agency, must write a new EIR.

PAPER WATER   Since the State Water Project can deliver less than half, on average, and much less in a really dry year (it delivered only 12% in 1991), the part that can be delivered on average is called "wet" or "real" water by many, while the other part, that which exists only on paper, is called "paper water." Paper water is now being marketed to developers for use in their environmental documentation to show that they indeed do have a water supply to serve their development projects. Over 100 new towns are being planned in the state to house our growing population, many of them with a paper water supply that will not be there when families move into the new homes being built. The Newhall development, of 21,000 homes in Santa Clarita in northern Los Angeles County, is one such new town. Several lawsuits are pending over this issue.

The two laws that require documented water supplies before any development of size can go forward begin to address this issue. They are also stimulating lawsuits. It will be interesting to see if and how these new laws are interpreted by the courts and implemented statewide.

The Napa Proposition

Another secret attempt at creating additional paper water to sell occurred in the northern California city of Napa, involving water industry officials in cooperation with the U.S. Bureau of Reclamation and the state Department of Water Resources. These agencies met to find ways of managing the CVP and State Water Project more closely together. The federal government has excess storage capacity, while the state has more pumping and conveyance capacity out of the delta. By combining these assets, they figure they can pump an additional 27%, or an additional million acre-feet, out of the delta without regard for water quality, habitat, or endangered species issues. They hoped they could get away with it by meeting and agreeing in secret. But now that the word is out, they are being challenged in court.

The changes in the State Water Project contracts (the Monterey Amendments described earlier) and the Central Valley Project Improvement Act, which permits transfers, are two examples of the strong movement to privatize water in the state, to deregulate it. Farmers and others are buying farmland for the water resources attached and are pushing the state legislature and Congress to help facilitate their ability to market water. Multinational corporations are also buying farmland for the water rights in order to sell water on the open market. And they are looking for other ways to grow their water business by selling a variety of services. Some farmers, suffering from global competition and increasing costs, would rather sell their water than farm.

Barron's Financial Weekly, in its March 5, 2001, issue, featured water on its cover as the next big business to get into. *Fortune* magazine calls water the oil of the twenty-first century, and the World Bank predicts that future wars will be fought over water.

EUROPEAN MULTINATIONALS DOMINATE   Three huge multinational corporations dominate the water business: Vivendi Environmental of France, now called Veolia Environnement (also owner of Universal Movie Studios), Ondeo, formerly Suez Lyonnaise des Eaux of France, which was kicked out of Atlanta, Georgia in 2003, and RWE of Germany, which also owns the largest British and American water companies, Thames Water and American Water Works Company. It is the state's fourth-biggest private water supplier, with 480,000 customers. Veolia also owns the largest U.S. manufacturer of water equipment (USFilter), and Ondeo owns the two largest American water chemical companies (Nalco and Calgon). USFilter, of Palm Desert, has become the biggest water-related company in the country by rapidly buying up small water companies, water service equipment firms, and bottled-water firms as well as by signing contracts to build and manage wastewater systems. It has won nine contracts to run publicly owned wastewater systems in California, including those in Petaluma, Richmond, and Rialto, just east of Los Angeles. RWE and Connecticut-based Poseidon Resources have been pitching desalination plants in Moss Landing, Huntington Beach, and Carlsbad. Enron had a water marketing subsidiary called Azurix.

The Bass Brothers of Texas bought a large spread in the Imperial Valley to ranch the water, only to learn that the landowners do not own the water rights. The water rights belong to the Imperial Irrigation District (IID). IID has agreed to sell San Diego 200,000 acre-feet of water its farmers will conserve. This deal is also the subject of multiple lawsuits.

If the United States should list water delivery as a service that falls under the General Agreement on Trade (GAT) or the North American Free Trade Agreement (NAFTA), then multinational giants such as Veolia Environnement and Germany's RWE would have the ability to challenge the public ownership and operation of most United States water systems.

Today about 160 private distributors, most of them small, supply about 20% of the state's residents. The biggest of these is the 77-year-old San Jose–based California Water Services Company (Cal-Water), serving 2 million people. Not all investor-owned utilities are multinational corporations.

Bills before Congress as this is written would make federal assistance to upgrade water systems conditional on the recipients' consideration of privatization.

AT THE RETAIL LEVEL   These same multinationals are looking for water and sewerage agencies or city water departments to buy. They are interested in agencies that either treat and deliver drinking water through retail water delivery systems or manage wastewater collection and treatment facilities. As our cities age, the infrastructure, the pipes in the ground, leak and need replacing. Keeping up with ever-stricter water quality regulations also costs money. Elected officials are loath to raise water rates to pay for these necessities. Some are finding it easier to be wooed by giant corporations who dangle a big buyout check in front of them and promise not to increase water rates—for a time. According to the Reason Public Policy Institute Policy Brief 17 (2001), about 15% of city utilities are turning to private firms for technical management. Once the system has been purchased or management services contracted for, there is no guarantee that rates will stay low or that the system will be managed for the health and welfare of those it serves. Of necessity the system will be managed for the financial health of the corporation and its shareholders.

In 2001, Cal-Am, owned by the multinational RWE-Thames, bought Chualar's water system. Chualar, population 1,440, is located amidst the lettuce fields in Monterey County. Its residents are almost entirely Latino farm workers, many Spanish-speaking only, with low or very low incomes. Monthly water bills had been a flat $21 a month until the takeover; then their bills soared to between $200 and $430 a month. The local school faced a monthly water bill of $2,753.13, up from a previous average of $180 a month, to serve 300 students. These rates were imposed without the required public notification process, forcing residents to choose between having water or food for their families. Complaints went to customer service representatives in Illinois who speak only English.

This is only one story told in a study issued by the Environmental Justice Coalition for Water called *Thirsty for Justice: A People's Blueprint for California Water,* June 2005. The study documents several other water system acquisitions, mergers, and rate increases that are outrageous, including a 34% increase in rates for the Monterey Peninsula. The small town of Felton, near Santa Cruz, is involved in a lengthy legal process to buy back their water system from Cal-Am (http://www.ejcw.org/our_work/blueprint.html).

RWE's American Water Works, of which Cal-Am is a part, has 2.6 million customers in 23 states. Philadelphia Suburban is also engaged in acquisitions. It is 17% owned by Veolia and is operating across six states with 600,000 customers. Water supply businesses generate about $400 billion in revenue worldwide. As small investor-owned utilities and other agencies are being bought up, they are being purchased by even bigger companies, with headquarters perhaps in Europe. "We are not going to know with whom we're dealing, one month to the next," said John Wilson, chair of the employee group that bid against a takeover in New Orleans.

BENEFITS AND DANGERS OF PRIVATIZATION   Private industry does have much to offer and can help some water utilities become more efficient. It can provide strong financial backing, the capital needed to do the job; the technical know-how needed to keep up with ever more stringent water quality standards in both drinking water and wastewater arenas; advanced management practices; economies of scale needed in procurement of supplies and chemicals, etc.; construction know-how; the ability to make critical improvements more quickly than government.

But there are dangers. With sufficient government oversight, privatization may work well, but several considerations must be kept in mind.

Private companies are not always more efficient in managing water and wastewater systems. They are natural monopolies, without competitors, just like a government-run utility. With private management, accountability/responsibility is blurred. Where does the buck stop? Who is really responsible for the system and keeping on top of water quality regulations?

Private companies are experienced in negotiations and have well-heeled trade associations and interest groups for support. Government employees and elected officials often have little or no negotiation experience. Complex privatization deals are often poorly understood by government officials, even in the United States and Europe. Conflicts of interest are inherent in the consulting/contracting business. An active interest is not always retained in the job beyond negotiations.

Privatization often means the loss of local expertise—and therefore the inability to monitor adequately how well a job is being done. Underrepresented communities can be bypassed. The poorest must be protected. Some agreements may discourage efficiency and conservation efforts. Money is made from sales, not by reducing sales. Some agreements may fail to protect important natural resources, such as habitat. And it is extremely difficult to make profitability dependent on performance.

In spring 2002, the Pacific Institute published a study of privatization called *The New Economy of Water: The Risks and Benefits of Globalization and Privatization of Fresh Water.* It concludes that much more public oversight is needed if privatization is to take place, because no formal guidelines are in place. Many communities have had bad experiences. Prices have soared and water quality has deteriorated. The inevitable results are heightened environmental and health risks and blurred accountability. Canada seems to have become the epicenter of protest. The Canadian Union of Public Employees is so angry that they publish an annual report on the privatization of water and sewerage systems in their country (www.cupe.org.ca). Another Canadian organization is working to protect against water privatization (www.blueplanetproject.net). The nonprofit Food and Water Watch is fighting privatization in the United States (www.fwwatch.org).

Some public employees are challenging takeover schemes. They are reorganizing the operation and management of their water and/or wastewater systems under continued local and public control. By "reengineering" they are saving money, rewarding employees, improving water quality, and keeping the money in the community. The City of Phoenix set a goal of reducing costs by $60 million and saved $77 million. San Diego saved $37 million in the first two years, nearly double the targeted savings amount. They are expanding the program to other parts of the city government. Other success stories come out of Miami-Dade Water and Sewer Department and King County, Washington. Reengineering can be done much more quickly than negotiating complicated purchase agreements as well as providing all the benefits of local control.

Using markets to manage important public resources can sometimes lead to disastrous consequences. The deregulation of the power industry resulted in massive abuses of the public trust and highly inflated energy costs. Water agencies and cities are at a disadvantage regarding professional knowledge and the complex web of professional interactions that are a part of all negotiations. They can get involved in playing games with unknown players, for which they are not trained and are totally unprepared. Privatization has enormous implications for the public health and for the health of our natural world. Water is far too important for our health and welfare to be placed entirely in the private sector.

Of course, not all private, investor-owned utilities behave badly. Some are ethical and perform valuable services at reasonable cost, as promised. In California, it is the Public Utilities Commission's (PUC) job to prevent unjustified rate increases. The PUC provides an open and accountable forum, but it does not address all the issues at stake.

Publicly operated utilities are supposedly more open and fair, with environmental stewardship as a goal. Private business is supposedly more efficient, innovative, and entrepreneurial. Where does the truth lie? Where and how should the debate on the ethical questions raised occur? Under what circumstances should privatization be encouraged? When should it be discouraged? In which instance is there more corruption?

PLANNING PROCESSES

Despite the importance of water for the health and welfare of everyone in the state, there are no effective statewide planning processes. These is no one officially recognized process to establish policies that apply to everyone or that sets priorities for land use, for water use, and for how water can or should be distributed around the state to meet local needs. Nor is there the political will to do so, though interest is increasing in finding a way to do so.

Part of the reason for this lack of coordinated planning is the often-stated concern by local water agencies that they must maintain local control over their own resources. Many local agencies resent being told what and how to do anything that does not originate within their own board or staff. As a result, there is great resistance to any effort by the legislature, for example, to impose groundwater management requirements on local government or even to establish one set of criteria, one software system, for recording and reporting water information. It took a 10-year struggle to pass the legislation that requires any new town or new development of size to have identified a long-term water supply to serve that new community.

Senator Sheila Kuehl introduced another bill, SB 820, in the 2005 session of the legislature that would require agricultural water management plans, groundwater management plans, better urban water management plans, and a more open process for adopting these plans. They could provide the necessary information to begin to regulate these resources. SB 820 was passed by both houses of the legislature after garnering support from many water agencies and the environmental community, only to be vetoed by Governor Schwarzenegger at the behest of the Farm Bureau and the state Chamber of Commerce.

DWR's Reliability Report

In theory, several planning processes could do part if not all of the job. Most if not all of them depend on a Reliability Report issued by DWR every two years. This report attempts to predict the amount of water state contractors can expect during the next two years. It assumes historical precipitation and depends on a computer model, Calsim II, which has been the subject of severe criticism when peer reviewed (www.baydeltaoffice.water .ca.gov/ and http://science.calwater.ca.gov/workshop/calsim_05.shtml).

These planning processes discussed next have some influence on how water managers think, but they have no teeth.

State Department of Water Resources B-160

The state publishes a *California Water Plan*, known as Bulletin 160, which is supposedly updated every five years. It "guides the orderly and coordinated control, protection, conservation, development, management, and efficient use of the water resources of the state" (Water Code 10005(a)). It is supposed to act as a master plan, with estimates of future supply and demand.

Historically it assembled information from all of the water agencies, compiled it, and published it as the plan, a very difficult thing to do because each agency has its own system of accounting, its own methodologies for reporting, and different software and mapping systems. Bulletin 160-1998 was written for and by the water purveyors in a process that was not open and transparent. It projected higher State Water Project and CVP water usage while at the same time projecting reduced groundwater overdraft in the San Joaquin Valley. The document praised DWR's capability to construct additional infrastructure to meet future water needs that the water purveyors wanted. Every state plan in the last century identified a shortage and then provided plans to build our way out of that shortage. There were no economic or affordability studies—and no environmental concerns.

However, the process for writing Bulletin 160-2003, now labeled Bulletin 160-2005, was handled in a much more open, transparent, and inclusive manner. A large advisory committee of 65 people, representing all of the parties of interest, was assembled, as was a review panel of 350, with an additional 2,000 people to represent the public at large. With such an open and inclusive process, the results are much different than before. Its Framework for Action promotes three fundamental actions (water use efficiency, water quality improvement, and environmental stewardship) and two key initiatives (integrated regional water management to ensure reliability and improved state water management systems). It envisions for the state a vital economy, a healthy environment, and a high standard of living.

More efficient use of water is the primary way to meet increasing demand, and integrated management should be based on regional partnerships. It recommends sustainability, regional self-sufficiency, environmental justice, coordination and collaboration, and sound science. For the first time, global warming and climate change are given credence, even if not included fully in this planning document. The review draft contains essays that examine many aspects of water management in the state from many viewpoints.

Even though the Bulletin 160-2005 planning process was so much more open and transparent than before, it remains a wish list of policies and programs. There are no mandates and no funding attached. It depends on the legislature and on the various water agencies to implement the recommendations. It does have a real vision of what the California water future could or should be, contains goals and objectives and a measurable action plan, but has no teeth. It sets the agenda for any agency that wants to comply. The Framework for Action is a summary of the plan. It can be viewed, together with all the planning documents, at www.waterplan.water.ca.gov.

The Pacific Institute analyzed the public review draft of Bulletin 160-2005 in a study entitled *California Water 2030: An Efficient Future* and has concluded that it delays action on efficiencies by at least five years by not advocating an aggressive, high-efficiency approach that will pay many dividends in environmental protection, increased reliability, and lower costs. It details how smart technology, strong management, and appropriate rates and incentives can allow the state to meet its needs well into the future with less water and without harm to the economy or the quality of life of the people of California (www.pacinst.org/reports/california_water_2030).

CALFED

CALFED is the process that was established to restore the Sacramento–San Joaquin Delta, to provide for a reliable supply of good-quality water for those dependent on the State Water Project and the Central Valley Project, and to encourage habitat restoration and levee system integrity in the delta. The parts of the state affected by CALFED include the watershed of the entire Central Valley and the watersheds of all the other parts of the state that contract for state water, including southern California. The contractors cover much of the San Joaquin Valley, the San Francisco Bay Area, the service area of the MWD, and a few other smaller communities. The north coast and most of the inland deserts are not included.

A plan, the Record of Decision (ROD), was adopted in August of 2000 to achieve the goals that were worked out over years of meetings and discussion and vetted through an environmental impact report process. The openness of this process set the stage for the openness of the Bulletin 160-2005 process. CALFED is partially responsible for administering Propositions 50, 13, and 204 matching funds. The availability of money to invest in watersheds and efficiencies and the openness of the process have helped to stimulate investments. CALFED also initiated an extensive science program to understand better how the delta and its ecosystem work. Its work plans are designed to take small incremental steps toward improvements and to use adaptive management techniques to refine the plans as they go.

CALFED holds regular meetings in each region of the state with those who serve in local water agencies, consulting firms, and the environmental community. The meetings explore local water issues, help bridge gaps in understanding, and keep a dialogue going. In the Los Angeles Area, the meetings are held at MWD headquarters, cochaired by Frances Spivy-Weber of the Mono Lake Committee and Tim Worley, Assistant Manager of External Affairs at MWD.

CALFED started out as a cooperative and open way to solve problems. However, it has become highly politicized and therefore ineffective. As a result, the funding needed to continue its efforts has not been forthcoming. Neither the state nor the federal government is willing to devote the financial resources needed, because the debate has descended once again into whether to fund more dams and reservoirs or to fund the CALFED program of restoring the ecosystem and improving efficiencies while studying the economics and environmental impact of building additional dams and conveyances. Compounding the debate are lawsuits to require the implementation of water quality standards in the delta.

As summarized by Dana Wilkie of the Copley News Service, April 5, 2002, "Seven years and millions of taxpayer dollars later, many of those intimate with the peacekeeping effort known as 'CALFED' complain that key negotiators have given up and gone to court. Some are filing lawsuits, challenging various provisions of this plan and provisions in both the Monterey Agreement and the Napa Proposition. Others have abandoned negotiating for political arm-twisting as they ask Congress to approve water plans that may ignore years of delicately crafted deals. As Mark Twain is credited with stating, 'Whiskey is for drinking, water is for fighting.' This continues to be what the state lives by."

As funding is drying up at both state and federal levels of government, the water industry is also fighting the agreed-on policy that the beneficiary pays for improvements to the system. It is clear that the principle beneficiaries will be those who use the water and that the money should come from user fees or water bills. The industry is also intent on pumping ever more water out of the delta, as evidenced by the secretive Monterey

Agreement and the Napa Proposition—this despite the facts that the ecosystem is collapsing and scientists who have been studying the delta to develop restoration plans have left CALFED.

One of the many lawsuits filed has been decided in the Third Court of Appeals. In an October 2005 decision, the court threw out the entire CALFED Record of Decision (ROD). It found that the environmental documentation was insufficient because it did not include as an alternative reducing the amount of pumping from the delta, nor has it identified the sources of water needed to fill the new dams and reservoirs that CALFED promised to study, nor has it analyzed the Environmental Water Account and its potential alternatives or impacts. Should this decision be upheld by the U.S. Supreme Court, CALFED will have to go back to square one and totally rewrite the EIS/EIR. And any project that is based on the ROD (such as the studies for more storage and conveyance) will no longer be able to go forward.

Because all of these issues are now front and center, the entire governance structure of CALFED is up for grabs. The Little Hoover Commission was charged to study just how effective CALFED has been and to make recommendations regarding its ability to do the job. It has recommended a complete restructuring, where authority is clearly in the hands of the Secretary for Resources or a water czar, instead of an advisory Bay Delta Authority with no regulatory or taxing authority. It recommends that a Policy Group of leaders from all the state and federal agencies be reconstituted, with a scientific advisory group and a public advisory group providing advice. Success should be measured, based on performance and the ability to mediate disputes. These recommendations have now been mostly adopted by the governor. The Little Hoover Commission report can be found at www.lhc.ca.gov/.

Delta Vision for the Future

Because the delta is not sustainable as it is now managed, a number of studies have been instituted that will lead to a delta vision of what the delta will look like and how it will function 100 years from now. The original landscape has been dramatically changed, and the delta has evolved to serve many purposes other than agriculture. The waterways also serve as a major recreational destination for boating and fishing. Highways, towns, railroad tracks, power and natural gas lines, and telephone lines now crisscross the delta. Scientists are struggling to figure out how to deal with sea level rise, the continuing subsidence of the delta islands, water quality, ecosystem protection, and the unstable levees to ensure the long-term viability of the delta as the hub of the state's water system and as a sustainable asset for everyone in the state. This visioning process is scheduled for completion by January 2008.

To view the ROD, CALFED annual reports, and many other pertinent materials, visit http://calwater.ca.gov.

United States Bureau of Reclamation

The Bureau of Reclamation's planning role in California centers on the Colorado River and the Central Valley Project (CVP), both of which it built and manages. Contracts between the CVP farmers and the bureau have been coming up for renegotiation. In the early 1990s, Congress passed the Central Valley Project Improvement Act. It requires the federal government to set aside 800,000 acre-feet of water for the environment, and, before renewing any of the contracts, farmers must develop conservation plans for using less water. It also permits water marketing. Many aspects of this law and its implementation are in the courts.

The Bureau of Reclamation also has responsibilities to conserve and to develop new water supplies. Therefore it has performed studies such as the water reuse studies for both southern California and the San Francisco Bay Area and is taking a leading role in the Water Augmentation Study of capturing local stormwater for groundwater recharge with the Los Angeles & San Gabriel Rivers Watershed Council and others.

Both Reclamation and the California Department of Water Resources created a water purchase program in 2001. As part of both agencies' efforts at managing droughts and facilitating water transfers, both are asking for willing sellers to make water available for purchase by others, especially in dry years. To ensure cooperation among all involved agencies, the following guidelines were established: work with local leadership, ensure that local areas had adequate supply before water is sold outside the region, minimize third-party impacts, protect the environment, and help all areas of the state.

Additional State Planning Documents: Urban
Water Management Plans, SB 221 and SB 610

The state legislature, in an effort to begin to rationalize how water is used in the state, passed a law in 1983 (a number of amendments have since passed) that requires each agency serving more than 3,000 connections or 3,000 acre-feet a year to prepare a plan that spells out its water supplies, its use, its projected growth, and how that growth is to be met. The plan must also detail the response to a 50% cutback in times of drought.

There are 418 utilities that qualify: 26 wholesale only, 373 retail, and 19 mixed. They serve 86% of the state's population.

These plans are updated every five years. They range from full-fledged 100-page documents to short six- or eight-page reports of just charts and numbers. In the year 2000, the State Department of Water Resources established a checklist to evaluate the adequateness and completeness of the plans submitted and filed. Other amendments describe tools to maximize local supplies, minimize imports, require sharing the document with other local government agencies, and require more information about recycled water, water quality, and groundwater resources when they are identified as a water source. It also requires more data sharing between suppliers. State bond money and low-interest loans will be given only to those who comply.

According to *Water for Growth: California's New Frontier* (July 2005) a study by the Public Policy Institute of California, one-sixth of the required agencies did not submit plans and more had little detail. Some lacked internal consistency. Many are counting on paper water. And only 6 out of 10 "have some form of local oversight policy" to connect new development to water supply. This study also projects potential savings of over 1 million acre-feet a year each from urban efficiencies, from groundwater storage, and from reuse and 0.9 maf from agricultural conservation. It projects a drop of 5–10% a year in agricultural irrigation due to the urbanization of agricultural land. It recommends conservation pricing policies (inclined block rate) and calls for greater regional collaboration among utilities to build a broader portfolio of water supply options. It also calls for more and better consultation with citizens and the public. However, most utilities are not projecting substantial savings between now and 2020 and are counting on new supplies, such as groundwater and reuse, to meet their growth needs (www.ppic.org).

Because of the growing concern that some new towns planned in California will not have an adequate water supply to serve the needs of the people who will live there, two other very significant bills were passed. SB 221 (Kuehl) took effect January 1, 2002. It requires that developments of over 500 units must identify a 20-year, long-term water supply and be able to meet water needs even during multiple dry years for all existing and planned developments. Another bill, SB 610 (Costa), requires that much more information be made available to developers regarding water supply in water planning documents (urban water management plans) and in environmental impact reports.

In 2001, a lawsuit was filed challenging the accuracy and honesty of these planning documents in northern Los Angeles County outside the Los Angeles Area as defined for this book. Newhall Land and Farming is planning a 21,000-home development along the Santa Clarita River and is claiming both paper water and a contaminated groundwater basin as water supply. How this suit will be settled as well as other, similar challenges to existing water supplies remains to be seen.

Wholesale Agencies

The Metropolitan Water District is the de facto planning agency for its service territory. It established a much more open and inclusive planning process with its first integrated resource management plan (IRP), initiated in 1996, which was updated July 2004. The basic information contained in the IRP is developed in close consultation with its member agencies. MWD established targets for conservation, storage, recycling, and transfers in the context of its own urban water management plan. Its local resource programs provide incentives for using local resources more effectively. These programs are routinely oversubscribed. It is currently heavily engaged in promoting a landscape ethic called "Heritage Gardens." MWD takes its role as de facto planner seriously. However, it can only plan, recommend, and offer incentives.

In northern California there are two (there may be more) large wholesale agencies that can serve this same purpose, though both serve much smaller populations: the San Francisco Public Utility District, which manages the pipeline that brings water from Hetch Hetchy Reservoir to the Bay Area (65% of San Francisco Bay Area water is imported), and the Santa Clara Valley Water District (SCVWD), which serves the County of Santa Clara with both water supply and stormwater management. The SCVWD is one of the state's leaders on a wide range of issues. Working with its 15 cities and the county, it has developed guidelines for local land use planning that takes into account water supply reliability, flood management, and riparian corridor protection. Each planning and building permitting department in the county has the "Standards and Guidelines" on their desks, to be used in the permitting processes (http://www.valleywater.org/).

As part of the Drinking Water Source Assessment and Protection Program (DWSAP), the California Department of Health Services administers a voluntary Source Water Protection Program for public or community water systems. The goal of the program is to identify, develop, and implement local projects that will advance the protection of drinking water supplies from contaminants such as bacteria, nitrates, disinfection by-products, and other chemicals. Those who initiate these projects are encouraged to establish a technical or advisory committee, gather data, designate a protection zone, develop an inventory of possible contaminating activities, prepare a report, and develop a source protection plan. The department has funded 57 multiyear projects as of April 2001, totaling almost $26 million. Not a single project is located in Los Angeles County. Most of the projects are in northern and central California. Much of this work has already been accomplished in Los Angeles under the guise of a sanitary survey program established several years ago.

Drought Management

NATIONAL POLICY   The National Drought Policy Act of 1998 established a 15-member National Drought Policy Commission to assist in the creation of an integrated federal policy to prepare for and respond to drought emergencies. Historically, about 18% of the nation experiences drought each year. In the 100-year period between 1896 and 1995, severe or extreme drought was recorded somewhere in the country every single year and in 10–25% of the country in 72 of those years. Studies of federal response during past droughts showed that $6 billion and more was spent on recovery from the droughts of 1976–1977 and 1988–1989. Being adequately prepared can reduce these expenditures. The lack of a comprehensive drought policy has been called a "hydro-illogical cycle."

The commission adopted a policy statement that recommends that the federal government support but not supplant or interfere with state, regional, local, tribal, and personal efforts to reduce drought impacts. The guiding principles would favor preparedness over insurance, insurance over relief, and incentives over regulation; research priorities based on the potential of the research results to reduce drought impacts; and coordinating the delivery of federal services through cooperation and collaboration with nonfederal entities.

The study suggests that preparedness may well reduce the social, economic, and environmental impacts of drought and the need for federal emergency relief expenditures. Preparedness may even lessen conflicts over competition for water during drought. More research is needed into basic weather patterns, soil moisture, snowfall, and climate change, with an accessible gateway or point of contact where standardized, comprehensible current information and historical weather data are available. A more comprehensive insurance program is needed that would more equitably distribute relief. Crop insurance, a central feature of any drought relief program, covers only major field crops in all locations. It does not include all vegetable and lesser field crops in all locations, nor does it cover livestock.

The federal government has over 80 drought-related programs and no central point of contact concerning all of the federal programs. Even within the same federal department, there is no one contact to help people access programs, information. and products. The western, southern, and national governors' associations support the adoption of these recommendations by Congress. This final report can be accessed at www.fsa.usda .gov/drought.

The National Drought Mitigation Center has developed the handbook *A Methodology for Drought Planning* (http://enso.unl.edu/ndmc/handbood/10step/process.htm).

STATE POLICY Managing water supplies during times of drought is an important responsibility for all water agencies. Drought action plans, developed by local water agencies such as MWD and by the state and federal governments attempt to reduce water consumption during times of drought in a variety of ways. The state plan includes requiring agencies to set and publicize a goal to reduce demand by a certain percentage from nondrought levels. Wholesale water agencies may offer retail agencies a rebate if water demand is reduced in the retail agencies' service area. Customers receive water conservation packages containing such items as shower flow restrictors, dye tablets to check for toilet leaks, drought-resistant plant seeds, soil polymers to hold water in the plant's root zone, and other information on water conservation.

Public education plays an important role. Via various media, the public is educated on the severity of the drought and on how best to conserve. Feature articles and artwork are provided to local newspapers. Weathercasters are supplied with supplemental drought information. Special cards are even placed on restaurant tables to inform customers why water is served only on request. Hotels are encouraged to change sheets and towels only on request for guests that stay more than one night.

The state requires that before urban areas can take delivery of water from the State Water Bank, those areas must implement conservation best management practices.

The State Department of Water Resources (DWR), under former Governor Pete Wilson, developed a Drought Water Bank. During times of drought, DWR purchases water from those with excess water supplies and sells it to parties with critical needs, such as farmers with investments in permanent crops such as fruit and nut trees or vines. During the drought year of 1991, DWR transferred 800,000 acre-feet of water through the Drought Water Bank.

As part of the CALFED process, former Governor Gray Davis convened an Advisory Drought Planning Panel. It was charged with identifying all available sources of water, to build on the governor's Drought Water Bank, to recommend appropriate funding, and to appeal to all of the CALFED agencies to help facilitate any transfers not already a part of CALFED. In its report, *Critical Water Shortage Contingency Plan* (December 29, 2000), the panel recommended that all of the efficiency goals already established as part of CALFED be implemented and that a more streamlined (web based?) drought bank be established for willing buyers and willing sellers based on the further mining of groundwater and land fallowing while remaining sensitive to third-party impacts (http://watersupplyconditions.water.ca.gov/).

The more recent planning processes, such as CALFED, urban water management plans, and the planning for DWR's Bulletin 160, seem to have supplanted drought management planning. The impact of climate change and the need to prepare for the likelihood of earthquakes in the delta have also taken on much more importance since the 2005 hurricanes on the Gulf coast.

Effective planning is extremely important in order to reduce the severity of water shortages. Conservation, conjunctive use, wastewater reuse,

TABLE 15. Planning and Conservation
League Investment Strategy

ADDITIONAL NEEDS (MAF)	
Additional population	2.0–2.4
Environmental restoration	1.0
Total additional needs	3.0–3.4

FIRST-PRIORITY MANAGEMENT OPTIONS (MAF)	
Urban water conservation	2.0–2.3
Agricultural water conservation	At least 0.3–0.6
Recycled water	1.5
Groundwater treatment and desalination	At least 0.29
Total first-priority potential	At least 4.09–4.69

SOURCE: "An Investment Strategy for California Water," Water for California and the Planning and Conservation League. Full publication available at www.pcl.org.

and the various aspects of watershed management and restoration are all important ways to prepare for drought. Expanding existing reservoirs or building new reservoirs can increase water storage for the region and reduce the adverse effects of shortages during times of drought. But doing so means the loss of additional habitat or farmland and further stresses many already-listed species.

AT THE LOCAL LEVEL MWD has built southern California's largest surface reservoir in Diamond Valley, four miles southwest of the City of Hemet. This reservoir is designed to hold 800,000 acre-feet of water, providing a six-month emergency water supply for southern California. It will evaporate an estimated 12,000–14,400 acre-feet a year that could have been conserved if this reservoir had been established underground.

Los Angeles Area groundwater basins can hold an additional 1.78 million acre-feet. The Chino Groundwater Basin, nearby, can store an estimated 2 million acre-feet of water underground, with no evaporation. The water agency that serves the area, the Inland Empire Utility Agency, has developed a plan to weather three consecutive dry years without the need to import a drop and is working on a plan to eliminate the need for any imported water. They are building four reclamation plants that together will make it possible to reuse 70,000 acre-feet a year. The Santa Ana Water Project Authority is also able to be self-sufficient in multiple dry years.

Planning and Conservation League

The Planning and Conservation League (PCL) is a nonprofit that lobbies in Sacramento on a wide range of environmental issues. It has developed it own plan, an *Investment Strategy for California Water*, dated October 2004, that concludes that there is enough water in the state to take care of all our needs and restore the environment, too. It could provide the basis for a new statewide water bond in the future (www.pcl.org).

Table 15 was developed by PCL as part of its Investment Strategy for California Water. It is very conservative, based on proven resources (http://www .pcl.org/pcl/pcl_files/Investment%20Strategy_11_18_04.pdf).

Issues Neglected in the Planning Process

Issues not sufficiently covered in any of the planning processes, though given lip service in some, include the need to integrate surface water, groundwater, stormwater, wastewater, and water quality. It is the wave of the future. Forward-thinking water managers like Rich Atwater, of the Inland Empire Utility Agency, located near Chino, and the Los Angeles Bureau of Sanitation have been working toward this kind of integration because of the tremendous efficiencies that can be achieved by holistic thinking. Many agencies could band together to fund integrating projects that each individual agency could not afford on its own and create multiple benefits.

First and foremost, there must be one comprehensive system and methodology for data collection, with comparable data, using the same software and software language both statewide and at the federal level.

The proliferation of water agencies is just as egregious at the state level as within the Los Angeles Area, if not more so, with all the financial inefficiencies that go with a multitude of small agencies. Each one wants to maintain its independence, yet many lack the financial resources to meet water quality standards or other regulations on their own. The perks that go with being a director of a water agency are too good to be given up easily. The unwillingness by many, especially the smaller agencies, to give up the smallest amount of control to regional planning processes is shortsighted.

It creates institutional barriers to good policy such as integrated planning, groundwater management, and the consideration of consolidation.

The governor or the legislature have not been able to plan for where new towns should be located, in places where water supplies and other infrastructure already exist, to accommodate our growing population. New towns should not be located in floodplains or in the delta, where the risks of flooding are great.

The proper role for the public, whose very lives are at stake, is given the least amount of lip service. The people of California have historically been left out of local water issues and concerns and therefore are ill prepared to be involved with regional or statewide policy matters. And the industry likes it that way.

POLITICAL CONSENSUS

In response to the problems facing the state's water world, a political consensus is growing, especially in some of the larger urban water agencies, in Sacramento, and among those who study our water resources. This consensus revolves round two ideas about how best to meet the future needs of the state: the need to maximize the use of local resources first before thinking about any other new sources of water; and the need to plan in a better, more integrated way for the future. The more flexibility and adaptability we can build into our waterworks, the better we will be able to adapt to extremes.

Effective planning is extremely important in order to reduce the severity of water shortages. Better integration of groundwater and surface water management will also be a must as both water sources are stressed by droughts and floods. A healthier ecosystem adapts better than a weakened one. Moving people out of the floodplains, curbing urban sprawl, and reducing fossil fuel consumption and the resulting greenhouse gas emissions are just some of the measures that should be taken. We cannot assume that the future will look like the past.

This consensus is reflected in a great number of places. The Metropolitan Water District started an Integrated Planning Process in the mid-1990s and brought together the member agencies with environmentalists and community groups to figure out how to manage their limited resources in a better way. An increased emphasis on local resources was the direct result of this exercise. This document was recently refined and updated, though in not as open a manner. The City of Los Angeles instituted an integrated planning process to integrate drinking water supply, stormwater management, and wastewater management into one plan—an amazing document.

DWR's California Water Plan Bulletin 160-2005 spells out several scenarios. The one that would utilize resources much more efficiently is given by far the most ink. And the state has already called a meeting to begin the process of figuring out how to encourage local regional planning as a part of B160-10. The whole idea behind CALFED is to foster this kind of cooperation—to develop better information and therefore better planning.

The federal Bureau of Reclamation has performed studies of the wastewater reuse potential of both southern California and the San Francisco Bay Area, identifying tremendous opportunities for reuse while also identifying the institutional constraints that will prevent much from happening. The Bureau of Reclamation has been working with nine other groups/agencies in southern California to explore watershed management opportunities to increase our local water supply.

Even the legislature has been pushing us to do a better job, first by requiring urban water management plans that are updated every five years so that we all have better information about what exists, and what doesn't exist and where, in order to do better land use planning. In the 2005 session, the legislature passed SB 820 (Sheila Kuehl), which would have required the same kind of information about groundwater management, agricultural management, and the interrelationship between water and energy, and it would have established a more open process for gathering all of this data. The bill was vetoed by the governor at the urging of the Farm Bureau and the state Chamber of Commerce.

All of the drought management plans developed over the past couple of decades at both the state and federal levels conclude that local resources are much more dependable in times of drought and must be maximized. They also point out the lack of coordination among those agencies and programs that actually deal with the consequences of drought, especially at the federal level.

Four congressmen from the Central Valley are actually calling for a long-term plan that will deal with water supply, water quality, the environment, and flood control in the Central Valley: two Republicans (Jim Costa and Devin Nunes) and two Democrats (George Radanovich and Dennis Cardoza). They have asked the California Water Institute at Fresno State to prepare four reports that would recommend how best to plan for the future of the Central Valley.

The state is also encouraging local cooperation and integration by requiring interagency cooperation and regional plans in order to qualify for Proposition 50 grants and for other sources of funding as a way of helping to push these processes along.

The whole idea of watershed management is an outgrowth of these ideas. It requires getting people around the table to think and plan cooperatively and to use local resources to the best of their ability. In the north, this usually revolves around the protection of endangered species and habitat restoration. In the Southland, it revolves around making better use of local supplies, such as stormwater, so as to reduce our dependence on imported water while accomplishing a whole host of other goals.

The Bay Area Water Agencies Coalition, composed of 29 cities, water agencies, and others in the San Francisco Bay Area, was formed in 2002 to promote conservation and cooperation.

The Sacramento Water Forum is a group of business, agricultural, and citizen groups, environmentalists, water managers, and local government that came together to plan for a reliable, safe water supply for the region's economic health and development to 2030 and to preserve fish and wildlife and the recreational and aesthetic values of the lower American River. They reached agreement in 1999 to integrate the actions needed for a regional solution to water shortages, environmental damage, groundwater contamination, and limited economic prosperity. Its recommendations have not been adopted (www.waterforum.org).

Institutional barriers, those placed in the way of proceeding, are rampant. Yet ways to overcome them are being found.

CONCLUSION

Many uncertainties face the state, including an enormous growth in our population, for which we must plan. Future water needs are based on projected population multiplied by the amount per person of water consumed daily. Should either of these two numbers change over time, and of course they will, then the total amount of water needed to serve these people will also change dramatically.

Every source of water is already oversubscribed, and, as in the case of local groundwater, some is overdrafted and/or contaminated. Pressures are growing to leave more water in rivers and streams to protect fish and wildlife, to guarantee the survival of a growing list of threatened and endangered species, and to protect water quality. Climate change will only exacerbate these concerns.

Conservation has become well accepted in the water world as an important part of our water future. CUWCC has identified a suite of best management practices (BMPs) and how much can be conserved by each at what cost and is looking to adopt additional cost-effective BMPs. But a quick look at CUWCC's website shows both that not very many of the thousands of water agencies in the state have signed on and how poorly, by their own admission, many of these agencies are doing with implementation. The Pacific Institute has concluded that over a third of indoor urban water use can be conserved cost effectively with current technology and that there is really enough to rewater our rivers and the delta without impacting the quality of our lives. Conservation has been adopted by CALFED as an important part of its program and is also given great importance in DWR's Bulletin 160-2005.

The agriculture sector uses about 80% of the developed water in the state and has formed an organization similar to CUWCC. Because the cost of water to agriculture is so low, it is using about half of its developed water to grow water-intensive but low-value crops: alfalfa, irrigated pasture, cotton, and rice. Cotton and rice are also subsidized by the federal government. As a result, agricultural water is targeted for transfer, to be marketed, to provide water to our growing cities, despite the adverse impacts on the areas of origin, both environmental and economic, and on the growth implications in both sending and receiving areas.

The amount of treated wastewater that is being reused is growing, pushed by examples from the Los Angeles Area. Also contributing to wastewater reuse are studies led by the Bureau of Reclamation and cost shared by many local agencies. Treated wastewater is now used mostly for irrigation of landscaped areas, such as parks and golf courses, and for industrial process water, such as in oil refineries. The most efficient way to reuse such highly treated water, instead of throwing it away, is to pump it up to spreading basins so that it can percolate slowly through the soil into our drinking water supply. Percolating through the soil helps purify the water. Then the infrastructure already in place can be used to chlorinate and distribute it. One such project has been in existence in the Whittier Narrows area for over 40 years with no known adverse health effects. The potential for the future is enormous, as enormous as the institutional barriers to reclamation and reuse.

Using our groundwater more effectively and efficiently in conjunction with surface water is also beginning. All the important groundwater basins in the Los Angeles Area have been adjudicated and are being managed to save wet-season rain for dry-season use. More can be done saving wet-year surpluses against dry-year need. The Association of Ground Water Agencies has studied southern California and found opportunities to store millions of acre-feet of water underground. However, it is impossible to require groundwater management, even in areas with massively overdrafted groundwater basins, such as the San Joaquin Valley. These overdrafted basins are pumped even more during droughts to sell to the governor's Drought Water Bank. This will change as shortages increase and local agencies determine that, to be sustainable, they must do a better job of resource management.

Watershed managers are beginning to explore the many local opportunities available to them. The advantages and possible disadvantages of capturing more rainwater by putting it into the ground where it falls are being studied. Better management of our dams and spreading grounds are under constant study and refinement. Establishing a landscape ethic, using native plants (preferably) or other Mediterranean plant materials is being promoted. Low-water-use plant materials, not necessarily natives, are now required by law for new large installations. On average, about half of the water delivered to single-family homes is used outside, more than is necessary to maintain current landscaping. Even small improvements in home landscaping irrigation practices can conserve a lot of water. Computerized irrigation controllers are invaluable.

And last of all, new technologies are being explored, such as waterless urinals, dry composting toilets, and desalination facilities. Desalination is a proven technology for brackish or other groundwater that does not quite meet potable standards. It is coming down in price as better membranes are developed. The best use for reverse osmosis is to clean tertiary treated wastewater further and to put it underground to be pumped up into existing distribution systems, instead of throwing away an almost-potable water supply. A few jurisdictions permit the use of gray water for home landscaping.

As a few forward-thinking agencies, such as the Inland Empire Utilities Agency, the Santa Ana Watershed Project Authority, and Orange County in southern California and the Santa Clara Valley Water District and the East Bay Municipal Utility District in northern California find ever more creative ways to deal with local problems, more and more local solutions will present themselves. It is critically important for agencies to work much more closely together to reap the benefits of planning comprehensively and cooperatively for the benefit of everyone. Especially needed is some cooperation and coordination among water and land use planning agencies.

Land use management agencies and developers have not yet gotten the message, for they continue to build, and allow to be built, such totally unsustainable water features as ski lakes and golf courses in the desert and then plant lush tropical gardens to promote their developments. They also insist on building housing on the floodplains and in the delta. A statewide land use policy is needed to determine where the new towns will go and why. Housing developments should not be built on prime agricultural land or where there is insufficient water. Urban sprawl and the financing needed for new infrastructure, such as water, sewers, libraries, parks, schools, and hospitals, are not viable without subsidies from existing cities. Cities would benefit greatly from rebuilding their inner cores, where infrastructure already exists. Then transportation planners could plan for a transit system that would work. Rebuilding a denser city will use less water and will not destroy precious native habitat or further decimate our rivers. And the resources of our precious state can be utilized more reasonably and beneficially.

The thousands of small water agencies in the state prefer to preserve their own local control. Many are unable to keep up with water quality regulations or their own infrastructure needs. Privatization, selling out to investor-owned utilities, is one way of upgrading old systems and meeting ever more stringent water quality standards that can have unforeseen consequences. And water marketing has evolved as the politically expedient way to reallocate a limited resource, in direct contradiction to the state's responsibility to allocate water to benefit the health and welfare of all the people. Privatization and water marketing raise serious questions about the ethics of buying and selling a public resource for profit, the abilities of local agencies to negotiate the complexities of dealing with multinational corporations, and how to assess the true benefits that might or might not accrue from giving control of this life necessity away from public ownership to private investors.

In conclusion, a great deal of water in our region and in the state is not being used efficiently or effectively. It is difficult to measure and to quantify because there is no uniform system for doing so. But that does not mean that it does not exist. There *is* sufficient water to meet our growing population needs, to meet the needs of agriculture, and to restore much of our decimated rivers and wildlife if we were to adopt the programs outlined earlier in a comprehensive manner, statewide, with all agencies cooperating to do so. Watershed management agencies or nonprofits may be the best vehicle for encouraging the regional planning that is so important for the future.

What is needed is strong political leadership, strong enough to overcome the campaign contributions of giant agribusiness and privateers in the state as well as the terrible inertia and unwillingness to move that is so prevalent. California must remain green and golden, with a future that is truly healthy and sustainable.

ELEMENTS OF A SUSTAINABLE STATEWIDE WATER POLICY

The need for an integrated, comprehensive, and cooperative statewide water policy is obvious. The lessons learned from this book can be summed up by defining some of the elements of what such a water policy should and could look like. Getting these elements adopted into law will take a long and very difficult political process that can only be successful if people of goodwill all over the state organize to take on the hydraulic brotherhood that controls Sacramento. What follows are some elements of what such a comprehensive water policy could look like.

1. Local water resources are the most dependable, least costly, and most drought resistant. Therefore they must be carefully managed, protected, and used sustainably.

2. Conservation is the cheapest next source of water, resulting in the least environmental damage. This applies to both urban and agricultural sectors.

3. Groundwater is closely tied to surface water and must be managed conjunctively with surface water and in a sustainable way, preventing any further overdrafts. Groundwater must not be exported until safe yield has been determined as well as the social and economic impacts of such an export.

4. DWR computer models of both surface water and groundwater must first of all be consistent, with one data collection and mapping system used statewide. The data collected and the models for predicting the future must be subjected to peer review, be predictable and accurate, and truly reflect realities. The current Calsim II model was constructed to maximize exports given certain hydrology and constraints. It is being used as the preferred tool for environmental impact analyses. One problem with Calsim II is that it does not recognize the connections between groundwater and surface water. Therefore there is no current limit on what can be sucked from the ground, as if groundwater were infinite.

5. Reuse of highly treated wastewater, especially for groundwater recharge and even direct potable reuse, must be encouraged. This is the most economical way to reuse massive amounts of water.

6. A portion of water saved by conservation and reuse must be reserved for the environment. We must find a way to assign water rights to fish, for stream and habitat restoration, and possibly to recharge overdrafted groundwater basins. The City of Los Angeles has established the precedent of leaving behind a third of the water formerly taken from the eastern Sierra for environmental purposes. Therefore, at least a third of what is saved is a good place to start.

7. Delta water quality standards and minimum stream flows must be determined and enforced. This means no more pumping out of the delta or exporting water from rivers that are already decimated by transfers.

8. There is great need to consolidate local water supply agencies and to consolidate them with other water management agencies, to

make them more accountable, more responsive, and more responsible in their behavior. Minimally they must plan cooperatively. With thousands of agencies in the state, it is impossible for citizens to monitor and have input on water decisions or to even know what many of these agencies do. The experience of the Los Angeles Area is that larger agencies do a much better job of conservation, planning, and public accountability than many smaller agencies. And many economies of scale are to be had, along with savings from not having to support so many boards of directors and their lifestyles. Regional agencies, perhaps at the watershed level, is a goal to pursue.

9. Watershed management, with all that it implies, must be moved front and center. It includes more and better communication between and among the various kinds of water agencies, capturing stormwater where it falls for recharge, especially in urban areas, and a host of other management techniques, including permeable paving, land use planning, habitat restoration, water quality improvements, and improving local quality of life and property values.

10. Agriculture is facing international competition for some basic crops, such as cotton, that consume much of the developed water in the state. J. G. Boswell has predicted that 10 years from now cotton will no longer be grown in the San Joaquin Valley. This will free up an enormous amount of water that can be earmarked to restore the San Joaquin River and the delta or be taken back by the state for reallocation.

11. Some farmers manage their land in ways that are environmentally beneficial. Some rice growers flood their fields after harvest so that migratory birds can feed on the leftover rice and fertilize the fields for next year's crop. Other farmers should be encouraged to find ways to benefit themselves and the environment as well.

12. Some agricultural land should be retired to protect against naturally occurring boron and selenium, which are toxic and wash out of the soil, or because there is a clay lens under the surface that causes water to collect in the root zone of what is grown. An agricultural drain is not the answer. It has no place to drain to. The

water saved by retiring this land should be returned to the state for reallocation where best needed.

13.   The areas of origin must be protected so that they have the option to grow as they wish.

14.   Multinational corporations and others are looking to turn our water resources into a commodity to be sold to the highest bidder. Our publicly owned water must remain in public hands and be used only for the health and welfare of the people of California, not the bottom line of multinational or other corporations.

15.   The public, the people of California, must have a prominent voice in the development of any water policy. There must be an end to water officials meeting behind closed doors and deciding our fate in their own interest, not in ours.

16.   The public trust doctrine is the best tool to require that water is used in the best interests of all the people of California.

There is enough water for our growing population, for agriculture, and to restore much of our ecosystems decimated by water transfers. We are that inefficient. We can have it all. We just need the political will to make it happen.

Postscript

These 16 elements have been refined by the California Water Impact Network, the only statewide nonprofit working solely on water issues, into 16 Principles for a Sustainable Water Future. These principles, the facts that support each of them, and more about the organization and the water world can be found at www.c-win.org. The website is designed to serve as an organizing tool and a network for all the people and small groups around the state interested in water issues. It is the first step toward developing the political will needed to make the changes that are so necessary.

GLOSSARY

$10^6 \, g\text{-}l = 2\frac{1}{2} \, AF$

ACRE-FOOT   A measure of water; 43,560 cubic feet, 325,900 gallons, or a football field one foot deep in water.

ACTION LEVEL   The level of a contaminant that, if exceeded, triggers treatment or other requirements that a water system must follow.

ACUTE EXPOSURE   A single exposure to a hazardous material for a brief length of time.

ACUTE HEALTH EFFECT   An immediate effect (i.e., within hours or days) that may result from exposure to certain drinking water contaminants (e.g., pathogens).

ADJUDICATION   A process performed by the courts that determines ownership of groundwater and assigns a Watermaster to manage or enforce pumping rights and sometimes water quality. This is a multiyear process.

ADVERSE HEALTH EFFECTS   Effects of chemicals or other materials that impair one's health. They can range from relatively mild temporary conditions, such as minor eye or throat irritation, shortness of breath, or headaches, to permanent and serious conditions, such as cancer, birth defects, or damage to organs.

AERATION   Passing air through a solid or liquid, especially a process that promotes breakdown or movement of contaminants in soil or water by exposing them to air.

AIR STRIPPING TOWER   Air stripping removes volatile organic chemicals (such as solvents) from contaminated water by causing them to evaporate. Polluted water is sprayed downward through a tower filled with packing materials while air is blown upward through the tower. The contaminants evaporate into the air, leaving significantly reduced pollutant levels in the water. The air is treated before it is released into the atmosphere.

ALKALINITY   As opposed to acidity. Measured by pH.

ANADROMOUS FISH   Those fish that spend part of their life cycle in freshwater (to spawn) and part of their life cycle in the ocean, such as salmon and steelhead.

APPROPRIATIVE WATER RIGHTS   Holders can use available water that is not taken by anyone else. It originated during the gold rush, when streams were redirected into hoses that washed the mountains down in search of gold. These rights belong to whomever got there first—first in time, first in right.

AQUIFER   A natural underground layer, often of sand or gravel, that contains water.

ARTESIAN WELL   A well that flows up like a fountain because of the internal pressure of the aquifer.

BASIN PLAN   A planning document produced and updated every five years by regional water boards that establishes the beneficial use for each water body and the water quality for each use.

BEST AVAILABLE TECHNOLOGY   The water treatment(s) that the EPA certifies to be the most effective for removing a contaminant.

BEST MANAGEMENT PRACTICES (BMP)   Structural, nonstructural, and managerial techniques that are recognized to be the most effective and practical means to control nonpoint-source pollutants yet are compatible with the productive use of the resource to which they are applied. BMPs are used in both urban and agricultural areas.

BIOACCUMULATION   The storage and buildup of chemicals in wildlife and plants. This process can take place in one of two ways: through direct consumption of chemicals or when one organism consumes another that has already consumed these chemicals. The second method contributes to the level of these substances in the organism that is higher in the food chain.

BIOREMEDIATION   A process whereby microorganisms change toxic compounds into nontoxic ones.

BLACK WATER   Water that comes from toilets or other highly contaminated sources.

CANCER RISK   A number, generally expressed in exponential form (e.g., 1×10^{-6}, which means 1 in 1 million), that describes the increased probability that an individual will develop cancer from exposure to toxic materials. Calculations producing cancer risk numbers are complex and typically include a number of assumptions that tend to cause the final estimated risk number to be conservative.

CAPITOL STORM   A design storm used for sizing storm drain systems. Los Angeles County Public Works uses a 50-year storm as its capitol event.

CARCINOGEN   A substance or agent that may produce or increase the risk of cancer.

CHECK DAM   The small dams built to capture debris flows during storm events to prevent clogging of a storm drain system, which can cause floods.

CHRONIC EXPOSURE   Repeated contact with a chemical over a period of time, often involving small amounts of a toxic substance.

CHRONIC HEALTH EFFECT   The possible result of exposure over many years to a drinking water contaminant at levels above its maximum contaminant level.

CLEAN WATER ACT (CWA)   A federal law regulating the pollution that will reach surface waters (rivers, lakes, ponds, and streams). The law prohibits a point source from discharging pollutants into the water unless the discharge meets certain permit requirements.

COLIFORM   A group of related bacteria whose presence in water may indicate contamination by disease-causing microorganisms.

COLOR CODING OF VARIOUS QUALITIES OF WATER   Water from toilets and other highly contaminated sources is called BLACK WATER. GRAY WATER comes from showers, sinks, and washing machines and can be used for irrigation if distributed underground. PURPLE PIPES are used for reclaimed water, to prevent cross-connections with potable water.

COMMUNITY WATER SYSTEM   A water system that supplies drinking water to 25 or more of the same people year-round in their residences. Examples are mobile home parks and small towns that have their own wells.

COMPREHENSIVE ENVIRONMENTAL RESPONSE, COMPENSATION, AND LIABILITY ACT (CERCLA)   A federal law, enacted in 1980 and nicknamed SUPERFUND, that provides the authority through which the federal government can compel people or companies responsible for creating hazardous waste sites to clean them up.

CONCENTRATION   The amount of a chemical in a given volume of air, water, or other medium. An example is 15 parts of carbon in a million parts of air.

CONJUNCTIVE USE   Surface water is managed together with (conjunctively with) groundwater.

CONSENT DECREE   A legal document, approved and issued by a judge.

CONTAMINANT   Anything found in water (including microorganisms, minerals, chemicals, radionuclides, etc.) that may be harmful to human or aquatic health.

CONTRACTUAL WATER RIGHTS   Contracts between water agencies and the government agency that builds dams, aqueducts, or other infrastructure to capture and move water.

CRYPTOSPORIDIUM   A microorganism commonly found in lakes and rivers; highly resistant to disinfection.

DEBRIS BASIN   A man-made facility consisting of a dam behind which the sediment and debris that washes off hillsides is caught so as not to clog up rivers or streams. It is periodically cleaned out.

DETENTION BASIN   A man-made facility to hold stormwater temporarily until such time as there is room in the storm drain system to release it safely.

DISINFECTANT   A chemical (commonly chlorine, chloramine, or ozone) or physical process (e.g., ultraviolet light) that kills microorganisms such as bacteria, viruses, and protozoa.

DISINFECTION BY-PRODUCTS   When a disinfectant such as chlorine or ozone are added to drinking water, they combine with naturally occurring substances in the water to produce other compounds, some of which are of concern.

DISSOLVED SOLIDS (TDS)   Total dissolved solids, minerals, or salts in water. A measure of hardness.

DOWN-GRADIENT   The direction in which groundwater flows.

EFFLUENT   Wastewater, treated or untreated, that flows out of a treatment plant, sewer, or industrial outfall. Generally refers to wastes discharged into surface waters.

EXPOSURE   Coming into contact with a substance through inhalation or ingestion or directly through the skin; may be acute or chronic.

FINISHED WATER   Water that has been treated and is ready to be delivered to customers.

GIARDIA LAMBLIA   A microorganism frequently found in rivers and lakes that, if not treated properly, may cause diarrhea, fatigue, and cramps after ingestion.

GRADIENT   The natural slope of groundwater that flows downhill or down-gradient.

GRAY WATER   Water from sinks, showers, and washing machines that is fit for landscape irrigation if delivered underground.

GROUNDWATER   Water found beneath the earth's surface that fills pores between materials such as sand, soil, and gravel.

GROUNDWATER BASIN   An underground basin formed by the natural geology of an area that contains groundwater.

HAZARDOUS WASTE   By-products or waste materials of manufacturing and other processes that have some dangerous property; generally categorized as corrosive, ignitable, toxic, or reactive or in some way harmful to people or the environment.

HEAVY METALS   Metals such as lead, chromium, copper, and cobalt that can be toxic at relatively low concentrations.

HYDROGRAPH   How streams, seas, lakes, and rivers are measured with reference to utilization of their waters.

HYDROLOGY   The science of how water moves in the environment.

IMPAIRMENT   Failure to meet applicable water quality standards or to protect designated beneficial uses (such as fishing and swimming).

IMPORTED WATER   Water supply that is conveyed from one watershed to be used in another.

IN-LIEU REPLENISHMENT   Replenishing groundwater by trading water for this purpose from another source.

INFLUENT   Water or other liquid—raw or partially treated—flowing into a reservoir, basin, treatment process, or treatment plant.

INJECTION WELL   A well used to inject potable water into the ground to prevent seawater from intruding into the groundwater and contaminating it.

INORGANIC CONTAMINANTS   Mineral-based compounds, such as metals, nitrates, and asbestos. These contaminants occur naturally in some water but can also get into water through farming, chemical manufacturing, and other human activities. The EPA has set legal limits on 15 inorganic contaminants.

LEACHATE   Typically, water that has come in contact with hazardous wastes. For example, water from rain or other sources that has percolated through a landfill and dissolved or carries various chemicals and thus could spread contamination. Current landfills have systems to collect leachate.

LEAD AGENCY   A public agency with the principal responsibility for ordering and overseeing site investigation and cleanup or for writing an environmental impact report (EIR).

MAXIMUM CONTAMINANT LEVEL (MCL)   A contaminant level for drinking water, established by the California Department of Health Services, Division of Drinking Water and Environmental Management, or by the U.S. Environmental Protection Agency. These levels are legally enforceable standards based on health risk (primary standards) or nonhealth concerns such as odor and taste (secondary standards).

MAXIMUM CONTAMINANT LEVEL GOAL (MCLG) The level of a contaminant at which there would be no risk to human health. This goal is not always economically or technologically feasible, and is not legally enforceable.

MICROGRAMS PER GRAM (µG/G) A measurable unit of concentration for a solid. A mercury level of 1.0 µg/g means that 1 microgram (one millionth of a gram) of mercury was detected in 1 gram of sample. It is equivalent to 1 part per million.

MICROORGANISMS Tiny living organisms that can be seen only with the aid of a microscope. Some microorganisms can cause acute health problems when consumed in drinking water. Also known as MICROBES.

MONITORING Testing that water systems must perform to detect and measure contaminants. A water system that does not follow the EPA's monitoring methodology or schedule is in violation and may be subject to legal action.

MONITORING WELL A well drilled to collect groundwater samples for analysis to determine the amounts, types, and distribution of contaminants in the groundwater.

NATIONAL PRIORITIES LIST (NPL) The EPA's list of the most serious uncontrolled or abandoned hazardous waste sites, identified as candidates for long-term cleanup using money from the Superfund trust fund.

NONPOINT SOURCE A pollution source that is diffuse and lacks a single point of origin or is not introduced into a receiving stream from a specific outlet. The pollutants are generally carried off the land by stormwater runoff. The common categories for nonpoint sources are agriculture, forestry, urban, mining, construction, dams and channels, land disposal, and saltwater intrusion.

NONPOTABLE WATER Water considered unsafe and/or unpalatable for drinking.

NONTRANSIENT, NONCOMMUNITY WATER SYSTEM A water system that supplies water to 25 or more of the same people at least six months per year in places other than their residences. Some examples are schools, factories, office buildings, and hospitals that have their own water systems.

ORGANIC COMPOUNDS Molecules that typically contain carbon, hydrogen, oxygen, or nitrogen.

ORGANIC CONTAMINANTS Carbon-based chemicals, such as solvents and pesticides, that can get into water through runoff from cropland or discharge from factories. The EPA has set legal limits on 56 organic contaminants.

OVERDRAFT The pumping out of the ground of more water than nature can replenish.

PARTS PER BILLION (PPB)   A unit of measure used to describe levels or concentrations of contamination. A measure of concentration, equaling 0.0000001%. For example, 1 part per billion is the equivalent of one drop of impurity in 500 barrels of water. Most drinking water standards are ppb concentrations.

PARTS PER MILLION (PPM)   A unit of measure for the concentration of one material in another. When looking at contamination of water and soil, the toxins are often measured in parts per million. One part per million is equal to one thousandth of a gram of substance in one thousand grams of material. One part per million would be equivalent to one drop of water in 20 gallons. See MICROGRAMS PER GRAM.

PATHOGEN   A disease-causing organism.

PERCHED GROUNDWATER   Water that accumulates beneath the earth's surface but above the main water-bearing zone (aquifer). Typically, perched groundwater occurs when a lens of harder, less permeable soil is "perched" on otherwise-porous soils. Rainwater moving downward through the soil stops at the lens, flows along it, and then seeps downward toward the aquifer.

PERCOLATION   The movement of water downward and radially through subsurface soil layers, usually continuing downward toward groundwater.

PERMEABILITY   The degree to which water can move freely through soils.

PH   A measurement of an acidic or alkaline substance. The values range from 0 to 14, with a pH of 7 corresponding to neutral. Tap water pH may lie between 6 and 8. Strongly acidic waste solutions (pH less than 2) and strongly basic ones (pH greater than 12.5) are defined as hazardous wastes because of their corrosive effect on metals and on skin.

PLUME   A body of contaminated groundwater flowing from a specific source. The movement of the groundwater is influenced by such factors as local groundwater flow patterns, the character of the aquifer in which the groundwater is contained, and the density of contaminants. A plume may also be a cloud of smoke or vapor. It defines the area where exposure would be dangerous.

POINT SOURCE   A stationary location or fixed facility from which pollutants are discharged; any single identifiable source of pollution (e.g., a pipe, ditch, ship, ore pit, or factory smokestack).

POTABLE WATER   Water that is safe and clean for drinking and cooking.

POTENTIALLY RESPONSIBLE PARTIES (PRPS)   Any individual or company who may have contributed to contamination at a Superfund site. Under CERCLA, PRPs are expected to conduct or pay for site cleanup.

PRECIPITATION   Rain, snow, or heavy fog.

PRESCRIPTIVE RIGHTS   A form of water rights achieved by trespass or unauthorized taking that can yield title if allowed to continue longer than the five-year statute of limitations. It is also the water commandeered by the state and federal governments to fill their aqueduct systems for which contracts have been signed.

PRETREATMENT   Required before any substance that could upset the bacteriological processes of a sewage treatment plant can be discharged into the sewage system.

PUBLIC HEALTH GOAL   The level of a contaminant that is not expected to cause human health problems; set by the Office of Environmental Health Hazard Assessment of CalEPA.

PUBLIC WATER SYSTEM (PWS)   Any water system that provides water to at least 25 people for at least 60 days annually. There are more than 170,000 public water systems providing water from wells, rivers, and other sources to about 250 million Americans. The others drink water from private wells. Standards for public water systems differ by their size and type.

RADIONUCLIDES   Any man-made or natural element that emits radiation and that may cause cancer after many years of exposure through drinking water.

RAW WATER   Water in its natural state, prior to any treatment for drinking.

REACTIVE SUBSTANCE   A substance capable of changing into something else in the presence of other chemicals, usually violently, or producing a hazardous by-product.

RECHARGE   Process by which rainwater (precipitation) seeps into the groundwater system.

RECHARGE AREA   Usually a shallow pond or basin used to store water temporarily until the water can soak or percolate into the underlying aquifer.

RECLAMATION OR REUSE WATER   Wastewater that has been treated sufficiently so that the treated water can be safely used for landscape irrigation, industrial process water, and other nonpotable purposes.

RECORD OF DECISION (ROD)   A public document that records a decision reached after much due process, such as the CALFED ROD or that used in the Superfund cleanup process.

RECYCLED WATER   Wastewater that has been cleaned up for reuse is also recycled.

REMEDIAL ACTION (RA)   The phase in Superfund site cleanup following the remedial design (RD) phase, where the actual construction or implementation occurs. The RA is based on the specifications described in the Record of Decision (ROD).

REMEDIAL DESIGN (RD)   The phase in Superfund site cleanup where the technical specifications for cleanup remedies and technologies are designed. It is based on the specifications described in the Record of Decision (ROD).

REMEDIAL INVESTIGATION/FEASIBILITY STUDY (RI/FS)   Performed at a site after it is listed on the National Priorities List (NPL). This study collects data and evaluates alternative remedies.

REMEDY   The method selected to clean up a Superfund site.

RESERVOIR   A man-made water storage facility often called a lake.

RESOURCE CONSERVATION AND RECOVERY ACT (RCRA)   A federal law whose primary goals are to protect human health and the environment from the potential hazards of waste disposal, to conserve energy and natural resources, to reduce the amount of waste generated, and to ensure that wastes are managed in an environmentally sound manner. Management of solid waste (e.g., garbage), hazardous waste, and underground storage tanks holding petroleum products or certain chemicals is regulated by RCRA.

RETENTION BASIN   A man-made place to retain water so that it might percolate into the groundwater aquifer.

REVERSE OSMOSIS   The process of forcing water through a special membrane to remove salts and other pollutants.

RIPARIAN RIGHTS   Water rights that are pertinent to the land next to a flowing river. The rights are attached to the land. The landowner has rights to use the water as long as she or he does no harm to those downstream who also have riparian rights. The right is lost if it is not used. Use it or lose it.

RISING GROUNDWATER   As aquifers fill (are replenished), the level of the groundwater rises relative to the surface.

RUNOFF   The water that flows off the land, not from a single source. In cities, urban runoff consists of water from car washing, overirrigation, and animal waste or illegal dumping of toxic materials.

SAFE DRINKING WATER ACT (SDWA)   A federal law that ensures that our tap water is fit to drink.

SAFE YIELD   The amount of water that can be pumped each year from an aquifer without causing any reduction in stored water.

SALINITY   The amount of salts or minerals in water.

SANITARY SURVEY   An on-site review of the water sources, facilities, equipment, operation, and maintenance of public water systems for the purpose of evaluating the adequacy of the facilities for producing and distributing safe drinking water.

SEAWATER INTRUSION   When groundwater basins are overdrafted near the coast, sea water moves in to fill the void.

SEAWATER-INTRUSION BARRIER   To prevent seawater intrusion into a potable aquifer, potable water is injected into the ground to prevent the sea water from contaminating the potable aquifer.

SECONDARY DRINKING WATER STANDARDS   Nonenforceable federal guidelines regarding cosmetic effects (such as tooth or skin discoloration) or aesthetic effects (such as taste, odor, or color) of drinking water.

SEDIMENT   The soil, sand, and minerals at the bottom of surface waters, such as streams, lakes, and rivers. Sediments capture or adsorb contaminants. The term may also refer to solids that settle out of any liquid.

SEDIMENTATION   The process whereby sediment that is carried by a stream flow is captured behind a dam or in a recharge basin and settles out.

SITE ASSESSMENT   The process by which the EPA determines whether a potential site should be placed on the National Priorities List.

SLUDGE   The solids removed at wastewater treatment plants.

SOURCE WATER   Water in its natural state, prior to any treatment for drinking.

SOURCE WATER ASSESSMENT PROGRAM   Program under the federal Safe Drinking Water Act that requires states to determine the water quality safety of drinking water sources. California satisfies this requirement with the California Drinking Water Sources Assessment and Protection Program (DWSAP).

SPREADING GROUND, BASIN   Basin used to impound water to allow for slow percolation of water into the ground in order to recharge the underlying groundwater aquifer.

STATE REVOLVING FUND   Program that evolved from the federal Clean Water Act that provides funds for the construction of municipal sewage treatment works.

STORMWATER   Precipitation that can infiltrate into the ground or run off.

SUBSTRATE   A geological term that refers to the area below the surface of the soil.

SURFACE WATER   Bodies of water that remain above ground, such as lakes, ponds, rivers, streams, bays, and oceans.

TOTAL MAXIMUM DAILY LOAD (TMDL)   How much of each pollutant a water body can assimilate is determined by a process that then assigns the reduction of each pollutant back to its sources.

TOTAL DISSOLVED SOLIDS (TDS)   All of the solids dissolved in water.

TOXIC   Poisonous.

TRANSIENT, NONCOMMUNITY WATER SYSTEM   A water system that provides water in a place such as a gas station or campground where people do not remain for long periods of time. These systems do not have to test or treat their water for contaminants that pose long-term health risks because fewer than 25 people drink the water over a long period. They still must test their water for microbes and several chemicals.

TURBIDITY   The cloudy appearance of water caused by the presence of tiny particles. High levels of turbidity may interfere with proper water treatment and monitoring.

UNDERGROUND STORAGE TANK (UST)   An underground tank storing hazardous substances or petroleum products. Under the Resource Conservation and Recovery Act (RCRA), Congress directed the EPA to establish regulatory programs that would prevent, detect, and clean up releases from UST systems containing petroleum or hazardous substances.

UP-GRADIENT   The direction from which water flows in an aquifer. In particular, areas that are higher than contaminated areas and, therefore, are not prone to contamination by the movement of polluted groundwater.

VOLATILE ORGANIC COMPOUNDS (VOC)   A group of chemicals composed primarily of carbon and hydrogen that have a tendency to evaporate (volatilize) into the air from water or soil. VOCs include substances contained in common solvents and cleaning fluids. Some VOCs are known to cause cancer.

WASTEWATER   The used water and solids that flow to a treatment plant through its sewer system. Stormwater, surface water, and groundwater infiltration also may enter a wastewater treatment plant. Wastewater can also be cleaned via a constructed wetland.

WASTEWATER RECLAMATION PLANT   A facility that receives and treats wastewaters to produce less harmful by-products. Also known as a POTW (publicly owned treatment works) or a sewage treatment plant.

WATER TABLE   The top of the water-saturated portion of an aquifer.

WATERMASTER   A person or agency appointed by the courts to manage an aquifer that has been adjudicated, usually by administering pumping rights and sometimes water quality.

WATERSHED   The land area from which water drains into a stream, river, or reservoir.

WELL   A bored, drilled, or driven shaft whose purpose is to reach underground water supplies.

WELLHEAD PROTECTION PROGRAM   A program under the federal Safe Drinking Water Act that requires states to determine the water quality safety of the area around a drinking water well or well field. California satisfies this requirement with the California Drinking Water Sources Assessment and Protection Program (DWSAP).

NATIVE PLANT RESOURCES

Rancho Santa Ana Botanical Garden, 1500 N. College Avenue, Claremont, 91711. 909-625-8767. Twice yearly sales, but always some interesting plants for sale at the bookstore and gift shop. Mostly concerned with research. www.cgu.edu/inst/rsa

Theodore Payne Foundation specializes in growing native plants for sale and teaching people how best to care for and maintain them. This nonprofit was established to promote the restoration of our natural habitat. It can be found at 10459 Tuxford Street, Sun Valley, 91352, or call 818-768-3582. www.theodorepayne.org

California Native Plant Society publishes a monthly magazine and has twice yearly sales of native plants. For information: www.cnps.org.

Mediterranean Garden Society, a nonprofit that encourages the use of Mediterranean plants. www.mediterraneangardensociety.org

Los Angeles & San Gabriel Rivers Watershed Council maintains a website where native plant images and information are available. www.theplantprofiler.com

Los Angeles River plant guidelines and plant palette for the County: www.ladpw.org/wmd/watershed/LA/LAR_planting_guidelines_webversion.pdf

Metropolitan Water District: www.bewaterwise.com

There are a few commercial nurseries that specialize in natives in southern California:

Tree of Life Nursery, a commercial grower, is located at 33201 Ortega Highway, San Juan Capistrano, 92693. It can be reached by phone at 949-0728-0685 or through their website: www.treeoflifenursery.com

Las Pilitas Nursery, 3232 Las Pilitas Road, Santa Margarita, 93453. 805-438-5992; or in Escondido at 8331 Nelson Way, 92026. 760-749-5930. They have a very complete website with tons of information. www.laspilitas.com

Matilija Nursery, 8225 Waters Road, Moorpark, 93021. 805-523-8604. They are open on Fridays and Saturdays, midweek by appointment. www.matilijanursery.com

Natural Landscapes, 16 Limetree Lane, Rancho Palos Verdes, 90275. 310-377-2536, by appointment. All plants are grown from local seed. www.natural-landscapes.com

El Nativo Growers, a wholesaler, has a website full of useful information. www.elnativogrowers.com

Native Sons, a Mediterranean plant specialist and wholesaler, provides extensive native plant descriptions on their website, with a list of nurseries in southern California that sell their stock. www.nativesons.com

WEBSITES OF INTEREST

FEDERAL AGENCIES

Bureau of Reclamation: http://www.usbr.gov
    for groundwater quality: http://www.lc.usbr.gov/~scao/planpgm2.htm
    for CVP operations: http://www.ewg.org/reports/virtualflood
    for reclamation study: http://www.sawpa.org/projects/planning/
      socal-recyc.htm
    US Bureau of Reclamation Drought Planning Guidebook:
      http://www.usbr.gov/mp/watershare/documents/Contingency-
      DroughtPlanning.pdf
FEMA flood maps: http://www.myfloodzone.com
National Drought Policy Commission: http://www.fsa.usda.gov/drought
US Army Corps of Engineers: http://www.usace.army.mil
USEPA: http://www.epa.gov
    http://www.epa.gov/safewater
    Superfund: http://www.Yosemite.epa.gov.r9/sfund/overview.nsf
US Geological Survey analysis of Central and West Basins:
    http://www.water.usgs.gov/ogw/gwrp

CALIFORNIA DEPARTMENT OF WATER RESOURCES
http://www.dwr.water.ca.gov

Bay Delta Authority, Calsim, etc.: http://www.baydeltaoffice.water.ca.gov
CALFED ROD and much more: http://www.Calwater.ca.gov
California Water Plan, Bulletin 160-05: http://www.waterplan.water.ca.gov
Calsim: http://www.science.calwater.ca.gov/workshop/calsim_05.shtml

Desal Task Force, 2003:
   http://www.owue.water.ca.gov/recycle/desal/Docs/FinalReport.htm

Drought and preparedness: http://www.watersupplyconditions.water.ca.gov

Groundwater Bulletin 118: http://www.groundwater.water.ca.gov/bulletin118

Landscape Task Force:
   http://www.cuwcc.org/ab2717_landscape_task_force.lasso

Recycling Task Force and Desalinization Branch:
   http://www.owue.water.ca.gov/recycle

Reliability Report: http://www.baydeltaoffice.water.ca.gov

State Water Project, Bulletin 132-04: http://www.water.ca.gov

Watermaster Services: http://www.dpla.water.ca.gov/sd/watermaster/
   watermaster.html

Water transfers: http://www.watertransfers.water.ca.gov

OTHER CALIFORNIA AGENCIES

California Department of Health Services: http://www.dhs.ca.gov
      Drinking water programs: http://www.dhs.cahwnet.gov/ps/ddwem

Caltrans: http://www.dot.ca.gov

Department of Toxic Substances Control:
   http://www.calepa.ca.gov/About/History01/dtsc.htm

State Water Resources Control Board: http://www.swrcb.ca.gov

FOR POLLUTION INFORMATION

http://www.waterboards.ca.gov/losangeles/html/programs/programs.html

WHOLESALE WATER AGENCIES

Central Basin Municipal Water District: http://www.centralbasin.org

Foothill Municipal Water District: http://fmwd.com

Metropolitan Water District of Southern California:
   http://www.mwdh2o.com

San Gabriel Valley Municipal Water District:
   http://home.onemain.com/~ymcvicar

Santa Clara Valley Water District: http://www.valleywater.org

Three Valleys Municipal Water District:
   http://www.threevalleys.com

Upper San Gabriel Valley Municipal Water District:
   http://www.usgvmwd.org

Water Replenishment District of Southern California: http://www.wrd.org

West Coast Basin Municipal Water District: http://www.westbasin.org

RETAIL AGENCIES

American States Water Company: http://www.aswater.com

American Water Works: http://www.amwater.com/awpr1/default.html

California American Water:
   http://www.calamwater.com/awpr1/caaw/default.html

California Water Services Group: http://www.calwater.com

City of Azusa: http://www.ci.azusa.ca.us

City of Beverly Hills: http://www.beverlyhills.com

City of Burbank: http://www.ci.burbank.ca.us/PublicWorks/index.htm

City of Compton: http://www.comptoncity.org

City of Glendale: http://www.ci.glendale.ca.us

City of Long Beach: http://www.lbwater.org

City of Pasadena: http://www.ci.pasadena.ca.us/waterandpower

City of San Marino: http://www.ci.san-marino.ca.us

City of Santa Monica: http://www.santa-monica.org

City of Torrance: http://www.ci.torrance.ca.us

Golden State Water Company: http://www.aswater.com/Organization/
   Company_Links/Regions/Region_2/region_2.html

Las Virgenes Municipal Water District: http://www.lvmwd.dst.ca.us

Los Angeles County Department of Public Works: http://www.ladpw.org

Los Angeles Department of Water and Power: http://www.ladwp.com

Southwest Water Company: http://www.southwestwater.com

SANITATION DISTRICTS

City of Los Angeles Bureau of Sanitation: http://www.lacity.org/SAN

Sanitation Districts of Los Angeles County: http://www.lacsd.org

WATER QUALITY AUTHORITY

San Gabriel Basin Water Quality Authority: http://www.wqa.com

WATERMASTERS

Main San Gabriel Basin Watermaster: http://www.watermaster.org

ASSOCIATIONS OF WATER AGENCIES

Association of California Water Agencies (ACWA): http://www.acwa.com

Association of Ground Water Agencies: http://www.agwa.org

California Urban Water Agencies: http://www.cuwa.org/publications.html#
conservation

California Water Association (of investor-owned utilities): http://www
.calwaterassn.com

Central and West Basin Association of Pumpers: no website

Covina Irrigation Company: no website

Groundwater Resources Association of California: http://www.grac.org

San Gabriel Valley Protective Association: no website

San Gabriel Valley Water Association: http://www.sgvwa.org

San Gabriel Valley Water Committee: no website

Southeast Water Coalition (SEWC): no website

Water Industry Coordinating Council: no website

NONPROFITS WORKING ON WATER EDUCATION

Agricultural Water Management Council: http://www.agwatercouncil.org

Blue planet on international privatization: http://www.blueplanetproject.net

California Urban Water Conservation Coalition: http://www.cuwcc.org

California Water Impact Network: http://www.c-win.org

Canadian Union of Public Employees on privatization:
http://www.cupe.org.ca

Environmental Working Group: http://www.ewg.org/reports/watersubsidies

Food and Water Watch: http://www.fwwatch.org

The Ground Water Foundation: http://www.groundwater.org

Pacific Institute: http://www.pacinst.org/reports/california_water_2030

Planning and Conservation League: http://www.pcl.org

Public Policy Institute of California: http://www.ppic.org

Sacramento Water Forum: http://www.waterforum.org

The Water Education Foundation: http://www.watereducation.org

SUGGESTED READINGS

Arax, Mark and Rick Wartzman. *The King of California.* Public Affairs, New York, 2003. The story of J. G. Boswell and agriculture in the San Joaquin Valley.

Barlow, Maude and Tony Clarke. *Blue Gold: The Battle Against Corporate Theft of the World's Water.* March 2002.

Barlow, Maude. *The Global Water Crisis and the Commodification of the World's Water Supply.* International Forum on Globalization (IFG), June 1999.

Blomquist, William. *Dividing the Waters: Governing Groundwater in Southern California.* Institute for Contemporary Studies, October 1992.

Brechin, Gray. *Imperial San Francisco, Urban Power, Earthly Ruin.* University of California Press, 1999.

Brown, Lester. *Population Growth: Sentencing Millions to Hydrology Poverty.* Worldwatch Institute Issue Alert 2000-4.

Carle, David. *Drowning the Dream.* Praeger Publishers. February 2000. The impacts of imported water on the landscape of southern California.

Carle, David. *Introduction to Water in California.* University of California Press, 2004.

Clark, Alfred. *War over the San Gabriels* and *A Century of Dividing the Waters.* Unpublished. Available at Cal Poly Pomona and at the Azusa Public Library.

Davis, Cheryl K. and Robert E. McGinn. *Navigating Rough Waters: Ethical Issues in the Water Industry.* American Water Works Association, 2001.

Dawson, Robert and Gray Brechin. *Farewell Promised Land: Waking from the California Dream.* University of California Press, 1999. An environmental history of the state, with many photographs.

Deister, Ane. *Working Toward an Active National Drought Policy.* Journal, American Water Works Association. March 2001.

Fradkin, Philip. L. *A River No More: The Colorado River and the West,* Alfred A. Knopf, 1981.

Gleick, Peter et al. Published by the Pacific Institute:

> *The World's Water: Biennial Report on Freshwater Resources.*
>
> *Threats to the World's Freshwater Resources.*
>
> *The New Economy of Water: The Risks and Benefits of Globalization and Privatization of Fresh Water.*
>
> *Waste Not, Want Not: The Potential for Urban Water Conservation in California,* November 2003.
>
> *California Water 2030: An Efficient Future,* May 2005.

Glennon, Robert. *Water Follies: Groundwater Pumping and the Fate of America's Fresh Waters.* Island Press, 2002.

Gottlieb, Robert and Margaret Fitzsimmons. *Thirst for Growth: Water Agencies as Hidden Government in California.* University of Arizona Press, 1994.

Gumprecht, Blake. *The Los Angeles River: Its Life, Death, and Possible Rebirth.* The Johns Hopkins University Press, 1999.

Haddad, Brent. *Rivers of Gold: Designing Markets to Allocate Water in California.* Island Press, Covelo, CA., 2000. Pro transfers and marketing.

Helperin, Alex, David Beckman, and Dvora Inwood, *California's Contaminated Groundwater: Is the State Minding the Store?* Natural Resources Defense Council. April 2001.

Hundley, Jr., Norris. *The Great Thirst: Californians and Water—A History,* Revised Edition. University of California Press, 2001. The classic text on the subject.

Kahrl, William and others. *The California Water Atlas.* Prepared by the Governor's Office of Planning and Research in cooperation with the Department of Water Resources, 1978–79.

Kahrl, William. *Water and Power.* University of California Press, September 1983. The story behind the building of the Los Angeles Aqueduct from the Owens Valley and Mono Lake.

McPhee, John. *The Control of Nature.* Noonday Press, 1990. Describes the San Gabriel Mountains, how erodable they are, and how difficult it is to manage stormwater.

Mulholland, Catherine. *William Mulholland and the Rise of Los Angeles.* University of California Press, 2000. A biography written by Mulholland's granddaughter.

Postel, Sandra. *Last Oasis: Facing Water Scarcity.* The Worldwatch Environmental Alert Series, W. W. Norton and Company, 1997.

Reisner, Mark. *Cadillac Desert: The American West and its Disappearing Water.* Penguin Books, 1993. This book is also a classic, describing in very readable language the development of water resources in the West.

Robinson, John W. *The San Gabriels.* Published by the Santa Anita Historical Society, 1991.

Rozengurt, M. A. *The Agonizing San Francisco Bay Ecosystem.* In Proceedings of the 22nd Annual American Geophysical Union, April 1–4, 2002, Colorado State University, Fort Collins, CO.

Shiva, Vandana. *Water Wars: Privatization, Pollution and Profits.* South End Press, 2002. Written by an Indian water activist.

Simon, Ted. *The River Stops Here.* Random House, 1994. The fight to save Round Valley from being dammed and flooded changed the fate of California.

University of California Cooperative Extension, California Department of Water Resources, et al. *A Guide to Estimating Irrigation Water Needs of Landscape Plantings in California.* Available from DWR.

Vickers, Amy. *Water Use and Conservation.* WaterPlow Press, 2001. A comprehensive guide to water conservation in every sector.

Ward, Diane Raines. *Water Wars, Drought, Flood, Folly and the Politics of Thirst.* Riverhead Books, 2002.

Water Education Foundation publishes *Layperson's Guides to California Water* and water maps that are continually being updated. They also publish *Western Water*, a bimonthly publication that usually takes on one subject at a time and treats it in some depth. 717 K Street, Suite 517, Sacramento, 95814. 916-444-6240. www.water-ed.org

Text: 11/14 Adobe Garamond
Display: Gill Sans
Compositor: Michael Bass Associates
Indexer: Herr's Indexing Service
Printer and binder: Maple-Vail Book Manufacturing Group